PARENT-CHILD RELATIONS: NEW RESEARCH

PARENT-CHILD RELATIONS: NEW RESEARCH

DOROTHY M. DEVORE
EDITOR

Nova Science Publishers, Inc.
New York

For permission to use material from this book please contact us:
Telephone 631-231-7269; Fax 631-231-8175
Web Site: http://www.novapublishers.com

Library of Congress Cataloging-in-Publication Data
Available upon request.

ISBN 1-60021-167-4

Published by Nova Science Publishers, Inc. ✢New York

CONTENTS

PREFACE

In the life of a person, there are probably no events, outside influences or genetic characteristics even approaching the significance of the broad category of acts and actions called parent-child relations. These include decisions and actions and lack thereof from the first day of life and sometimes throughout the lifespan. They include learning by example, schooling, disciplining, coping skills, behavioral practices, eating habits, communication skills, conflict management and a plethora of other actions. This book presents new research in this dynamic field.

The studies presented in chapter 1 examined whether or not adolescents' scoring-patterns on the IPPA (*Inventory of Parent and Peer Attachment*) would converge with a 3-way classification of attachment styles (i.e., secure, avoidant, and ambivalent). Data were used from two survey projects in the Netherlands. The first sample consisted of 508 adolescents aged 12-18 and their parents, the second sample consisted of 1,012 youths aged 11-14. Multi-informant and longitudinal analyses showed that reports of problem behaviors and social-emotional functioning from ambivalently and avoidantly attached youths could not be differentiated unambiguously on the basis of IPPA scores. Furthermore, IPPA-based attachment classifications did not have predictive power above conventional scale values, and results from cluster analyses - based on conventional scale values - did not always converge satisfactorily with the IPPA-based attachment classifications.

Chapter 2 proposes a new perspective on the evolution of attachment and of representation formation in general. This perspective compliments Bowlby's emphasis on the centrality of the infant's proximity-seeking behavior with respect to his caretaker, a behavior shaped primarily by an evolutionary instinct that operates to safeguard the child's physical survival and to regulate his experience of an external fear or of an internal anxiety. This same instinctual mechanism of proximity-seeking behavior reemerges during the rapprochement phase of development. During this phase, however, early forms of representation, primarily organized by the infant's sensorimotor experiences, achieve a new and higher level of reorganization governed by language. This chapter proposes that the child's need for the mother's proximity during rapprochement constitutes a new and crucial developmental stage of attachment, serving to ensure the survival of the child's mind. The mother's failure to respond appropriately to her child's emerging need at this time will result in both the toddler falling back into his original attachment organization patterns and the disruption of the toddler's ability to make appropriate use of the emerging representation organization mechanism. Importantly, the history of relationships during infancy do not distinguish or impoverish this instinct since this instinct is a universal one prompted by the ever-changing brain; only the quality of the reunion is affected by the history of these relationships. This chapter discusses the rapprochement developmental stage in the light of this new developmental theory and also suggests that during rapprochement, under appropriate conditions, symbolic activity takes prominence over sensorimotor activity to guide and regulate affective experience. The outcome of this transition can be seen in the subconscious when affective and sensorimotor experiences fail to formulate into a retrievable symbolic form.

Chapter 3 describes the impact of maternal postpartum depression during the first two years of infant life on children's behavioural growth trajectories between two and eight years of age. Analysis data from 3533 Canadian children reveals that children of mothers who experienced postpartum depression have higher levels of anxiety, hyperactivity and aggression than children of non-depressed mothers at age two. Over time, anxiety increases, while hyperactivity and aggression decrease at the same rate for children of depressed and non-depressed mothers. However, a constellation of other factors including parenting qualities of the mother-child relationship, social support, family structure, sex of the child, and socioeconomic variables also predict initial levels and rates of behavioural change.

The purposes of chapter 4 were to investigate the frequency, intensity, and subjects of arguments that Hmong second-generation adolescents have with their immigrant parents, and to explore whether the relationships of these conflicts and acculturation have any effect on the adolescent adjustment, as measured by self-esteem, depression, delinquent behaviors, and school performance. One hundred eighty-one adolescents (105 males, 76 females) of Hmong descent, ages 12 – 24 years (M = 15.82, SD = 2.00) participated in the study. The results indicate that 74% of the adolescents reported at least one conflict with their parents and an average of 4.47 (SD = 4.78) conflicts over the past month. The most frequently mentioned conflict issues with fathers and mothers were helping around the house, getting low grades, talking back to parents, watching television, and telephone calls. Conflicts with mothers, but not fathers, were significantly related to adolescents' reports of depression and delinquent behavior. Some educational approaches are discussed when professionals intervene parent-adolescent conflicts in Hmong immigrant families.

Chapter 5 will examine the interactions that occur between parents and their young children as they navigate through one of the most difficult stages of development. In particular, this chapter will review the normative developments that occur for young children during toddlerhood, such as rapid cognitive development, the development of a sense of self, and the first signs of growing autonomy. Certainly, a common consequence of young children reaching these developmental milestones is that they will demonstrate frequently testing of the limits placed upon them by their mothers and fathers (Campbell, 1990) and a certain level of negativity (Keenan and Wakschlag, 2000). Next, the types of discipline that parents use with their young children in response to these behaviors will be described and critiqued. Unfortunately, mothers and fathers frequently report problems and uncertainties in disciplining their young children (Campbell, 1990; Jenkins, Bax, and Hart, 1980). This fact is concerning, in that children below the age of 4-years tend to be most vulnerable to poor quality parenting (Loeber, 1990). Finally, the possibilities of parent-young child interactions going off-course at this stage and young children demonstrating the beginning signs of a disruptive behavior disorder will be examined. To summarize and put this information into context, suggestions regarding the promotion of a healthy parent-young child relationship and positive adaptation for young children will be offered.

Although parents who live in the same household parent their children concurrently, research often approaches parenting as if mothers' and fathers' behavior were independent rather than interdependent. Yet in practice parents do seem to coordinate their parenting, organizing parenting activities to reinforce shared beliefs and to avoid redundant tasks. The nature and success of such arrangements, however, has not been extensively studied. During the sometimes-turbulent toddler period successful joint parenting efforts should result in interparental agreement on whether their child's behavior is normal or problematic, as this is the starting point for family decisions about socialization and discipline. Chapter 6 reviews theory and research about parenting configurations that individual and systemic theories predict should promote agreement about child behavior. New data are presented that explored different configurations of parenting styles, and which of these parenting configurations best predicted consensus about child behavior. Participants were parents from 51 families with 30-month-old children. Primary and secondary caregivers reported on their toddlers' behavior problems and on their own parenting activities. Results indicated that parents agreed moderately on both parenting and child behavior. Specific configurations of parenting styles did predict agreement on child behavior problems. Parents with similar but non-optimal parenting styles showed the lowest levels of agreement about their children. The highest levels of agreement about child behavior were predicted by parenting configurations that provided balanced parenting coverage, even if their individual parenting styles seemed dissimilar. This relation could not be accounted for by marital consensus more generally.

Research on parent-child relations has often focused on the quality of interactions (e.g., parental nurturance) or magnitude of a characteristic present in the interaction (e.g., parental warmth). Chapter 7 focuses on the *predictability* (i.e., consistency) of parenting characteristics and family life rather than the *degree* (i.e., amount) of that characteristic. Thus, family unpredictability is defined as a lack of consistency in the behaviors and regulatory systems of a family (Ross and Hill, 2000). How family unpredictability relates to family functioning is reviewed and summarized. Theoretical foundations are described, including attachment theory and learned helplessness. Several possible correlates pertaining to origins of family unpredictability are highlighted, namely parental transitions, residential instability, parental divorce, and parental alcoholism. It is possible that the negative outcomes of these family patterns may be due in greater part to the unpredictability associated with them, rather than the condition per se. Particular attention is given to the research conducted by the author over the past decade, including the development of the Family Unpredictability Scale (FUS) and the Retrospective Family Unpredictability Scale (Retro-FUS). Finally, future research ideas are suggested and prevention, treatment, and policy implications are discussed.

Contentious family conflicts may frequently arise when families provide care to dependent elders. However, few studies have examined caregiving conflict according to specific theoretical models; sparse research has been conducted on caregiving conflict among aging parent and adult child caregivers. The purpose of chapter 8 was to investigate caregiving conflict and relationship strategies of aging parent and adult child caregivers using Rusbult's relationship investment model as the conceptual framework. A total of 16 aging parent caregivers and adult child caregivers participated in individual or joint interviews about caregiving conflict. Content analysis of the interview data showed that 56% of parent and child caregivers reported the presence of conflict. Parent and child caregivers favored constructive approaches in dealing with caregiving conflict. Fear, protection, and relationship history guided caregivers in their reactions to caregiving conflict. Implications of these findings for theoretically driven research on intergenerational ties are discussed.

Chapter 9 is concerned with the psychological and/or behavioral problems that children of stroke patients suffer. The study is designed to assess the clinical course of children's functioning during the first year after parental stroke, and to discover factors which predict children's suffering at 1 year post-stroke. Results show that depression of the healthy parent was the most significant predictor of all outcome scores, and that support was most frequently given to children with a more severely disabled parent. These findings confirm the need of a family-centered rehabilitative process in which all family members take part.

Chapter 10 describes an empirically supported approach for collaborating with parents in the design and implementation of communication intervention for children with developmental and physical disabilities. The approach includes four phases: (a) identifying and verifying prelinguistic behaviors, (b) non-directive collaborative consultation with parents, (c) parent use of functional communication training procedures, and (d) feedback on implementation of intervention strategies. Each phase of the approach is described. This description may enable clinicians to collaborate more effectively with parents. Emerging evidence suggests that this approach may enhance the communicative interactions and social relations between parents and their child with developmental and physical disabilities.

In chapter 11, school-wide surveys in five middle schools were used to measure educational aspirations, attitudes toward sexual health risk behaviors and drug use, and perceptions of parental interactions and disapproval of risk behavior and one year later. Participants were male and female students of Black ($n = 222$), Hispanic ($n = 317$), White ($n = 216$), and Asian or other heritage ($n = 85$), ages 11 to 14. Analyses were performed for three factors with Cronbach's alpha coefficients ≥ 0.65 (youth's attitudes, discourse with parents, and parents' disapproval of risk behavior), and three single items inquiring about use of alcohol, use of marijuana, and sexual behavior. Generalized Linear Model (GLM) with logit link was used to evaluate the contribution of these measures at baseline as predictors of educational aspirations at the one-year follow-up. Results showed race/heritage ($p < .001$), attitudes toward health risk behaviors ($p < .01$), extent to which youth talked with parents about use of drugs and other health risk behaviors ($p < .05$), and perceptions of their parents' disapproval of risk behavior ($p < .05$) each made significant contributions in predicting educational aspirations. Gender did not contribute to the prediction of educational aspiration nor did self-report of actual risk behavior. These results indicate that youths' interactions with parents regarding health risk behaviors is worthy of further exploration to develop interventions to reduce adolescent health risks and increase educational aspirations.

In: Parent-Child Relations: New Research
Editor: Dorothy M. Devore, pp. 1-27
ISBN 1-60021-167-4

Chapter 1

PARENTAL ATTACHMENT IN ADOLESCENCE BASED ON THE IPPA: MULTI-INFORMANT AND LONGITUDINAL RESEARCH IN TWO DUTCH SAMPLES

Geertjan Overbeek[1], Rutger C. M. E. Engels[1] and Marc J. Noom[2]
[1]Radboud University Nijmegen, Nijmegen, The Netherlands
[2]University of Leiden, Leiden, The Netherlands

ABSTRACT

The studies presented in this chapter examined whether or not adolescents' scoring-patterns on the IPPA (*Inventory of Parent and Peer Attachment*) would converge with a 3-way classification of attachment styles (i.e., secure, avoidant, and ambivalent). Data were used from two survey projects in the Netherlands. The first sample consisted of 508 adolescents aged 12-18 and their parents, the second sample consisted of 1,012 youths aged 11-14. Multi-informant and longitudinal analyses showed that reports of problem behaviors and social-emotional functioning from ambivalently and avoidantly attached youths could not be differentiated unambiguously on the basis of IPPA scores. Furthermore, IPPA-based attachment classifications did not have predictive power above conventional scale values, and results from cluster analyses - based on conventional scale values - did not always converge satisfactorily with the IPPA-based attachment classifications.

An attachment relationship is generally referred to as a close, enduring, affectional bond between infant and caretaker (Schaffer, 2000). The main characteristics are that it provides the individual with a sense of security and comfort, that it involves proximity seeking toward attachment figures – especially in times of distress – and that it produces feelings of anxiety

[1] Geertjan Overbeek and Rutger C.M.E. Engels, Behavioral Science Institute; Marc Noom, Department of Intercultural Studies. Address correspondence to: Geertjan Overbeek, PO box 9104, 6500 HE - Nijmegen, The Netherlands, Phone: +31 24 361 27 05, Fax: +31 24 361 27 76, E-mail: g.overbeek@pwo.ru.nl

and grief with the actual or threatened loss of an attachment figure (Colin, 1996). These features point to the existence of two basic functions of attachment relationships: to provide support and protection in times of distress and to facilitate the autonomous exploration of the environment (Ainsworth, 1989). In other words, support and autonomy are important dimensions in individuals' intimate relationships – even beyond childhood. More specifically, earlier attachment experiences, in these respects, form the core of 'internal working models' that influence children's understanding of, and participation in, future relationships (Parkes and Stevenson-Hinde, 1982), and remain crucial to individuals' social-emotional adjustment. Despite this strong theoretical claim, however, the present body of research does not permit scholars to make clear-cut statements about the links between attachment concepts in childhood and later life stages (Vivona, 2000). This is mainly due to the existence of different assessment techniques aimed at the construct attachment across different life phases.

The bulk of attachment research has focused on individual differences between young children aged 10 to 18 months in a strange-situation procedure (Ainsworth, Blehar, Waters, and Wall, 1978). This experimental procedure consists of eight periods, which last about three minutes. During the successive periods, the child's behavior is observed while alone with its mother, confronted with a strange adult, left by the mother with the stranger, left completely alone, and reunited with its mother. Using this procedure, about 65% of all children can be classified as *securely attached* – actively achieving proximity and/or interaction with mother upon her return. About 20% of the children fall into the category *avoidantly attached* – not disturbed by mother's absence in their intense and active exploration of the environment, but actively avoiding mother when she returns, or showing neutral behavior toward her. Finally, about 10% of the infants can be classified as *ambivalently attached* – showing both contact seeking behavior and avoidance when the mother returns. This threefold typology had been identified in many subsequent studies, performed in many different cultures (Van IJzendoorn and Kroonenberg, 1988). Later, eight subcategories were differentiated within this threefold typology, and a category of 'disorganized attachment' was added that could be assigned in conjunction with one of the three primary classifications (Main and Solomon, 1985). The validity of the strange situation has been demonstrated by research showing cortisol levels and heart rates increase after the separation from mother (Spangler and Grossmann, 1999), and by research showing that outcomes in the strange situation procedure correspond to the mother's sensitivity to her child's attachment needs (Isabella and Belsky, 1991).

For obvious reasons, researchers interested in parental attachment during adolescence can not make use of a strange situation procedure. Instead, they have designed self-report measures to assess parental attachment in adolescents, such as a Parental Bonding Instrument (PBI; Parker, Tupling, and Brown, 1979), a Parental Attachment Questionnaire (PAQ; Kenny, 1990), and an Inventory of Parent and Peer Attachment (IPPA; Armsden and Greenberg, 1987). This has limited the study of attachment to parents across the life span, for none of these measures differentiates between the two insecure styles of avoidant and ambivalent attachment (Greenberger and McLaughlin, 1998). The PAQ and IPPA, for instance, exclusively provide rules for coding 'high security' or 'low security' in adolescents. In addition, the PBI relies on peoples' autobiographic memories concerning the first 16 years of life, which means that it does not exclusively focus on parental attachment in adolescence. Unfortunately, a solution to this problem cannot be found in adapting adult attachment measures (e.g., Hazan and Shaver, 1987; Collins and Read, 1990) for adolescent populations, for these instruments too may not be sufficiently sensitive to discriminate between the two insecure attachment styles, or in other cases focus exclusively on romantic attachment styles rather than parent-child attachment (Brennan, Clark, and Shaver, 1998). Although attachment interviews have been developed specifically for adolescent populations (Allen et al., 2005), these can not be used in large-scale population studies simply because they consume too much time. At present, we know of only one questionnaire – the Behavioral Systems Questionnaire (BSQ; Furman, Simon, Shaffer, and Bouchey, 2002) – that assesses 'relational styles' with parents, friends, and partners during adolescence.

Apart from the issue of incompatible measures of parental attachment across different life periods, however, one may also question the use of the term 'attachment' when adapting a measure such as the IPPA, for instance. Whereas some authors stringently define attachment as a variable that differentiates individuals on attachment behaviors (Crowell, Fraley, and Shaver, 1999), others have used the term attachment to refer to the affective quality of the parent-child bond (Noom, Deković, and Meeus, 1999). In a recent study, Vivona (2000) addressed this issue by using adolescents' IPPA scores to construct three attachment styles that converged with styles inferred from infants' behaviors in the strange situation procedure – secure, avoidant, and ambivalent attachment. However, the IPPA has been stated to be a measure of the general affective quality of late adolescents' relationships with parents (Heiss, Berman, and Sperling, 1996), and the three subscales of Alienation, Trust, and Communication are usually taken to provide information on the degree and quality of involvement with parents (Armsden and Greenberg, 1987). Nevertheless, Vivona defined three IPPA-based attachment styles that would match Ainsworth's original 3-way classification. The secure style is characterized by trust and respectful communication with parents, in a context of sufficient autonomy. In accordance, Vivona identified secure attachment as high Trust, at least medium Communication, and low Alienation. The avoidant style is characterized by a lack of trust which, in combination with feelings of anger, leads to avoidance of the attachment figure. Vivona accordingly identified avoidant attachment based on the IPPA as low or medium Trust, low Communication, and at least medium Alienation. Finally, an ambivalent attachment style is characterized by active engagement with parents on the one hand, and a diminished trust in parents and feelings of alienation toward them on the other. Thus, Vivona identified ambivalent attachment as low or medium Trust, and at least medium Communication and Alienation.

In a first study among 159 undergraduates aged 18 to 23, Vivona examined the construct validity of the 3-way IPPA classification by linking it to another measure of parental attachment, the PAQ (Kenny, 1990) and theoretically related constructs: worrying, depression, and anxiety. Vivona was able to identify 84% of all respondents as belonging to one of the three attachment styles – 50% were designated securely, 31% avoidantly attached, and 19% ambivalently attached. The results showed that securely attached youths had significantly higher scores than their insecurely attached peers on three PAQ dimensions of affective quality of attachment, fostering of autonomy, and emotional support. Furthermore, securely attached respondents had lower mean levels of worries, depression, and anxiety in comparison with the insecurely attached respondents. Ambivalent students did not differ from avoidant students in terms of fostering of autonomy in the ANOVA, however. In a second study among 170 first-year students aged 16 to 20, Vivona replicated most of these results. In total 74% of all respondents fell into one of the three attachment styles – 46% were designated securely, 33% avoidantly, and 21% ambivalently attached. Again, IPPA-based securely attached youths reported higher levels of quality of attachment, fostering of autonomy, and emotional support, and lower levels of depression and anxiety than insecurely attached youths. The results demonstrated that ambivalent students differed from avoidant students in terms of PAQ affective quality and support, but not with regard to PAQ fostering of autonomy – similar to Study 1. No differences were found between ambivalent and avoidant attachment with regard to youths' social-emotional adjustment, except for openness and comfort in relationships.

Importantly, previous studies demonstrated that measurement precision is not constant across the entire range of the concept of 'parental attachment' in different kinds of dimensional measures of adult attachment (Fraley, Waller, and Brennan, 2000). Thus, we may expect that the IPPA is – psychometrically speaking – more sensitive in distinguishing secure from insecure attachments (i.e., in the high-medium range of Trust and Communication, and in the low range of Alienation) than it is in differentiating between different types of insecure attachment (i.e., in the lower range of scores on Trust and Communication, and the medium-high range on Alienation). Until now, unfortunately, no information exists with regard to the IPPA in this respect. Other issues are to be resolved as well before the IPPA-scores can be used by researchers or clinicians to designate adolescents to attachment styles. Firstly, Vivona exclusively conducted her surveys among adolescents aged 16 to 23 – people involved in undergraduate college programs. At present, we do not know whether the IPPA can be used effectively to differentiate between three attachment styles in younger populations of early and middle adolescents (i.e., aged 12 to 16) who are enrolled in secondary schools. Secondly, in examining relationships between IPPA-based attachment styles and adolescents' psychosocial adjustments, Vivona exclusively focused on internalizing problem behaviors such as depression and anxiety. However, theoretically relevant constructs with regard to problem behavior may also be found in the domains of delinquency or conduct problems (Loeber and Stouthamer-Loeber, 1986; Goetting, 1994). Thirdly, the present empirical evidence is based entirely on adolescents' self-reports. Thus, the links between attachment styles and adjustment measures may be overestimated due to uni-rater bias, while people have a general tendency to respond positively to different types of questions – among other things about the quality of the relationship with parents and about themselves.

STUDY 1

In the present chapter we report on findings from two studies. The purpose of these studies was to examine whether adolescents' scoring-patterns on the IPPA would converge with a 3-way classification of attachment styles (i.e., secure, avoidant, and ambivalent), and whether an IPPA-based attachment classification would have sufficient construct and convergent reliability. To this aim, in Study I we used data from a sample of 508 Dutch adolescents aged 12-18 and their parents. First of all, we tested whether Vivona's IPPA-based attachment classification could be replicated in our Dutch sample, and to what extent this theoretically delineated classification would converge with an empirical differentiation made – by means of cluster analysis – between IPPA-based attachment styles. Then, we examined to what extent the IPPA-based attachment styles would be linked to theoretically related constructs in the realm of adolescents' social-emotional functioning (i.e., self-esteem, autonomy, social competence), and internalizing and externalizing problem behaviors (i.e., depressive moods, deviant behavior), and whether the IPPA-based attachment classification would have significant predictive power with regard to these variables above conventional IPPA scale values. Lastly, we examined whether youths' self-reports on the IPPA would be associated with parent reports of family cohesion, responsiveness, and fostering of autonomy.

Previous research showed significant associations between lower scores on the IPPA and lower social-emotional functioning in terms of social skills and competence (Engels, Finkenauer, Meeus, and Deković, 2001). Accordingly, we assumed that insecurely attached respondents would report lower levels of social competence as compared to securely attached respondents. We expected to find no differences, however, between ambivalently and avoidantly attached adolescents, because both groups were deemed to have encountered sub-optimal family environments to develop social skills. As for self-esteem and autonomy the literature suggested that, based on a 'distant' relationship with parents and feelings of parental rejection during their upbringing, avoidantly attached adolescents would be likely to develop a tendency toward self-reliance and self-awareness (Kobak and Sceery, 1988). This would cause them to report relatively high levels of autonomy. In contrast, ambivalent adolescents were expected to report lower levels of autonomy or self-esteem than their securely attached peers. Their parents' inconsistent behavior could have frustrated their development into autonomy and self-awareness (Cassidy and Berlin, 1994).

With regard to the associations between parental attachment and problem behaviors, many previous studies have shown significant linkages between lower-quality attachments and emotional maladjustment and depressive moods (e.g., Burbach and Bourduin, 1986; Nada Raja, McGee, and Stanton, 1992), and delinquent and deviant behaviors (Mak, 1990; 1994). Both avoidant and ambivalently attached youths are theorized to have experienced low-quality bonds with their parents during childhood. It has been suggested (Bretherton, 1985; Parkes and Stevenson-Hinde, 1982), that these low-quality bonds are incorporated into insecure 'working models' of intimacy in which people perceive themselves as unworthy of love, and others as emotionally unavailable or unresponsive. In turn, this may cause adolescents to interpret disappointments or conflicts as personal failures, contributing to the development of distress (Kenny and Rice, 1995) and depression (Dozier, Stovall, and Albus, 1999). As for deviant behavior and delinquency, we hypothesized that avoidantly attached adolescents would report higher levels of deviant and delinquent behavior than securely and ambivalently attached youths, because avoidantly attached individuals tend to downplay the importance of their intimate bonds and often exhibit relatively low self-and-other awareness (Kobak and Sceery, 1988; Vivona, 2000), which may be precipatory factors in the development of aggression and other types of externalizing problem behaviors.

Across the groups of secure, ambivalent, and avoidant attachments, we expected that there would be decreasing levels of family cohesion and responsiveness. Previous research demonstrated that parental responsiveness is a primary cause of differentiation between the three attachment styles (Isabella and Belsky, 1991). Similarly, we expect family cohesion – a variable that is positively associated with responsiveness of family members toward each other (Henry, Sager, and Plunkett, 1996) – to be highest in the families of securely attached respondents, intermediate in the families of ambivalently attached respondents, and lowest in the families of avoidantly attached respondents. Finally, we expected that fostering of autonomy would be highest in parents with avoidant offspring and in parents of securely attached children. The lowest levels of fostering of autonomy were expected to be found in families with ambivalently attached children.

Moreover, Bowlby (1988) stated that parental attachment would exert similar effects on the development of social-emotional functioning and problem behaviors for men and women. However, other scholars have provided evidence for the fact that men, generally, are affected to a greater extent by parental attachment than women (Berman and Sperling, 1991; Schultheiss and Blustein, 1994). Therefore, we examined gender main effects and gender x attachment style interaction terms by investigating the associations between attachment styles and the different outcome variables. In addition, because of the relatively wide age group involved in the present study (i.e., 12-18 years) we defined two separate age groups, one of 12-14 years and one of 15-18 years, and exploratively investigated whether the associations between attachment styles and each of the outcome measures would be different across age groups.

METHODS

Procedure and Sample

The sample consisted of 508 Dutch adolescents who participated in a national survey on family relationships and child development (i.e., 'Parenting in the Netherlands', Rispens, Hermanns, and Meeus, 1996). Participants were 254 boys and 254 girls aged 12 to 18 (*M* age = 14.7, *SD* = 2.0) and their parents. The sample consisted of 467 fathers (*M* age = 46.1, *SD* = 5.0) and 502 mothers (*M* age = 43.9, *SD* = 4.6). The data were collected via a questionnaire battery administered to the adolescents during a home visit. The adolescents were living with both parents. All subjects were pupils from various secondary schools – comparable to the high schools in the US – (11% with lower vocational education, 40% with intermediate general or vocational education, 25% with higher general or vocational education, and 24% with pre-university education). Respondents were predominantly white and from a wide range of socio-economic backgrounds. Socio-economic status was based on parental occupation and education, with 28 % of the families classified as blue-collar (i.e., unskilled labor, skilled labor, and lower-grade civil servants), 63% as white-collar (i.e., tradesmen, office workers, and higher-grade civil servants), and 9% as professional (i.e., managers, academic and technical occupations).

Measures

Parental Attachment. The Inventory of Parent and Peer Attachment (IPPA; Armsden and Greenberg, 1987) was used to measure parental attachment. The IPPA attempts to measure parental attachment by assessing the 'affectively toned cognitive expectancies' with regard to individuals' trust in the accessibility and responsiveness of an attachment figure (Lyddon, Bradford and Nelson, 1993). The IPPA in itself does not allow the classification of attachment styles. Rather, the subscales of the IPPA are indicative of the relative degree of perceived parental security by adolescents. For our present purposes, we used the translated and adapted version of the original 28-item IPPA parent subscale (Deković and Noom, 1996), with 24 items consisting of three subscales of 8 items each (4 items for each parent): Trust (e.g., 'My mother/father respects my feelings'), Communication (e.g., 'I always tell my mother/father about my problems and worries') and Alienation (e.g., 'I am angry with my mother/father'). Response categories ranged from 1 never to 5 always. Empirical research on the psychometric properties showed high internal consistencies (Nada Raja, McGee and Stanton, 1992; Papini, Roggman and Anderson, 1991; Paterson, Pryor, and Field, 1995) and a high 3-week test-retest reliability was reported. With regard to the construct and convergent validity of the instrument, several studies demonstrated a 3-factor structure to underlie the IPPA items (Armsden and Greenberg, 1987; McCarthy, Moller, and Fouladi, 2001) and showed that the IPPA correlated in the expected direction with different dimensions of well-being and adjustment (Benson, Harris, and Rogers; 1992; Cotterell, 1992; Helsen, Vollebergh, and Meeus, 1999). The alphas for the subscales in the present study ranged between .66 and .74. IPPA-subscales (Communication, Trust, and Alienation) were divided in the lowest third, middle third, and highest third. The same cut-off points were used for boys and girls. Attachment styles were based on the IPPA classification rules as previously set forward by Vivona (2000).

Autonomy. Adolescent autonomy was measured by using a self-report questionnaire (Noom, Deković, and Meeus, 1999; adapted from Bekker, 1993). This self-report questionnaire consisted of 15 items about the ability to exercise control over one's life. The items referred to the perception of goals by means of opportunities and desires (e.g., 'I know what I want'), the perception of independence through self-confidence and individuality (e.g., 'I have the tendency to give in to others easily' – reversely coded), and the perception of strategies by means of self-regulation and self-control (e.g., 'I always go straight for my goal'). Cronbach's alpha for this scale was .79. Adolescents were asked to respond to each item on a 5-point scale ranging from 1 a very bad description of me to 5 a very good description of me. Previous research (Noom and Deković, 1999) already provided evidence for a high internal consistency of the instrument and showed that the original factor solution of Bekker's instrument was retained in the Dutch adapted version.

Self-esteem. The Rosenberg Self-esteem Scale assesses the balance of positive and negative feelings toward oneself (Rosenberg, 1965; Van der Linden, Dijkman, and Roeders, 1983). Respondents provided information on their current self-esteem on a 4-point scale, ranging from 1 a very bad description of me to 4 a very good description of me (10 items, α = .86). A sample item is 'I am satisfied with my self'. Rosenberg's self-esteem scale is one of the most frequently used assessments of general self-esteem. Gray-Little, Williams, and Hancock (1997) carried out an extensive study on the psychometric properties of this scale, and found high internal consistencies (alphas between .72 and .85), and a high test-retest reliability of .82 with an interval of two weeks and one of .63 with an interval of six months. Furthermore, their study demonstrated a unidimensional factor structure to best fit their data, providing evidence for the construct validity of the instrument.

Social competence. The social competence subscale of the Adolescent Self-Perception Profile (Harter, 1985; Straathof and Treffers, 1989) includes 5 items, which question adolescents whether they perceive themselves as popular, as having many friends, and as making friends easily (α = .68). The participants are asked to read two alternatives (e.g., 'A: Some people do not easily make friends, B: Others make friends easily') and choose the one that fits one's personality best, with answers on a 4-point scale (1 A is very true for me, 2 A is moderately true for me, 3 B is moderately true for me, 4 B is very true for me).

Depressive mood. The Kandel and Davies depressive mood scale (6 items, α = .75) consists of 6 items that measure psychological symptoms of internalized distress during the past 12 months (Kandel and Davies, 1982). Answers are given on a 5-point scale, ranging from 1 never to 5 always. A sample item is 'How often did you feel nervous and tense in the last year?' The Kandel Depression Scale is extensively employed in adolescent surveys (see review by Compas, Ey and Grant, 1993). Previous studies have shown sufficient internal consistency reliability, test-retest reliability and stability of scores of this measure over time.

Deviant behavior. The measure of externalized problem behavior taps the frequency of involvement in deviant behaviors in the last 12 months such as theft, drug use, vandalism, and aggressive behavior (Deković, Noom, and Meeus, 1997). Three subscales were distinguished. Aggressive behavior (7 items) refers to violent behavior towards other persons (e.g., 'being actively involved in a fight'). Substance use (4 items) refers to the use of stimulants (e.g., 'smoking marihuana'). Antisocial behavior (6 items) refers to inappropriate behavior towards authority figures (e.g., 'ignoring your parents'). Problem behavior has been scaled on a 4-point scale, ranging from 1 never to 4 more than 10 times. Cronbach's alpha of the present study for the total deviant behavior-scale was .71.

Family cohesion. Family cohesion was defined as the emotional closeness that family members experience towards each other (Olson, Portner and Lavee, 1985; Buurmeyer and Hermanns, 1988). Both parents and adolescents answered to 20 items (e.g., 'Our family is more important to us than any friendship') on a 4-point scale, ranging from 1 never true to 4 always true. Higher scores on this instrument are generally indicative of healthy family functioning. Cronbach's alpha was .83 for adolescents and .80 for parents. In a review study of popular, often-used instruments for family assessments Skinner (1987) concluded that the family cohesion scale of Olson et al. had adequate construct validity.

Responsiveness. This concept was measured for both parents and adolescents by an 8-item questionnaire (Gerris et al., 1993). The instrument assessed the tendency of parents to be aware of the child's needs (e.g., 'My mother knows very well what I want or feel'). The answers were given on a 6-point scale, ranging from 1 I completely disagree to 6 I completely agree. Cronbach's alpha was .92 for adolescents and .85 for parents.

Fostering autonomy. This concept was measured using a 7-item questionnaire (Gerris et al., 1993). This instrument assessed the tendency of parents to stimulate independence and individual responsibility (e.g., 'My father encourages me to make my own decisions'). The answers were given on a 6-point scale, ranging from 1 I completely disagree to 6 I completely agree. Cronbach's alphas were .81 for adolescents and .72 for parents.

RESULTS

Attachment style was determinable for 417 (82%) of the 508 adolescents by using the cut-off points as proposed by Vivona (2000). Of this sample 227 adolescents (54%) were designated securely, 86 (21%) were designated ambivalently, and 104 (25%) were designated avoidantly attached. These percentages are roughly similar to those reported by Vivona (2000). Descriptive statistics for adolescent outcome scores are shown in Table 1. A K-means cluster analysis showed that the 3-way attachment classification could not readily be differentiated empirically on the basis of the conventional IPPA scale values for Communication [F = 488,85, p < .001], Trust [F = 421,13, p < .001], and Alienation [F = 177,02, p < .001]. The cluster solutions were generally in line with a secure – insecure differentiation across IPPA scores. Specifically, two clusters were found in which respondents scored around or above mean levels of Trust and Communication, and below the mean level of Alienation, and one cluster was found in which respondents scored below the mean level of Trust and Communication, and above average on Alienation.

Table 1. Means of Social-Emotional Functioning and Problem Behaviors for Secure, Ambivalent, and Avoidant Attachment in Adolescents (N = 417)

	Secure (n = 227)	Ambivalent (n = 86)	Avoidant (n = 104)	Univariate F-tests	Scheffe contrast tests
Social competence	3.03	3.01	2.91	1.27	ns
Autonomy	3.50	3.39	3.28	5.27***	S < Am, Av
Self-esteem	3.26	3.01	2.87	18.37***	S < Am, Av
Deviant behavior	0.28	0.43	0.60	23.15***	S < Am < Av
Depressive mood	2.16	2.41	2.57	16.94***	S > Am, Av

Note. ns = not significant, S = Secure, Am = Ambivalent, Av = Avoidant
*** p < .001

We then examined to what extent the *a priori* IPPA attachment classification would converge with respondents' cluster memberships based on the conventional IPPA scale values. The results from cross-tabulation analyses showed that there was a significant association between the theoretically delineated attachment classification and the empirically derived cluster memberships [T_1: χ^2 (4) = 266,30, p < .001]. Specifically, 100% of adolescents classified as securely attached belonged to one of the two empirically derived clusters of secure attachment. Furthermore, 76,9% of adolescents classified as avoidantly attached belonged to the insecure cluster (23,1% to one of the secure clusters – more specifically, the secure cluster in which only average, but not high levels of Trust and Communication were reported by the respondents). Of those youths classified as ambivalently attached, only 27,9% were correctly classified as insecurely attached (72,1% was assigned to one of the previously mentioned secure clusters).

A MANOVA for social competence, autonomy, self-esteem, deviant behavior, and depressive moods by attachment styles and gender (and an attachment style x gender interaction) was performed in order to examine whether the IPPA-based attachment styles were associated with adolescents' social-emotional functioning and problem behaviors. With regard to social competence, we found no significant effects for attachment styles [F(2, 417) = 1.27, p = .26, ns] or sex [F(1, 417) = .04, p = .84, ns]. A significant effect, however, was found for age [F(1, 417) = 4.63, p = .03]. Older adolescents had higher levels of social competence than younger adolescents. As for autonomy, significant effects were found for attachment styles [F(2, 417) = 5.27, p < .01], sex [F(1, 417) = 3.98, p < .05], and age [F(1, 417) = 4.48, p < .05]. Post-hoc tests for attachment styles indicated that the secure group showed a higher level of autonomy than the ambivalent and avoidant groups. In addition, boys reported higher levels of autonomy than girls, and older adolescents reported higher levels of autonomy than younger adolescents. With regard to self-esteem, significant effects were found for attachment styles [$F(2, 417) = 18.37, p < .001$], and sex [$F(1, 417) = 13.39, p < .001$], but not for age [$F(1, 417) = 1.97, p = .16$, ns.]. Post-hoc tests for attachment styles indicated that the secure group had a higher level of self-esteem than the ambivalent and avoidant groups. Furthermore, girls generally reported lower levels of self-esteem than boys.

Scores on the measures of deviant behavior were found to differ across attachment styles [$F(2, 417) = 23.15, p < .001$], sex [$F(1, 417) = 12.83, p < .001$], and age groups [$F(1, 417) = 22.43, p < .001$]. Post-hoc tests for attachment styles indicated that the secure group showed a lower level of deviant behavior than the ambivalent group, and the ambivalent group reported a lower level of deviant behavior than the avoidant group. In addition, girls had lower levels of deviant behavior than boys, and older adolescents had higher levels of deviant behavior than younger adolescents. With regard to depression, the results indicated significant effects for attachment styles [$F(2, 417) = 16.94, p < .001$], and sex [$F(1, 417) = 17.35, p < .001$], but not for age [$F(1, 417) = .56, p = .45$, ns.]. Post-hoc tests for attachment styles indicated that the secure group showed a lower level of depressive moods than both the ambivalent and the avoidant group. Girls reported higher levels of depressive moods than boys.

Notably, the Pearson correlations between the IPPA subscales of Communication, Trust, and Alienation ranged from .36 to .60 ($p < .001$). In order to examine whether the IPPA-based attachment classification would have significant predictive power above the conventional IPPA subscales, we performed a MANCOVA in which we predicted youths' social-emotional functioning and problem behaviors on the basis of the IPPA attachment styles as *factor* and the conventional IPPA scale-values as *covariates*. The results demonstrated that the IPPA attachment style-factor did not significantly predict social-emotional functioning and problem behavior above the conventional IPPA scales [$F(10, 414) = 0{,}65$, *ns*].

Next, a MANOVA was computed for both adolescent-reported and parent-reported family cohesion (see Table 2).

Table 2. Means (Adolescent and Parent Reports) of Family Cohesion and Parenting Behaviors for Secure, Ambivalent, and Avoidant Attachment in Adolescents (N = 417)

	Secure (n = 227)	Ambivalent (n = 86)	Avoidant (n = 104)	Univariate F-tests	Scheffe contrast tests
Adolescent Reports					
Cohesion	3.01	2.86	2.66	39.47***	S>Am>Av
Responsiveness	4.84	4.52	3.31	134.45***	S>Am>Av
Fostering autonomy	4.03	4.03	3.75	4.14**	S, Am>Av
Parent Reports					
Cohesion	3.14	3.10	3.00	13.93***	S, Am>Av
Responsiveness	4.97	4.79	4.70	12.12***	S>Am, Av
Fostering autonomy	4.35	4.32	4.43	ns	--

Note. ns = not significant, S = Secure, Am = Ambivalent, Av = Avoidant
** $p < .01$, *** $p < .001$

The results with regard to adolescent-reported cohesion scores by attachment styles, sex, and age indicated significant 'between subjects' effects for attachment styles [$F(2, 414) =$

39.47, $p < .001$] and age [$F(1, 414) = 9.07$, $p < .001$]. Post-hoc tests for attachment styles indicated that the secure group showed a higher level of family cohesion than the ambivalent group, and that the ambivalent group reported a higher level of family cohesion than the avoidant group. Furthermore, younger adolescents reported higher levels of family cohesion than older adolescents. As for parent-reported cohesion, the results indicated significant effects for attachment styles [$F(2, 417) = 13.93$, $p < .001$] and age [$F(1, 417) = 7.63$, $p < .001$]. Post-hoc tests for attachment styles indicated that the secure group and the ambivalent group reported a higher level of family cohesion than the avoidant group. In accordance with the reports of the children, the parents of younger adolescents experienced more family cohesion than the parents of older adolescents.

With regard to parental responsiveness, the MANOVA indicated that for adolescent-reported responsiveness, scores differed by attachment styles only [$F(2, 416) = 134.45$, $p < .001$]. Post-hoc tests for attachment styles indicated that the secure group showed a higher level of responsiveness than the ambivalent group, and the ambivalent group reported a higher level of responsiveness than the avoidant group. The parent-reported responsiveness scores differed for attachment styles [$F(2, 417) = 12.12$, $p < .001$] and sex [$F(1, 417) = 5.31$, $p < .002$], but not for age. The post-hoc tests for attachment styles indicated that the secure group reported a higher level of responsiveness than the ambivalent and avoidant groups. Additionally, parents reported somewhat higher levels of responsiveness towards daughters than towards sons. As for adolescent-reported fostering of autonomy, the results demonstrated a significant effect for attachment styles [$F(2, 417) = 4.14$, $p < .05$] and age [$F(1, 417) = 10.63$, $p < .001$]. Post-hoc tests for attachment styles indicated that the secure group and the ambivalent group reported a higher level of fostering of autonomy than the avoidant group. In addition, parents reported to grant more autonomy to their older children than to their young children. Finally, the MANOVA showed that there were no significant effects with regard to parent-reported fostering of autonomy scores by attachment styles, sex and age.

Discussion

With regard to an IPPA-based attachment classification, this study presented a pattern that was comparable to the pattern of Vivona (2000) – about 55% of the respondents were securely attached, 20% were ambivalently attached, and 25% were avoidantly attached. This is not surprising, however, considering the fact that we employed IPPA cut-off scores identical to those employed by Vivona. Furthermore, in accordance with Vivona's results our study shows that a 3-way IPPA classification enhances the number of identified cases (82%) in comparison with the original secure-insecure differentiation made by Armsden and Greenberg (1987), who classified only 66% of their sample.

The findings of the present study replicated Vivona's (2000) findings with regard to the construct validity of the IPPA-based attachment classification. As expected on the basis of attachment theory, ANOVA outcomes demonstrated significantly higher levels of self-esteem and autonomy in securely attached adolescents compared to ambivalently or avoidantly attached peers. In contrast, however, no significant differences were found between secure and insecure styles on our measure of social competence. This finding may be explained by looking at the specific item-content of the social competence measure. Perceiving oneself as popular and having many friends, for example, may not entirely be accounted for by one's competence in social interactions but may also be a consequence of the affiliation with one specific, popular peer group member. Also, socially competent children may not necessarily have many friends and do not necessarily make friends easily.

The present results indicate that distinctions between specific types of insecurely attached adolescents are, in most cases, not to be found. This actually replicates Vivona's (2000) results, who concluded that 'distinctions between types of insecurely attached adolescents were less pervasive' (p. 321). We found evidence for only one of the hypothesized group differences between ambivalent and avoidant attachments; avoidantly attached youths reported higher levels of deviant behaviors than ambivalently attached youths did. Overall, the absence of significant differences between these groups may suggest that the IPPA-based 3-way attachment classification does not yield a highly sensitive procedure for establishing group differences between avoidant and ambivalent attachment in adolescence. This conclusion is supported also by the fact that results from a cluster analysis yielded a differentiation between two secure groups and one 'general' insecure group.

The present study had a multi-informant character which enabled us to examine, more stringently than was done by Vivona, whether self-reports of parental attachment would be linked to parent reports of family cohesion, responsiveness, and fostering of autonomy. In contrast with a first uni-informant analysis – which showed that secure adolescents had higher levels of family cohesion and responsiveness – the multi-informant analyses provided us with results that opposed our *a priori* hypotheses. Specifically, securely attached adolescents did not have parents who experienced higher levels of family cohesion than ambivalently attached youths. In addition, no significant differences were found in parents' fostering of autonomy between the three IPPA-based attachment styles. Finally, although reliable group differences were obtained between securely and insecurely attached youths on parents' responsiveness, no differences were observed between ambivalently and avoidantly attached youths. Overall, these findings contradict those of Vivona, who found significant contrasts of IPPA avoidant versus ambivalent styles on the PAQ dimensions of affective quality of attachment, fostering of autonomy, and emotional support.

In order to rule out the possibility that the results described above would be specific for this one particular sample, a second study was performed. The primary objectives of Study 2 were to longitudinally examine the linkages between the IPPA-based attachment styles and adolescents' social-emotional adjustment and problem behaviors. In doing so, multiple dependent variables were assessed (i.e., social-emotional adjustment: loneliness and stress – problem behaviors: delinquency, depressive mood, and aggression). Notably, Study 2 concerned a larger sample ($N = 1{,}012$) than Study 1 and, in addition, was characterized not by a cross-sectional design but instead by a 3-wave longitudinal design. This allowed us to conduct a stringent test with regard to the role of the IPPA-based attachment styles at T_1 and T_2 in predicting outcome measures at T_3, by controlling for earlier levels of social-emotional adjustment and problem behaviors at T_1. In addition, the longitudinal design allowed us to investigate the stability of IPPA-based attachment styles, and to link the (in)stability in attachment styles to subsequent developments in social-emotional adjustment and problem behavior during adolescence.

STUDY II

In our second study, we again tested whether the IPPA-based attachment classification could be replicated and to what extent this theoretically based classification would converge with an empirical differentiation made – by means of cluster analysis – between IPPA-based attachment styles. Secondly, we again examined to what extent these attachment styles would be linked to adolescents' social-emotional functioning (i.e., self esteem, loneliness, low sociability, shyness) and internalizing and externalizing problem behaviors (i.e., depressive mood, delinquency, aggression), and examined whether the IPPA-based attachment classification would have significant predictive powers with regard to these variables above conventional IPPA scale values. In this second study, we employed a 3-wave longitudinal design in order to control for the adolescents' earlier levels of social-emotional functioning and problem behaviors at T_1.

In addition to providing a longitudinal replication of Vivona's findings, the 3-wave design of the second study provided us with a unique opportunity to investigate the stability of IPPA-based attachment styles in adolescence. Until now, several previous studies prospectively examined the stability of attachment-related constructs over time in populations of adolescents or young adults (Keelan, Dion, and Dion, 1994; Kirkpatrick and Hazan, 1994; Scharfe and Bartholomew, 1995; Zimmermann and Becker-Stoll, 2002). These studies have found attachment styles to be stable in about 64% to 80% of respondents, although Keelan et al. (1994) found a lower stability rate of 50% for ambivalently attached respondents. These findings fit with the core notion of 'continuity of adaptation' in attachment theory, which states that parental attachment styles are moderately stable across time (Sroufe, Carlson, Levy, and Egeland, 1999). However, previous research has mostly focused on college student populations of young adults. Thus, the strength of the present study partly lies in its ability to provide insight into the stability of IPPA-based 'attachment'.

METHODS

Procedure and Sample

Data for analyses were derived from a large-scale survey among 1,012 Dutch 11 to 14-year-olds, carried out in the autumn of 2000. A total of 5 schools in 2 different provinces of the Netherlands were selected. All students of the first grade of secondary education of these schools were included, with a total of 49 classes. Before questionnaires were administered, parents had been informed about the aims of the study and were given the possibility to return a form stating they did not want their child to participate (none of the parents returned this form). The questionnaires were filled out in the classrooms in the presence of a teacher. No explicit refusals were recorded; non-response was exclusively due to absence on the day of assessment. A second wave was carried out in the spring of 2001, six months after the first wave, and a third wave in the autumn of 2001, twelve months after the first wave. Attention was drawn to the confidentiality of the responses (Botvin and Botvin, 1992). Letters of introduction and questionnaires emphasized privacy aspects and clearly stated that no personal information would be passed on to teachers or parents. In order to motivate respondents to participate, adolescents were able to participate in a lottery in which CD vouchers could be won.

The analyses for Study 2 were restricted to adolescents who provided us with complete data at each of the three waves (1,232 respondents participated in T_1, total response after 3 waves was 82%). This longitudinal sample consisted of 520 (50%) boys and 492 girls. The mean age was 12.3 (*SD* = .51), ranging from 11 to 14. The majority (97%) of the adolescent respondents were of Dutch origin. Ninety percent lived together with both parents, 8% with their mother, 1% with their father, and 1% in other settings. With regard to secondary education, 6% of the participants followed lower education, 39% average education, and 49% were involved in higher education programs.

Measures

All measures described below were assessed at all three waves. The instruments assessing parental attachment, self-esteem and depressive mood are similar to those employed in Study I. Cronbach's alphas of Rosenberg's (1965) self-esteem scale in this study were .79 (T_1), .83 (T_2) and .85 (T_3); for Kandel and Davies' (1982) depressive mood scale these were .77 (T_1), .80 (T_2) and .83 (T_3); and for Armsden and Greenberg's (1987) IPPA the alphas for the different subscales ranged from .71 to .82 at T_1 and from .73 to .86 at T_2.

Stress. A short form of the Perceived Stress Scale (PSS; Cohen, Kamarck and Mermelstein, 1983) was employed to measure the degree to which the respondent perceived his/her life as unpredictable, uncontrollable, or overloaded. This form is a translation of the 2-factor solution examined by Hewitt, Flett, and Mosher (1992) that assesses perceived general distress (7 items) and the perceived ability to cope with current stressors (4 items). Items were rated on a 5-point scale ranging from 1 *never* to 5 *very often*. The items of the subscale 'perceived ability to cope' were recoded. Thus, higher scores were associated with increased stress on both scales. Cronbach's alphas were .80 (T_1), .82 (T_2) and .83 (T_3). The PSS has good predictive validity, as was shown in the study by Hewitt et al. (1992), in which PSS scores were found to be positively related to scores on the Beck Depression Inventory.

Loneliness. Loneliness was assessed using the revised UCLA Loneliness scale (Russel, Peplau, and Cutrona, 1980), which had been translated into Dutch using a translation-back-translation procedure. The scale consists of 10 statements concerning the extent to which people feel lonely (e.g., 'I feel left out'). Respondents rated the items on 5-point scales ranging from 1 *not at all true for me* to 5 *very true for me*. Adolescents' responses were averaged to yield a loneliness score; higher values indicated greater feelings of loneliness. Cronbach's alphas were .84 (T_1), .85 (T_2) and .86 (T_3). Research on the psychometric properties of this instrument indicates that the measure is highly reliable in terms of internal consistency and test-retest reliability (Russel, 1996). Furthermore, it has a high convergent validity as indicated by significant correlations with other measures of loneliness, and a high construct validity as indicated by significant correlations with measures of the adequacy of the individual's interpersonal relationships and confirmatory factor analyses (Hartshorne, 1993).

Delinquency. Delinquent behavior was assessed with a widely employed instrument in the Netherlands, aiming to measure the frequency of engagement in petty crime of non-institutionalized adolescents (e.g., Baerveldt and Snijders, 1994; Houtzager and Baerveldt,

1999). Respondents were asked how many times in the past 12 months they had committed one or more of 25 minor offences, such as shoplifting, petty theft, vandalism and unarmed fights. Response categories ranged from 1 *not in the past 12 months* to 4 *4 times or more in the past 12 months*. Cronbach's alphas were .81 (T_1), .92 (T_2) and .89 (T_3). Previous research had already shown that this instrument owned a high level of internal consistency (Overbeek and Van Voornveld, 2003).

Aggression. Adolescents answered 8 questions on direct aggression. Items were 'I am mean to others', 'I destroy my own properties', 'I attack others physically', 'I scream or yell a lot', 'I act funny to get attention', 'I threaten others that I will hurt them', 'I make things up, or act cool', and 'I destroy properties of others'. The response categories ranged from 0 *does not apply to me at all* to 1 *applies to me sometimes* to 2 *applies to me often*. Items were adapted from the YSR (see Verhulst, Achenbach, Ferdinand, and Kasius, 1993). Cronbach's alphas were .70 (T_1), .75 (T_2) and .82 (T_3).

RESULTS

Separate t-tests showed no significant differences between the scores on the three IPPA subscales of the 520 boys and 492 girls at T_1 and T_2. Thus, a single set of cut-off points was used to determine attachment styles for both boys and girls (cf. Vivona, 2000). Using the classification rules, attachment styles could not be computed for 25% of the respondents at T_1 (26% at T_2 and 23% at T_3). At T_1, 385 (50%) were designated secure, 243 (32%) were designated avoidant, and 133 (18%) were designated ambivalent. At T_2, 404 (54%) were designated secure, 225 (30%) were designated avoidant, and 120 (16%) were designated ambivalent. At T_3, 410 (52%) were designated secure, 239 (31%) were designated avoidant, and 135 (17%) were designated ambivalent. A K-means cluster analysis at T_1 indicated that this 3-way attachment classification could also be differentiated empirically on the basis of conventional IPPA scale values for Communication [F = 890,61, $p < .001$], Trust [F = 496,13, $p < .001$], and Alienation [F = 861,53, $p < .001$]. Overall, the cluster solutions were in line with Vivona's *a priori* classification for the secure and avoidant groups (i.e., secure: high trust - high communication - low alienation, avoidant: low trust - low communication - high alienation), but this was slightly different for the ambivalent group (i.e., low trust – low (not medium or high) communication – low (not medium or high) alienation). At T_2 and T_3 the K-means cluster analyses produced similar outcomes.

We then examined whether the a priori IPPA-based attachment classification would converge with respondents' cluster memberships based on the conventional IPPA scale values. The results from cross-tabulation analyses showed that at each measurement wave there was a significant association between the theoretically delineated attachment classification and the empirically derived cluster memberships [T_1: χ^2 (4) = 537,19, $p < .001$; T_2: χ^2 (4) = 687,37, $p < .001$; T_3: χ^2 (4) = 608,47, $p < .001$]. However, we also found relatively large percentages of misclassifications. At T_1, 88,3% of the adolescents classified as securely attached belonged to the empirically derived cluster of secure attachment (while 11,7% belonged to the ambivalently attached cluster). Furthermore, 78,6% of the adolescents classified as avoidant belonged to the avoidantly attached cluster (while 21,4% belonged to the ambivalently attached cluster). With regard to the classification of ambivalent attachment only 30,8% were 'correctly' classified as ambivalently attached, as 53,4% belonged to the avoidant category. At T_2 and T_3, the cross-tabulations showed similar outcomes – with similarly high percentages of misclassifications in the ambivalently attached cluster (i.e., 63,6% at T_2 and 61,5% at T_3), and higher percentages of 'correctly' classified adolescents in the secure and avoidant attachment categories (i.e., ranging from 66,1% to 100%).

Next, we examined whether the IPPA-based attachment styles were associated with adolescents' social-emotional functioning and problem behaviors at the three waves. For T_1 data, a MANOVA for self-esteem, loneliness, stress, depressive mood, aggression, and delinquency by attachment styles and gender (and an attachment style x gender interaction) revealed main effects for attachment styles [$F(6, 690) = 20.26, p < .001$] and for gender [$F(3, 693) = 23.60, p < .001$], but not for the attachment styles x gender interaction [$F(3, 693) = 1.60$, *ns*] (see Table 3). Contrast analyses demonstrated that the securely attached adolescents had lower scores on loneliness and stress and higher scores on self-esteem than their ambivalent and avoidant peers.

Table 3. Means of Social-Emotional Functioning and Problem Behaviors for Secure, Ambivalent, and Avoidant Attachment in Adolescents (N = 696)

Wave 1	Secure (n = 360)	Ambivalent (n = 116)	Avoidant (n = 220)	Univariate F-tests	Scheffe contrast tests
Self-esteem	3.36	3.09	2.96	52.43***	S > Am > Av
Stress	1.96	2.38	2.48	82.75***	S < Am, Av
Loneliness	1.39	1.66	1.96	88.00***	S < Am < Av
Depressive mood	2.04	2.42	2.61	59.26***	S < Am, Av
Direct aggression	1.18	1.30	1.34	31.46***	S < Am, Av
Delinquency	1.10	1.21	1.22	17.61***	S < Am, Av
Wave 2	Secure (n = 389)	Ambivalent (n = 113)	Avoidant (n = 219)	Univariate F-tests	Scheffe contrast tests
Self-esteem	3.40	3.12	2.93	68.31***	S > Am > Av
Stress	2.04	2.26	2.52	52.48***	S < Am < Av
Loneliness	1.43	1.65	1.93	67.05***	S < Am < Av
Depressive mood	2.11	2.44	2.60	41.32***	S < Am, Av
Direct aggression	1.18	1.32	1.38	38.66***	S < Am, Av
Delinquency	1.11	1.26	1.31	15.88***	S < Am, Av
Wave 3	Secure (n = 394)	Ambivalent (n = 130)	Avoidant (n = 230)	Univariate F-tests	Scheffe contrast tests
Self-esteem	3.48	3.16	2.99	84.72***	S > Am > Av
Stress	1.99	2.38	2.54	84.22***	S < Am < Av
Loneliness	1.39	1.65	2.01	94.81***	S < Am < Av
Depressive mood	2.03	2.52	2.52	51.67***	S < Am, Av
Direct aggression	1.19	1.37	1.42	38.80***	S < Am, Av
Delinquency	1.11	1.25	1.28	18.42***	S < Am, Av

Note. S = Secure, Am = Ambivalent, Av = Avoidant
*** $p < .001$

The avoidant and ambivalent youths also differed in self-esteem (ambivalently attached adolescents scoring higher than avoidant adolescents) and loneliness (ambivalently attached adolescents scoring lower than avoidant adolescents). In addition, girls reported lower levels of self-esteem than boys. With regard to depression, aggression, and delinquency, the secure group also differed from the avoidant and ambivalent groups in the expected direction, with securely attached adolescents scoring lower than avoidant or ambivalently attached peers.

For T_2 data, a MANOVA of the social-emotional functioning and problem behavior scales by attachment styles and gender (and the attachment styles x gender interaction) again revealed main effects for attachment styles [$F(6, 715) = 19.15, p < .001$] and for gender [$F(3, 718) = 15.61, p < .001$], but not for gender by attachment styles interaction [$F(3, 718) = 1.38$, *ns*]. Contrast analyses (Table 3) demonstrated that the securely attached adolescents had lower scores on loneliness and stress, and higher scores on self-esteem than their ambivalent and avoidant peers. Again, the avoidant and ambivalent youths also differed in these variables. Also in line with T_1 findings, again, the girls reported lower levels of self-esteem than boys. Concerning depression, aggression, and delinquency, the secure group differed from the avoidant and ambivalent groups in the expected directions. For T_3 data, a similar MANOVA revealed main effects for attachment styles [$F(6, 748) = 23.06, p < .001$] and for gender [$F(3, 751) = 20.22, p < .001$], but not for gender by attachment styles interaction [$F(3, 751) = 1.62$, *ns*]. Contrast analyses showed similar findings as the results from T_1 and T_2.

Notably, at each of the three waves Pearson correlations between the IPPA subscales of Communication, Trust, and Alienation ranged from .43 to .67 ($p < .001$). In order to examine whether the IPPA-based attachment classification would have significant predictive powers above the conventional IPPA subscales, we performed three MANCOVAs (i.e., for T_1, T_2, and T_3 separately) in which we predicted adolescents' social-emotional functioning and problem behaviors on the basis of the IPPA attachment styles as *factors* and the conventional IPPA scale-values as *covariates*. The results demonstrated that only at T_1 the IPPA attachment styles factors significantly predicted social-emotional functioning and problem behavior above the conventional scale values from the IPPA [F (12, 1372) = 1,84, $p < .05$].

Cross-tabulations were conducted to examine the stability of attachment styles over time (see Table 4).

Table 4. Cross tabulation of Attachment Styles Reported by Adolescents at T_1, T_2, and T_3

		Wave 1	
Wave 2	Secure	Ambivalent	Avoidant
Secure	246 (81,5%)	44 (43,1%)	30 (16,3%)
Ambivalent	28 (9,3%)	39 (38,2%)	24 (13,1%)
Avoidant	28 (9,3%)	19 (18,6%)	130 (71,6%)
		Wave 2	
Wave3	Secure	Ambivalent	Avoidant
Secure	265 (78,4%)	34 (39,1%)	28 (16,3%)
Ambivalent	41 (12,1%)	28 (32,2%)	25 (14,5%)
Avoidant			

Note. T_1 to T_2: χ^2 (4, 588) = 282.93, $p < .001$, T_2 to T_3 χ^2 (4, 593) = 240.71, $p < .001$

Relatively high stability was found for each IPPA-based attachment style, as was indicated by a high chi-square value [χ^2 (4, 588) = 282.93, p < .001]. The probability of belonging to the secure group at T_2 was 81,5% for the secure group at T_1, the probability of belonging to the ambivalent group at T_2 was 38,2% for the ambivalent group at T_1, and the probability of belonging to the avoidant group at T_2 was 71,6% for the avoidant group at T_1. Similar findings were obtained for the time interval between T_2 and T_3 [χ^2 (4, 594) = 240.71, p < .001].

In order to examine the longitudinal associations between IPPA-based attachment styles at T_1 on adjustment measures at wave 3 logistic regression analyses were conducted in which T_1 and T_3 measures of adolescents' social-emotional functioning and problem behaviors were dichotomized. We controlled for earlier levels of social-emotional functioning and problem behaviors by including the T_1 measures in the first step of the regression model simultaneously with gender. Dependent variables were dichotomized based on scores of ≥ 1 *SD* above the mean. The IPPA-based attachment classification was entered as a categorical variable in the third step of the regression model (i.e., with secure attachment as the reference category). The findings with regard to problem behavior (see Table 5) showed that these behaviors were highly stable over time. Youths reporting depression or delinquency or aggressive behavior at T_1 were 3 to 4 times more likely to report these problems at T_3 than other youths at T_1. Concerning the relationships between attachment styles at T_1 and problem behaviors at T_3, it appeared that avoidant – but not ambivalently attached – adolescents were more likely than securely attached respondents to subsequently report internalizing and externalizing problem behaviors. Thus, the avoidant group was more likely to show aggressive, delinquent, or depressed behavior at wave 3 as compared to the secure group. In contrast, however, Table 6 demonstrates that both the avoidant and ambivalently attached adolescents were less likely to have high self-esteem and more likely to suffer from stress and loneliness as compared with the secure group. Next, we examined whether especially the respondents who were stable-avoidant or stable-ambivalently attached in early adolescence would be most likely to report problem behaviors and experience difficulties in social-emotional functioning – more than those respondents who were insecurely attached at only one measurement point.

Table 5. Logistic Regression Analyses of Problem Behaviors T_3 on Attachment Styles T_1

	Depressive mood T_3		Aggression T_3		Delinquency T_3	
	OR	95% CI	OR	95% CI	OR	95% CI
Depressive mood T_1	4.17***	3.00 – 5.78				
Aggression T_1			3.68***	2.65 – 5.12		
Delinquency T_1					3.97***	2.79 – 5.64
Attachment styles T_1						
Secure	1.00		1.00		1.00	
Ambivalent	1.39	0.90 – 2.16	1.38	.88 – 2.15	1.14	.71 – 1.84
Avoidant	1.70**	1.17 – 2.45	1.94***	1.35 – 2.81	1.53*	1.05 - 2.25

Note. All analyses are controlled for the effects of gender. Estimates of the final step of the equation are presented. OR = odds ratio. 95% CI = 95% confidence intervals.

* p < .05, ** p < .01, *** p <. 001

Table 6. Logistic Regression Analyses of Social-Emotional Functioning T_3 on Attachment Styles T_1

	Self-esteem T_3		Stress T_3		Loneliness T_3	
	OR	95% CI	OR	95% CI	OR	95% CI
Self-esteem T_1	4.18***	3.01 – 5.81				
Stress T_1			3.70***	2.76 – 5.13		
Loneliness T_1					3.21***	2.31 – 4.46
Attachment styles T_1						
Secure	1.00		1.00		1.00	
Ambivalent	0.62*	0.40 – 0.96	1.62*	1.05 – 2.50	2.82***	1.84 – 4.32
Avoidant	0.50***	0.35 – 0.73	2.28***	1.57 – 3.31	3.40***	2.34 – 4.95

Note. All analyses are controlled for the effects of gender, estimates of the final step of the equation are presented, OR = odds ratio, 95% CI = 95% confidence intervals.
* $p < .05$, ** $p < .01$, *** $p < .001$.

We examined this assumption by computing a new variable 'Attachment Stability' consisting of 9 groups (e.g., from Secure T_1 to Secure T_2, from Secure T_1 to Avoidant T_2, etcetera). Then, we computed the effects on social-emotional adjustment and problem behaviors at wave three, controlling for earlier levels of social-emotional adjustment and problem behaviors at wave 1 and gender. The regression analyses depicted in Tables 7 and 8 show that (a) the most adequate social-emotional functioning and fewest problem behaviors are reported by those who are securely attached at both waves, (b) overall, respondents who are insecurely attached at T_1 but securely attached at T_2 are not worse off as compared to those who are securely attached at both waves – except for the elevated risk for loneliness [ambivalent T_1 - secure T_2: $OR = 3.60, p < .001$; avoidant T_1 - secure T_2: $OR = 2.28, p < .05$] –, and (c) the strongest negative effects on social-emotional functioning and problem behaviors were found for those who remained avoidantly attached between T_1 and T_2 or became avoidant at T_2.

Table 7. Logistic Regression Analyses of Problem Behaviors T_3 on Attachment Style Stability T_1-T_2

		Depression T3		Aggression T3		Delinquency T3	
	N	OR	95% CI	OR	95% CI	OR	95% CI
S – S	246	1.00		1.00		1.00	
S – Am	28	1.07	0.44 – 2.60	0.55	0.22 – 1.39	1.21	0.48 – 3.01
S – Av	28	1.58	0.68 – 3.64	0.46	0.18 – 1.20	2.11	0.84 – 5.30
Am - Am	39	2.20*	1.02 – 4.75	1.65	0.78 – 3.50	1.06	0.47 – 2.38
Am - Av	19	1.23	0.44 – 3.50	1.93	0.66 – 5.64	2.31	0.74 – 7.19
Am - S	44	1.60	0.80 – 3.21	1.06	0.51 – 2.17	0.74	0.33 – 1.65
Av - Av	130	3.00***	1.79 – 4.94	1.98**	1.22 – 3.23	1.71*	1.04 – 2.84
Av - Am	24	1.53	0.62 – 3.77	3.57*	1.28 – 9.20	1.21	0.47 – 3.14
Av - S	30	0.80	0.34 – 1.86	1.04	0.46 – 2.37	0.87	0.33 – 2.33

Note. All analyses are controlled for the effects of gender and adjustment at T_1. Estimates of the final step of the equation are presented. OR = odds ratio, 95% CI = 95% confidence intervals, S = Secure, Am = Ambivalent, Av = Avoidant
* $p < .05$, ** $p < .01$, *** $p < .001$

Table 8. Logistic Regression Analyses of Social-Emotional Functioning T_3 on Attachment Style Stability T_1-T_2

		Self-esteem T_3		Stress T_3		Loneliness T_3	
	N	OR	95% CI	OR	95% CI	OR	95% CI
S – S	246	1.00		1.00		1.00	
S – Am	28	0.96	0.39 – 2.36	1.13	0.47 – 2.68	1.25	0.53 – 2.97
S – Av	28	0.43	0.18 – 1.03	3.54**	1.53 – 8.22	2.40*	1.04 – 5.54
Am - Am	39	0.31**	0.15 - 0.66	3.68***	1.70 – 7.98	2.82**	1.36 – 5.85
Am - Av	19	0.23*	0.07 – 0.73	3.46*	1.24 – 9.66	4.85***	1.71 – 13.75
Am – S	44	0.70	0.35 - 1.44	1.36	0.68 – 2.73	3.60***	1.78 – 7.25
Av - Av	130	0.38***	0.23 -0.64	4.42***	2.58 – 7.56	5.43***	3.18 – 9.27
Av - Am	24	0.25**	0.09 – 0.69	1.91	0.78 – 4.69	2.82*	1.10 – 7.27
Av – S	30	0.89	0.39 – 2.03	2.01	0.89 – 4.51	2.28*	1.02 – 5.13

Note. All analyses are controlled for the effects of gender and adjustment at T_1. Estimates of the final step of the equation are presented. OR = odds ratio, 95% CI = 95% confidence intervals, S = Secure, Am = Ambivalent, Av = Avoidant.

* $p < .05$, ** $p < .01$, *** $p < .001$

General Discussion

Overall, Study II replicated Study I with regard to the associations between IPPA-based attachment styles and adolescents' internalizing and externalizing problem behaviors. Although significant differences were observed between securely and insecurely attached respondents on measures of depressive mood, aggression, and delinquency, no contrasts were found between ambivalently attached and avoidant youths. Again, this finding replicates the results of Vivona (2000), who also found no pervasive distinctions between specific types of insecurely attached adolescents.

However, the results with regard to adolescents' social-emotional functioning in Study II differed noticeably from the outcomes of Study I – and from Vivona's (2000) study. Both measures of self-esteem and loneliness showed significantly higher scores for avoidant versus ambivalently attached adolescents. This discrepancy may be a consequence of the different age ranges in the two samples that were used. Study I examined youths aged 12-18, whereas Study II focused on early adolescents aged 11-14. Parental attachment may be especially significant for social-emotional functioning in early adolescents, because in this period parents are the primary source of social support and intimacy, whereas during middle and late adolescence many attachment functions are being transferred to intimate peer relationships (Ainsworth, 1989), which usually gain importance as sources of social support or closeness and interdependence (Furman and Buhrmester, 1992; Laursen and Williams, 1997). Because of its high significance, parental attachment is probably linked to a greater variability in scores on outcome measures during early adolescence in comparison with later stages in adolescence. In accordance, then, it probably is relatively easy to detect differences between specific types of insecure attachment in early adolescence.

The longitudinal design of Study II enabled us to examine the predictive value of the IPPA-based attachment classification controlling for earlier levels of social-emotional functioning and problem behaviors in adolescents. This is a major advantage over the majority of cross-sectional studies that have been carried out over the past two decades. In line with the earlier findings of Study I and of Vivona (2000) insecurely attached adolescents were found to report higher levels of aggression, delinquency, depressive mood, and self-esteem and lower levels of stress and loneliness. Notably, these findings correspond with the outcomes of previous cross-sectional research, which has shown that insecure attachment is negatively associated with self-esteem (Paterson et al., 1995), depressive moods (Engels et al., 2001), and general levels of emotional adjustment (Nada Raja et al., 1992).

However, in line with the MANOVAs we conducted in Study I and II, the regression models did not provide compelling evidence in favor of a tripartite definition of IPPA-based attachment styles. In particular, the results showed that only avoidant youths were placed at higher risk for the development of internalizing and externalizing problem behaviors in comparison with their securely attached peers. This may indicate that it is more satisfactory to define the IPPA as a measure of the general affective quality of parental bonds (Heiss et al., 1996), instead of an instrument that captures 'the secure base function' (Vivona, 2000). In line with the results of Study I and Study II, ,this conclusion is also supported by the fact that in studying linkages with an empirical cluster delineation, many respondents appeared to be incorrectly classified on the basis of Vivona's system as ambivalently attached, and the IPPA-based attachment classification did not predict significant adolescents' social-emotional functioning or problem behaviors above the conventional IPPA scale values.

The impression that the IPPA does not adequately capture individual differences in attachments, but rather captures a global perception of the quality of one's relationship with his parents, is nourished also by the longitudinal results with regard to attachment style stability. Although we found relatively high levels of stability in the secure and avoidant attachment styles across a six months time interval, lower levels of stability were found for ambivalent attachments. For instance, the likelihood of staying in the ambivalent category at T_2, for adolescents who were previously assessed as being ambivalently attached at T_1, was not any higher than the chance of becoming securely attached. It appears, then, as though the IPPA-based 'ambivalent' category represents a transient state rather than a stable attachment style. Earlier prospective studies that examined attachment style stability in college students found that, overall, about 50% to 80% of the respondents endorsed the same attachment style over time – intervals ranging from 4 months to 3 years (Keelan et al., 1994; Kirkpatrick and Hazan, 1994; Scharfe and Bartholomew, 1994). These overall stability rates are well above the stability rates of the IPPA-based ambivalent category in this study.

A possible explanation may be that the complicated decision rules as set forward by Vivona (2000) do not reflect a theoretically valid differentiation. Specifically, some overlap exists on the IPPA-dimension Communication between the ambivalent and secure styles (i.e., both scored medium or high on Communication), and on the dimension Alienation of ambivalent and avoidant attachments (i.e., both scored medium or high on Alienation). This may explain why many ambivalently attached youths switch to another attachment style over time, and it may also explain why levels of social-emotional functioning and problem behaviors in ambivalently attached respondents resemble, in many instances, those of either securely attached or avoidant peers. Another explanation for these findings may come from research based on the item response theory (IRT), which has demonstrated that measurement precision is not constant across the entire range of the concept of 'parental attachment' as assessed in different kinds of dimensional measures of adult attachments (see Fraley, Waller, and Brennan, 2000). Although the IPPA was not incorporated in the study by Fraley et al., it is possible that the IPPA is more sensitive in distinguishing secure from insecure attachment than it is in differentiating between three different types of attachment that sometimes rely on (too) subtle differences in mean scores on the IPPA subscales of Trust, Communication, and Alienation.

The current results should caution scholars and counselors alike to use the IPPA to classify individuals in terms of attachment styles. Before such a classification can be implemented in research and counseling practices – apart from more convincing evidence in longitudinal surveys conducted among adolescents from the general population – several other issues need to be resolved as well. First of all, it is necessary to compare attachment classifications in pen-and-paper measures like the IPPA to attachment classifications in 'golden standard' methods like the Adult Attachment Interview for example (AAI; Main and Solomon, 1985). Such a comparison is not without problems, however, as AAI classifications – in contrast with the IPPA – are based not on the contents but rather on the manner in which people reflect on their childhood relationships with parents. Nevertheless, previous attempts have been made to link the outcomes of pen-and-paper measures of attachment to the AAI. For instance, Van IJzendoorn et al. (1991) found a rather low overall correlation between the lack of warmth or overprotection dimensions of the PBI (Parker et al., 1979) with AAI insecure classifications. In another study, Manassis et al. (1999) showed that information obtained from the PBI was only comparable to information obtained from the AAI for people with 'optimal' attachment histories. Similar data for the IPPA are yet to be provided.

Another issue that would need to be resolved refers to the specific characteristics of attachment relationships. One of the main characteristics, supposed to underlie parental attachment, is that under conditions of stress or anxiety children actively seek support and safety in their bond with parents (Colin, 1996). However, it may well be possible that adolescents, who report high Communication and Trust and low Alienation in their relationship with parents on the IPPA, do not necessarily rely on their parents as attachment figures in times of stress. Therefore, it may be interesting to examine whether or not IPPA-based attachment classifications are linked to specific behavioral constellations in naturally occurring 'strange situations'. For instance, one might think of validation studies in which bio-physical information (e.g., heart beats, galvanic skin response, pupil dilations) is obtained, or of studies that focus on behavior in naturally occurring stress-provoking settings, for instance with separation settings in which spouses separate from each other or divorce (Fraley and Shaver, 1998).

In conclusion, Vivona's earlier studies (2000) represent an attempt to overcome a major obstacle in attachment research: the incompatibility of measures used to assess parental attachment across childhood and adolescence. Although Vivona concluded that her results 'supported the utility of the new technique to classify parental attachment…' (2000, p. 327) our multi-informant and longitudinal tests do not provide evidence in favor of this statement. Although insecurely attached adolescents reported more problem behaviors and lower social-emotional functioning than their securely attached peers, reports from the ambivalently attached respondents could not be unambiguously separated from those of securely attached or avoidant respondents. Also, IPPA-based attachment styles had no significant predictive powers above conventional scale values, and linking theoretically based classification with an empirical 3-way differentiation of attachment clusters revealed a relatively large percentage of misclassifications. As a result, at present the value of IPPA-based attachment classifications for research and counselling practice remains questionable.

REFERENCES

Ainsworth, M.D.S. (1989). Attachments beyond infancy. *American Psychologist, 44,* 709-716.

Ainsworth, M.D.S., Blehar, M.C., Waters, E., and Wall, S. (1978). *Patterns of attachment.* Hillsdale: Erlbaum.

Allen, J.P., Porter, M.R., McFarland, F.C., Marsh, P., and McElhaney, K.B. (2005). The Two Faces of Adolescents' Success With Peers: Adolescent Popularity, Social Adaptation, and Deviant Behavior. *Child Development*, 76, 747-760.

Armsden, G.C., and Greenberg, M.T. (1987). The inventory of parent and peer attachment: Individual differences and their relationship to psychological well-being in adolescence. *Journal of Youth and Adolescence, 16,* 427-454.

Baerveldt, C., and Snijders, T. (1994). Influences on and from the segmentation of networks: Hypotheses and tests. *Social Networks, 16(3),* 213-232.

Bekker, M.H. (1993). The development of an autonomy scale based on recent insights into gender identity. *European Journal of Personality, 7,* 177-194.

Benson, M.J., Harris, P.B., and Rogers, C.S. (1992). Identity consequences of attachment to mothers and fathers among late adolescents. *Journal of Research on Adolescence, 2,* 187-204.

Berman, W.H., and Sperling, M.B. (1991). Parental attachment and emotional distress in the transition to college. *Journal of Youth and Adolescence*, 20, 427-440.

Botvin, G.J., and Botvin, E.M. (1992). Adolescent tobacco, alcohol, and drug abuse: prevention strategies, empirical findings, and assessment issues. *Journal of Deviant Behavior and Pediatrics, 13(4),* 290-301.

Bowlby, J. (1988). Attachment and loss: Retrospect and prospect. *American Journal of Orthopsychiatry, 52(4),* 664-678.

Bretherton, I. (1985). Attachment theory: Retrospect and prospect. *Monographs of the Society for Research on Child Development, 50* (1-2, Serial No. 209).

Brennan, K.A., Clark, C.L., and Shaver, P.R. (1998). Self-report measurement of adult attachment: An integrative overview. In: W.S. Rholes and J.A. Simpson (Eds.), *Attachment theory and close relationships* (pp.46-76). New York, Guilford Press.

Burbach, D.J., and Borduin, C.M. (1986). Parent-child relations and the etiology of depression: A review of methods and findings. *Clinical Psychology Review, 6,* 133-153.

Buurmeyer, F.A., and Hermanns, P.C. (1988). *Gezins Dimensie Schalen* [family dimension scales]. Lisse: Zwets and Zeitlinger.

Cassidy, J., and Berlin, L.J. (1994). The insecure/ambivalent pattern of attachment: Theory and research. *Child Development, 65,* 971-981.

Cohen, S., Kamarck, T., Mermelstein, R.A. (1983). A global measure of perceived stress. *Journal of Health and Social Behavior, 24(4),* 385-396.

Colin, V.L. (1996). Human attachment. New York: McGraw-Hill.

Collins, N.L., and Read, S.J. (1990). Adult attachment, working models, and relationship quality in dating couples. *Journal of Personality and Social Psychology,* 58 (4), 644-663.

Compas, B.E., Ey, S., Grant, K.E. (1993). Taxonomy, assessment, and diagnosis of depression during adolescence. *Psychological Bulletin, 114(2),* 323-344.

Cotterell, J.L. (1992). The relations of attachments and support to adolescent well-being and school adjustment. *Journal of Adolescent Research, 7,* 28-42.

Crowell, J.A., Fraley, R.C., and Shaver, P.R. (1999). Mesurement of individual differences in adolescent and adult attachment. In: P.R. Shaver and J. Cassidy (Eds.), *Handbook of attachment: Theory, research, and clinical applications* (pp.434-465). New York: Guilford Press.

Deković, M., and Noom, M.J. (1996). Vragenlijst hechting aan ouders en leeftijdgenoten – adolescentenversie [*Inventory of Parent and Peer Atttachment – Adolescent version*]. Intern Report: Utrecht University.

Deković, M., Noom, M.J., and Meeus, W. (1997). Expectations regarding development during adolescence. Parental and adolescent perceptions. *Journal of Youth and Adolescence, 26,* 253-272.

Dozier, M., Stovall, K.C., and Albus, K.E. (1999). Attachment and psychopathology in adulthood. In: J. Cassidy and P.R. Shaver (Eds.), *Handbook of attachment: Theory, research, and clinical applications* (pp. 497-519). New York: Guilford.

Engels, R.C.M.E., Finkenauer, C., Meeus, W., and Deković, M. (2001). Parental attachment and adolescents' emotional adjustment: The role of interpersonal tasks and social competence. *Journal of Counseling Psychology, 48,* 428-439.

Fraley, R.C., and Shaver, P.R. (1998). A naturalistic study of adult attachment dynamics in separating couples. *Journal of Personality and Social Psychology, 75 (5),* 1198-1212.

Fraley, R.C, Waller, N.G., and Brennan, K.A. (2000). An item response theory analysis of self-report measures of adult attachment. *Journal of Personality and Social Psychology, 78,* 350-365.

Furman, W., and Buhrmester, D. (1992). Age and sex in perceptioins of networks of personal relationships. *Child Development, 63,* 103-115.

Furman, W., Simon, V.A., Shaffer, L., and Bouchey, H.A. (2002). Adolescents' working models and styles for relationships with parents, friends, and romantic partners. *Child Development, 73,* 241-255.

Gerris, J.R.M., Van Boxtel, D.A.A.M., Vermulst, A.A., Janssens, J.M.A.M., Van Zutphen, R.A.H., and Felling, A.J.A. (1993). *Parenting in Dutch families.* Nijmegen: Institute of Family Studies.

Goetting, A. (1994). The parenting-crime connection. *The Journal of Primary Prevention, 14 (3),* 169-186.

Gray-Little, B., Williams, V.S.L., and Hancock, T.D. (1997). An item response theory analysis of the Rosenberg Self-Esteem Scale. *Personality and Social Psychology Bulletin, 23,* 443-451.

Greenberger, E., and McLaughlin, C.S. (1998). Attachment, coping, and explanatory style in late adolescence. *Journal of Youth and Adolescence, 27,* 121-139.

Harter, S. (1985). *Manual for the self-perception profile for children.* Denver: University of Denver.

Hartshorne, T.S. (1993). Psychometric properties and confirmatory factor analysis of the UCLA Loneliness Scale. *Journal of Personality Assessment, 61,* 182-195.

Hazan, C., and Shaver, P. (1987). Romantic love conceptualized as an attachment process. *Journal of Personality and Social Psychology, 52,* 511-524.

Heiss, G.E., Berman, W.H., and Sperling, M.B. (1996). Five scales in search of a construct: Exploring continued attachment to parents in college students. *Journal of Personality Assessment, 67,* 102-115.

Helsen, M., Vollebergh, W., and Meeus, W. (1999). Psychosociale problemen in de adolescentie: De samenhang met hechting aan ouders en vrienden en de identiteit [Psychosocial problems in adolescence: Associations with attachment to parents and peers and identity]. *Nederlands Tijdschrift voor de Psychologie, 54,* 256-275.

Henry, C.S., Sager, D.W., and Plunkett, S.W. (1996). Adolescents' perceptions of family system characteristics, parent-adolescent dyadic behaviors, adolescent qualities and adolescent empathy. *Journal of Applied Family and Child Studies, 45,* 283-292

Hewitt, P.L., Flett, G.L., and Mosher, S.W. (1992). The Perceived Stress Scale: Factor structure and relation to depression symptoms in a psychiatric sample. *Journal of Psychopathology and Behavioral Assessment, 14(3),* 247-257.

Houtzager, B., and Baerveldt, C. (1999). Just like normal: A social network study of the relation between petty crime and the intimacy of adolescent friendships. *Social Behavior and Personality, 27(2),* 177-192.

Isabella, R.A., and Belsky, J. (1991). Interactional synchrony and the origins of infant-mother attachment: A replication study. *Child Development, 62,* 373-384.

Kandel, D., and Davies, M. (1982). Epidemiology of depressive mood in adolescents. *Archives of General Psychiatry, 39,* 1025-1212.

Keelan, J.P.R., Dion, K.L., and Dion, K.K. (1994). Attachment style and heterosexual relationships among young adults. A short-term panel study. Journal *of Social and Personal Relationships, 11,* 201-214.

Kenny, M.E. (1990). College seniors' perceptions of parental attachments: The value and stability of family ties. *Journal of College Student Development, 31,* 39-46.

Kenny, M.E., and Rice, K.G. (1995). Attachment to parents and adjustment in late adolescent college students: Current status, applications, and future considerations. *Counseling Psychologist, 23,* 433-451.

Kirkpatrick, L.E., and Hazan, C. (1994). Attachment styles and close relationships: A four-year prospective study. *Personal Relationships, 1,* 123-142.

Kobak, R., and Sceery, A. (1988). Attachment in late adolescence: Working models, affect regulation, and representations of self and others. *Child Development, 59,* 135-146.

Laursen, B., and Williams, V.A. (1997). Perceptions of interdependence and closeness in family and peer relationships among adolescents with and without romantic partners. In: S. Shulman and W.A. Collins (Eds.), *Romantic relationships in adolescence: Developmental perspectives.* (pp. 3-21). San Fransisco: Jossey-Bass.

Loeber, R., and Stouthamer-Loeber, M. (1986). Family factors as correlates and predictors of juvenile conduct problems and delinquency In: M. Tonry and N. Morris (Eds.), *Crime and justice: An annual review of research* (vol. 7). Chicago: Univ. Chicago Press.

Lyddon, W.L., Bradford, E., and Nelson, J.P. (1993). Assessing adolescent and adult attachment. A review of current self-report measures. *Journal of Counseling and Development, 71,* 390-395.

Main, M., and Solomon, J. (1985). Discovery of an insecure disorganized/disoriented attachment pattern. In M. Yogman and T.B. Brazelton (Eds.), *Affective development in infancy.* Norwood: Ablex.

Mak, A.S. (1990). Testing a psychosocial control theory of delinquency. *Criminal Justice and Behavior, 17,* 215-230.

Mak, A.S. (1994). Parental neglect and overprotection as risk factors in delinquency. *Australian Journal of Psychology, 46 (2),* 107-111.

Manassis, K., Owens, M., Adam, K.S., West, M., and Sheldon-Keller, A.E. (1999). Assessing attachment: Convergent validity of the Adult Attachment Interview and the Parental Bonding Instrument. *Australian and New Zealand Journal of Psychiatry, 33 (4),* 559-567.

McCarthy, C.J., Moller, N.P., and Fouladi, R.T. (2001). Continued attachment to parents: Its relationship to affect regulation and perceived stress among college students. *Measurement and Evaluation in Counseling and Development, 33,* 198-213.

Nada Raja, S., McGee, R., and Stanton, W.R. (1992). Perceived attachments to parents and peers and psychological well-being in adolescence. *Journal of Youth and Adolescence, 21,* 471-485.

Noom, M.J., Deković, M., Meeus, W.H. (1999). Autonomy, attachment and psychosocial adjustment during adolescence: a double-edged sword? *Journal of Adolescence, 22,* 771-783.

Olson, D.H., Portner, J., and Lavee, Y. (1985). *FACES III: Family adaptability and cohesion evaluation scales.* St. Paul: University of Minnesota.

Overbeek, G., and Van Voornveld, I. (2003). *Longitudinal associations between perceived school climate and internalizing and externalizing problem behavior.* Internal Report: Radboud University Nijmegen.

Papini, D.R., Roggman, L.A., Anderson, J. (1991). Early adolescent perceptions of attachment to mother and father: A test of emotional distancing and buffering hypotheses. *Journal of Early Adolescence, 11(2),* 258-275.

Parker, G., Tupling, H., and Brown, L.B. (1979). A Parental Bonding Instrument. *Journal of Medical Psychology, 52,* 1-10.

Parkes, C.M., and Stevenson-Hinde, J. (Eds.) (1982). *The place of attachment in human behaviour.* London: Tavistock Publishing.

Paterson, J., Pryor, J., and Field, J. (1995). Adolescent attachment to parents and friends in relation to aspects of self-esteem. *Journal of Youth and Adolescence, 24(3),* 365-376.

Rispens, J., Hermanns, J., and Meeus, W. (1996). *Opvoeden in Nederland* [Parenting in the Netherlands]. Assen: Van Gorcum.

Rosenberg, M. (1965). *Society and the adolescent self-image.* New Jersey: Princeton University.

Russell, D.W. (1996). UCLA Loneliness Scale (Version 3): Reliability, validity, and factor structure. *Journal of Personality Assessment, 66,* 20-40.

Russell, D., Peplau, L.A., Cutrona, C.E. (1980). The revised UCLA Loneliness Scale: concurrent and discriminant validity evidence. *Journal of Personality and Social Psychology, 39(3),* 472-480.

Schaffer, H.R. (2000). The early experience assumption: Past, present, and future. *International Journal of Behavioral Development, 24,* 5-14.

Scharfe, E., and Bartholomew, K. (1995). Accomodation and attachment representations in young couples. *Journal of Social and Personal Relationships, 12,* 389-401.

Schultheiss, D.E., and Blustein, D.L. (1994). Role of adolescent-parent relationships in college student development and adjustment. *Journal of Counseling Psychology, 41,* 248-255.

Skinner, H.A. (1987). Self-report instruments for family assessment. In: J. Theodore (Ed.), *Family interaction and psychopathology: Theories, methods, and findings* (pp.427-452). New York: Plenum Press..

Spangler, G., and Grossmann, K. (1999). Individual and physiological correlates of attachment disorganization in infancy. In: J. Solomon and G. Carol (Eds.), *Attachment disorganization* (pp. 95-124). New York: Guilford.

Sroufe, L.A., Carlson, E.A., Levy, A.K., and Egeland, B. (1999). Implications of attachment theory for developmental psychopathology. *Development and Psychopathology, 11,* 1-13.

Straathof, M.A.E., and Treffers, Ph.D.A. (1989). *De adolescentenversie van de CBSK* [the self-perception profile for adolescents]. Oegstgeest: Curium.

Van der Linden, F.J., Dijkman, Th.A., and Roeders, P.J.B. (1983). *Metingen van kenmerken van het persoonssysteem en het sociale systeem* [Measurement of characteristics of the person system and the social system]. Nijmegen: Hoogveld Instituut.

Van IJzendoorn, M.H., Kranenburg, M.J., Zwart-Woudstra, H.A., Van Busschbach, A.M. et al. (1991). Gehechtheid over meer generaties. De gehechtheid van de ouder, de gehechtheid van het kind en diens sociaal-emotionele ontwikkeling [attachment through several generations: parental attachment, infant attachment and the child's socio-emotional adaptation]. *Kind en Adolescent, 12 (2),* 87-97.

Van IJzendoorn, M.H., and Kroonenberg, P. (1988). Cross-cultural patterns of attachment: A meta-analysis of the Strange Situation. *Child Development, 59,* 1020-1033.

Verhulst, F.C., Achenbach, T.M., Ferdinand, R.F., Kasius, M.C. (1993). Epidemiological comparisons of American and Dutch adolescents' self-reports. *Journal of the American Academy of Child and Adolescent Psychiatry, 32(6),* 1135-1144.

Vivona, J.M. (2000). Parental attachment styles of late adolescents: Qualities of attachment relationships and consequences for adjustment. *Journal of Counseling Psychology, 47 (3),* 316-329.

Zimmermann, P., and Becker-Stoll, F. (2002). Stability of attachment representations during adolescence: The influence of ego-identity status. *Journal of Adolescence, 25,* 107-124.

In: Parent-Child Relations: New Research
Editor: Dorothy M. Devore, pp. 29-44
ISBN 1-60021-167-4

Chapter 2

Talk to Me (Like Mothers Do): On an Evolving Theory of Attachment

Ilan Harpaz-Rotem
Yale University School of Medicine
Department of Psychiatry, 300 George St Suite 901
New Haven, CT 06511

Abstract

This chapter proposes a new perspective on the evolution of attachment and of representation formation in general. This perspective compliments Bowlby's emphasis on the centrality of the infant's proximity-seeking behavior with respect to his caretaker, a behavior shaped primarily by an evolutionary instinct that operates to safeguard the child's physical survival and to regulate his experience of an external fear or of an internal anxiety. This same instinctual mechanism of proximity-seeking behavior reemerges during the rapprochement phase of development. During this phase, however, early forms of representation, primarily organized by the infant's sensorimotor experiences, achieve a new and higher level of reorganization governed by language. This chapter proposes that the child's need for the mother's proximity during rapprochement constitutes a new and crucial developmental stage of attachment, serving to ensure the survival of the child's mind. The mother's failure to respond appropriately to her child's emerging need at this time will result in both the toddler falling back into his original attachment organization patterns and the disruption of the toddler's ability to make appropriate use of the emerging representation organization mechanism. Importantly, the history of relationships during infancy do not distinguish or impoverish this instinct since this instinct is a universal one prompted by the ever-changing brain; only the quality of the reunion is affected by the history of these relationships. This chapter discusses the rapprochement developmental stage in the light of this new developmental theory and also suggests that during rapprochement, under appropriate conditions, symbolic activity takes prominence over sensorimotor activity to guide and regulate affective experience. The outcome of this transition can be seen in the subconscious when affective and sensorimotor experiences fail to formulate into a retrievable symbolic form.

In recent decades, psychoanalytic research in child development has blossomed, especially in the area of infant studies. New collaborations have evolved and developmental psychologists such as Edward Tronick, Mary Main, and Karen Lyons-Ruth have made important contributions to the psychoanalytic literature that have had implications for psychoanalytic treatment, the nature of therapeutic action, and the mechanism of change (Beebe and Lachmann, 2002; Bruschweiler-Stern, et al., 2002; Lachmann, 2001; Lyons-Ruth, 2000; Tronick, 1998).

The aim of this chapter is to expand our understanding of early childhood relationships, specifically that of the toddler with his mother, by highlighting a previously under-appreciated event with the development of attendant rapprochement. This perspective augments attachment theory (Bowlby, 1969) by proposing a new phase in which the toddler uses the primary caregiver as a focal point in the regulation process, but in a form different from that of the infant's existing sensorimotor regulatory systems. These new forms of regulation, which impel the toddler to reach for his mother, are no less intense than the motivational factors of attachment that Bowlby describes. However, during this proposed phase, the toddler has a unique opportunity to rework previously existing, maladaptive forms of early mother-child interaction. This view of the mother-child relationship, therefore, provides a richer understanding of the developmental processes of representation formation and affect regulation than has been previously available.

As Hofer (1996) noted, existing developmental theory lacks a clear account of how the sensory physiology of early infant social interaction becomes transmuted into the complex patterns of symbolic behavior characteristic of inner experience, often referred to as mental representations (Blatt, 1995; Fonagy and Target, 2000) or as internal working models of attachment theory (Bowlby, 1969). To quote Hofer: the "developmental events through which this remarkable transition takes place are not yet established" (1996, p. 177). Moreover, as the infant matures, the influence of early maternal regulators gradually wanes as the child becomes more independent. In some respects, regulation of the infant's biological systems becomes increasingly autonomous, while in others, regulation remains primarily influenced by key features of the child's environment such as: light, time of day, temperature, and interactions with caregivers or social companions (Hofer, 1996). Until recently, it has been unclear how these early regulatory processes become incorporated into mental representations or how they shift from regulation at the sensorimotor level to regulation at the cognitive-affectual level. This chapter considers the developmental context within which this transition occurs.

It is suggested here that the key feature propelling the transition from the sensorimotor level of regulation to the cognitive-affectual level of representation and affect regulation is embedded in the rapprochement stage of development. In the context of the infant's growing cognitive capacities, language becomes a primary organizing agent for affective experience, and the child experiences a heightened and new need for the mother as a verbal interlocutor or interpreter of inner and outer experiences. The mother's role during this stage can be understood as helping the child to organize the self-object structure derived from sensorimotor experience into a new structure governed by language. Seen in this light, the anxiety observed during the rapprochement stage of development stems not only from the child's growing appreciation for mutual separateness but also from the child's intense need for the mother in a new way. Consequently, this chapter will introduce rapprochement as a means to explain how early representations of affect, self, other, and self in relation to other come to be conceptualized processes accessible (or potentially accessible, if unconscious) to analysis within a two-person developmental model.

BACKGROUND

Instruments such as the Adult Attachment Interview (AAI) (George, Kaplan and Main, 1985), Differentiation-Relatedness Scale (D-R) (Diamond, et al,, 1991), Reflective Functioning Scale (RF) (Fonagy, et al., 1998), or Object Relation Inventory (ORI) (Blatt, et al., 1981) assess adult respondents' ability to reflect on current or early emotional relationships and have provided rich empirical methods for examining individuals' implicit and explicit schema of self and of self in relation to others. The knowledge gained by the use of these instruments raises questions such as the following: What constitutes the ability to reflect on one's emotional life? How does one come to talk about feelings? What gives one person the ability to reflect accurately (as much as one can) on self and others while another will reflect almost exclusively on fantasies of self and others? Although some models of development root these capacities in the mother-child relationship during the first year of a child's life (Fonagy and Target, 2000), focusing on the context in which early forms of representations are formed, they fail to explain how the child develops access to sensorimotor experience.

Researchers agree that the unique emotional relationship between mother and child appears to crystallize in the first year of a child's life (Bowlby, 1980; Cassidy, 1994; Main, 1999; Sander, 1980; Sroufe, 1979; Tronick, 2002), creating a relatively stable organization that persists at least into early adulthood (Main, 1995). However, the mechanisms by which an infant represents emotional experience and the actions that an infant takes to regulate these experiences are different from those of adults. Therefore, a better understanding of the transition from infant to toddler forms of experiencing and understanding is necessary for the understanding of adult relationships, including the analytic dyad.

The idea that the early mother-child interaction lays the foundation for self-structure, in the form of early emotional representations of the dyad, originated in Stern's theory of the structure of the self (1983). Stern and other psychoanalytic and developmental researchers on infancy argued that early preverbal forms of interaction provided the basic structure of the self. Stern claimed that mood, style, quality and rhythm of the mother-child dyad allowed for the creation of RIGS (Representations of Interactions that have been Generalized), which are the foundation of the self. Lachmann and Beebe (1989) also suggested that the patterns of these early representations were the basic forms of identity. In later work, Lachmann and Beebe (1991) described the principles by which representations take form: ongoing regulations, rupture and repair of the dyadic activity, and heightened affective experience.

However, an essential component in the formation of identity is self-reflexivity – the ability to make transitions between subjective and objective perspectives of the self (Bach, 1994). The capacity for self-representation, inherent in emerging self-awareness, appears as the ability to reflect on oneself as an object. As a result, self-awareness has two main facets (Blatt and Bers, 1993): subjective self-awareness and objective self-awareness. The ability to consolidate these two forms of self-awareness appears to emerge between 18 and 24 months (Blatt and Auerbach, in press). Fonagy and Target (1996) explained that this type of consolidation normally begins in the second year of a child's life and is largely completed by the sixth year. Mayes and Cohen (1996) argued that although the child experiences his body separate from his mother's at around the second year, it is only by the fifth or sixth year that the child fully understands that his mind is distinct from his mother's.

This description of emergent self-awareness (Blatt and Auerbach, in press; Fonagy and Target, 1996) appears to parallel the rapprochement phase of development described by Mahler, Pine, and Bergman (1975). It also coincides with the start of pretend play (Piaget, 1945) and with the use of transitional objects (Winnicott, 1971). All of this evidence points to the centrality of the child's transition into the third year of life and calls for a closer look at the mother's relationship to the child at this time. The observations of Mahler, Pine, and Bergman (1975) provide a rare opportunity to better understand this transitional period, during which the child's capacity to view his mind as separate from his mother's emerges out of a dialectical process.

Empirical investigations of visual self-recognition, assessed by observing infants' reactions to their images in mirrors, photos, and movies (Amsterdam, 1972; Berenthal and Fischer, 1978; Bullock and Lutkenhaus, 1990; Johnson, 1983; Lewis, Brooks-Gunn, and Jaskir, 1985; Lewis, Sullivan, Stanger, and Weiss, 1989; Priel and DeSchonen, 1986; Schulman and Kaplowitz, 1977), provide further data on the emergence of self-awareness during the rapprochement phase of development. These studies indicate that from 3 months of age infants are both attentive and positive toward their own images. By 9 months of age, infants begin to show awareness of contingency cues and use these cues for play and imitation. They also appear to show some understanding of the reflective properties of mirrors and, at this age, will turn to locate reflected objects and people. However, only by 18 months of age, the beginning of the rapprochement phase, do toddlers appear to have full self-recognition of the mirror image as their own. It is at this age, for instance, that children first respond to a spot of rouge covertly applied to their noses by touching their own rather than the mirror image of their noses.

Early psychological differentiation of self and other begins over sharing affective states between mother and child, a type of sharing that is preverbal and dialectical, fluctuating between mutually gratifying involvement and experienced incompatibility. This view is shared by Anna Freud (1965) who stressed the role of the dyadic exchanges between mother and child around issues of pleasure and pain as crucial experiences for cognitive growth and development. The centrality of preverbal affective processes in the formation of the self is also apparent in the writing of Bion (1962), Fairbairn (1952), Kohut (1977), and Winnicott (1956). The child's early ability to form mental representations of self and others are, then, rooted in early object relationships and are initiated in the early process of mirroring that occurs between infant and caregiver (Fonagy and Target, 1997). Fonagy and Target (1997) have suggested that infants gradually learn that they have feelings and thoughts and, in particular, feel that their caregivers respond to their internal experiences. Through this learning, primary representations of experience are organized into secondary representations of mind and body. Flawed parental responsiveness, though, leads to delay or absence of secondary representations of affect, with serious consequences for the development of the child's psychic reality.

Integrating various theories of intersubjectivity (Aron, 1998; Blatt and Auerbach, 2001; Benjamin, 1995), Blatt and Auerbach (in press) propose that children become independent subjects only when regarded as such by their parents and can only complete the process of separation when they recognize their parents' subjectivity – that is, when children understand that their parents have minds independent of their own. According to Blatt and Auerbach, "this basic intersubjective situation, this mutual recognition by caregiver and infant of each other's independent subjectivity, is just as crucial as are phylogenetic processes to the child's development of reflexive self-awareness and of the theory of mind that enables a child to understand the beliefs and desires of others" (p. 82).

It is suggested that the transition between early forms of representation of affect and the newly emerging organizing forms of verbally mediated thoughts occurs at rapprochement and are the product of the dialogue between self and other, a crucial component in the capacity for intersubjectivity (Blatt and Auerbach, 2001; Behrends and Blatt, 1985; Benjamin, 1995; Ogden, 1994) that should be at the heart of the investigation into the formation of mind. The centrality of the transition from a preverbal to a verbal level of representation is also seen as the child's growing capacity for verbalization, increased ego control over drives and affects, and the ability to test reality (Katan, 1961). The resolution of rapprochement, which will be described below, although different from the resolution offered by Mahler, Pine, and Bergman (1975), further emphasizes the significance of this stage of development.

WORDS AS TRANSITIONAL OBJECTS

Although development is a continuous process, there are several milestones that mark the achievement of each stage of organization (Piaget, 1970; Erickson, 1982; Freud, 1957). Each stage allows for not only the assimilation of new information but also the reorganization of previously integrated representations, both of which give the child the opportunity to look back, to derive new understanding and meaning, and to create more complicated mental constructs. During rapprochement, the role of language acquisition and language use, particularly in dialogic contexts, marks a major transition period from sensorimotor to linguistic representational forms of experience.

Vygotsky (1978) offered a dialectical approach to linguistic development that provides a model for understanding the child's psychological development during rapprochement. His dialectical approach to development integrates well into the line of thinking presented here regarding the formation of higher-level representations of affect and interactions that emerge during rapprochement. The relationship between psychoanalysis and Vygotsky's developmental theory was examined by Wilson and Weinstein (1990, 1992a, 1992b and 1996). They saw the psychoanalytic investigation of word meaning and sense, as providing clues to the context and affective conditions under which word meanings were originally created, and thus opening a window into hidden emotional climates (1992a).

Vygotsky (1978) claimed that higher mental functions develop through social interaction rather than solely as a result of internally generated cognitive change. More specifically, social interaction fosters cognitive growth by providing the child with the necessary tools for higher thinking. Vygotsky (1966; 1978) observed that just as humankind has developed tools to master the environment it has also created psychological tools to master its own behavior. He called the various psychological tools that people use to aid their thinking and behavior *signs*. Vygotsky went on to argue that we cannot understand human thinking without examining the signs that cultures provide. For Vygotsky, the most important sign system was undoubtedly speech. According to Vygotsky, when humans use signs, they engage in mediated behavior. That is, they do not just respond to environmental stimuli, their behavior is also mediated by their sign system.

Speech, according to Vygotsky (1966), is more than just a communication tool which enables a child to participate in social life; it also facilitates the child's own individual thinking. As speech develops children begin to carry out with themselves the kinds of dialogues they have previously had with others. At first this is done aloud; by about six years of age they carry on such dialogues more inwardly and silently. To talk to ourselves is to think with the help of words. The general model underlying cognitive development, according to Vygotsky (1978) is one of the internalization of social interactions, and the means for such internalization is speech, at first guided by others, but ultimately becoming an intrapsychic process.

Egocentric speech, with which at first the child talks aloud to himself, was observed by Vygotsky as helping and directing the child's behavior. Slowly, as speech becomes inner speech, the child develops the ability to have a silent dialogue within himself. Vygotsky (1987) saw this as a "verbal self-regulation process". Words, for Vygotsky, have a power through which the child masters his behavior. I believe that verbal self-regulation evolves to replace sensorimotor level of representation primarily during rapprochement. Moreover, verbal self-regulation which is first guided by parents and then becomes an intrapsychic process not only serves to regulate the child's behavior but most importantly assists both the child and the parents to regulate emotional states.

Harris (1992) has integrated Winnicott's (1971) concept of transitional objects with Vygotsky's notion that words are tool to perform cognitive and social tasks. As interpreted by Harris (1992), Winnicott's (1971) developmental theory suggested that language could serve as a transitional object. Winnicott highlighted the importance of the mother-child relationship as the context for the child to experience symbolic thought and creativity. The mother provides the child with the environment to learn how to distinguish self and other, a function that she performs through verbal and non-verbal interactions with her child. Increasingly, as the infant grows, she uses language as a means of communication and, in the process, provides him with a tool for achieving independence and subjective autonomy.

The notion of language as a transitional phenomenon is crucial to the chapter's argument. With language as a transitional object, the child can use language for a successful transition between different modes of organizing experience and between different patterns of relating to others. As Harris (1992) noted, it is the transitional experience between early *subjective omnipotence* – where the mother's response to the child produces the illusion that the child's wish creates the object of his desire (and which later on allows for the experience of spontaneous desires and gestures as real, important, and deeply meaningful even though they must be integrated in adaptive negotiations with another person) – and *objective reality*, where the child employs language to negotiate.

Entry into the speech system can be viewed as one of the greatest milestones in the child's developmental process. There is no doubt that verbally-mediated thinking designates a new level of conscious and unconscious representation and that language use marks a significant leap in the child's capacity to organize, reorganize, and regulate his experiences. The absence of language capability in the child's first year of life limits the organizational structuring of emotional experience to a more primitive level of representation. Although these internalized representations are crucial to the child during the first year of his life, the question the chapter seeks to address is how these experiences become available and reworked by the child as he later develops the capacity to give voice to his experience, past and present.

THE MOTHER'S ROLE DURING TODDLERHOOD

The unique space for enacting the transition between early forms of sensorimotor representation and the child's newly emerging verbal capacities for organizing experience in the form of thoughts constitutes the rapprochement phase of development. The contention is that what was originally thought to be anxiety associated with the loss of the child's love object can, in fact, also be understood as anxiety mainly associated with the emergence of the child's new capacity for organization and new need to put previous experience into verbally-mediated representational form. In this context, the child's need to return to the mother reflects a desire and need for the mother as an organizing agent for his emotional experiences and as a narrator or interpreter for both new experiences and those that were formerly constructed and internalized. During rapprochement, then, the child not only begins to separate from the mother but also starts to seek her out so that she can put his current and earlier experiences into words.

Separation-individuation processes appear to play a significant role in the formation of representational organizations of self and other and to be present almost from birth (Lachmann andBeebe, 1991). Not only physical separation and reunion but also understanding and misunderstanding are a crucial arena in which differentiation seems to occur. These events take place through various forms of ruptures and repairs on a daily basis and evoke anxiety, as the child must find new ways to understand self and other. This anxiety propels the developmental process and, if appropriately contained, leads to a new and more accurate view of self, other, and the world.

Identified by Mahler, Pine, and Bergman (1975), the rapprochement phase of development constitutes a crucial way station in the separation-individuation process. Given that the process of separation-reunion is ongoing from birth, why does heightened anxiety accompany the rapprochement phase as Mahler and her colleagues maintained? One would expect that the child's growing capacity for self-regulation would, over time, lead to a decrease in the anxiety associated with this process. Mahler and her colleagues proposed, for instance, that the child's increasing capacity for locomotion creates the occasion for physical separateness by making it possible for him to dart away from the mother. Because the child actively leaves and returns to the mother at this age, one might also expect that the child's initiated, intentional moves away from the mother would be less anxiety provoking than the mother's moves away from the child. Moreover, I believe that there is no reason to suspect that the child experiences increased anxiety associated with losing the object of love immediately after the practicing stage, when the child shows no signs of intense anxiety if he moves away from the mother. Indeed, there is a rich body of developmental literature indicating that before rapprochement, by 16 – 18 months, the child achieves evocative constancy (Fraiberg, 1969; Piaget, 1954; Werner, 1957; Werner and Kaplan, 1963). Since the child's anxiety does not seem to decrease as expected, it is suggested that the anxiety observed during the rapprochement phase deserves fresh examination and broader explanation than has been offered by Mahler and her colleagues.

The most striking observation made by Mahler, Pine, and Bergman (1975), an observation that therefore defines rapprochement, was that all of the children in their study wanted to return to their mothers after leaving them. During the prior practicing stage, the children approached their mothers in what was described as the *"refueling" type of bodily approach*. But during rapprochement, the child's approach was observed to be compounded by a much higher level of symbolic engagement, characteristically governed by the use of language, play, and other forms of intercommunication. Consequently, coming back to the mother during rapprochement has significantly richer features than those observed during refueling. Separation anxiety was a new feature of the child's experience at this stage, as was the child's tendency to approach the mother more frequently when she was present, often filling her lap with objects from the environment. Sharing, both physically and linguistically, became one of the most distinctive characteristics of their interaction. Furthermore, the child demanded the mother's full attention to his wish to share experiences, orienting the mother into a dyadic state of emotional exchange. No matter how the mother was previously experienced by her child, separation anxiety, which coincided with the child's practice of returning to the mother, was observed during the rapprochement phase in all of the children in Mahler's study. As a result, the transition from the practicing stage to rapprochement deserves further investigation since the child's need to return to the mother seems to emerge suddenly and vigorously. Additionally, the implications of this need require attention, as the child initiates a new type of engagement with the mother during rapprochement and as the effects of the child's engagement with the mother at this time may influence adult emotional relationships.

Secondly, Mahler, Pine, and Bergman (1975) found a change at the *beginning of rapprochement* in children's reactions to their mothers' locations, observing increased distress or emotional sadness in response to separation together with signs of greater vulnerability, impotent rage, and helplessness. For instance, Mahler, et al. noted that, for her child, the mother was no longer just "home base," but she had become a person with whom the child wished to share the world. It was important for the child to give the mother novel objects and to show her, by gestures or by words, that he needed her to be interested. Toward the end of the child's second year of life and the beginning of the third year, Mahler, Pine, and Bergman (1975) identified the *rapprochement crisis*, which was marked by a child's increased need for the mother and increased anxiety about the mother's whereabouts. Dependent on her presence and her responsiveness, the child's crisis led, Mahler and her colleagues speculated, to the discovery that the child had to function alone. They argued that, on the one hand, the children in their study strove to get to their mothers as quickly as possible and, on the other, the children's impulses to reach their mothers were compromised by their previous mental representations of them. This observation is crucial, since it indicates that the new intensified instinct to reach out to the mother is not compromised by the history and quality of the relationship between the mother and child prior to rapprochement.

Mahler, et al.'s (1975) observations support the notion that rapprochement is a crucial phase of development marked by reorganization of the child's representations of self, other, and self in relation to other. This reorganization process not only replaces previous sensorimotor representation but also lays the foundation for structuring new experiences in language. During the rapprochement crisis the child must approach the mother with what must be seen as an internal instinct similar to the one operating in the child's first year of life when the child seeks the mother in order to reduce fear associated with internal or external stimuli (Bowlby, 1980). During rapprochement, however, the child needs the mother not less urgently, but at this time, the child needs the mother as an interlocutor to reorganize current and past experiences, thus allowing the child to internalize and to later retrieve a new form of representation. This instinct to reach for the mother as interlocutor is not solely dependent on previous experiences of her as either a good or bad responder. Rather, it is biologically generated as part of this developmental phase. In other words, the toddler *must* approach the mother during rapprochement, even if she was previously experienced as a source of fear or anxiety or was not emotionally available.

As Mahler, Pine, and Bergman (1975) noted, the child's need to seek the mother during rapprochement is not compromised by the quality of their previous relationship; it is an instinct. However, previous attachment classifications manifest themselves and mediate the child's reaction to the mother as reunion is achieved, an event that Mahler and her colleagues described as the *splitting mechanism*. Because biologically driven and a part of the rapprochement developmental phase, this new need to reach for the mother as interlocutor cannot be muted in its initial stage by the child's previous experiences; however, these earlier experiences undoubtedly influence how the next developmental phase will be negotiated. Therefore, only the quality of the reunion during rapprochement will be affected by the previous attachment classification. The emergence of new attachment and reaction patterns during rapprochement create the opportunity for therapeutic intervention in adulthood, which has the unique potential to correct maladaptive interpersonal and representational patterns derived from this phase of childhood development.

With the new theoretical understanding, it is clear that the splitting mechanism recognized by Mahler and her colleagues (1975, p. 99) was insufficiently explored. We can now understand the splitting mechanism, which operates during rapprochement, as a manifestation of previous mental representations that coincide with the emergence of the new need for the mother. During this period, the child experiences intense need for the mother, and as he approaches her, the child's original sensorimotor-affective schemas are activated and interfere with the fulfillment of the child's new need for the mother as interlocutor and interpreter of his experiences.

This view of rapprochement differs from not only that of Mahler, Pine, and Bergman but also that of Lyons-Ruth (1991), who suggested that the basic need for comforting contact with the caregiver during early childhood most likely stems from earlier attachment styles. The move toward the mother is a universal one and only after this need has been met do previous attachment patterns mediate the quality of the reunion. Lyons-Ruth argued that a more complex construction than Mahler's separation-individuation model was needed to elucidate underlying processes of adaptive emotional regulation during rapprochement. This chapter aims to present such a model. In some respects, this view of rapprochement is more in line with that of Horner (1985) who stated that, "rapprochement, then is not a process of dealing with lost symbiotic bliss but a process of restoring positive equilibrium following perturbations, a process of re-attaining basic love and security when frustrations and resistance/opposition, and their correlated affects, have been effectively dealt with" (p. 21). I do not share Horner's conviction, however, that the restoration of equilibrium is prompted by the clash between the child's growing capacity for willful assertiveness and the mother's expectations of greater obedience and self-regulation. In this view, it is the evolution of the attachment instinct during rapprochement that regulates the new emerging system of representation. Furthermore, the child's mature higher-order, verbally mediated means of self-regulation can only be achieved through the successful, mutual resolution of the rapprochement developmental stage. The child's achievement of self-regulation, then, requires his mother's involvement in the resolution of the child's rapprochement crisis.

Mahler, Pine, and Bergman (1975) argued that after several months the child's need to reach out to the mother appeared to diminish. Through the exchange of emotional experiences with the mother and the experience of her availability as an organizing agent, the child comes to an implicit conclusion at this time about how the mother satisfies, or fails to satisfy, his emotional needs. Most likely the same patterns of interaction present in the child's first year of life repeat themselves in this phase, leading him to fall back upon pre-existing cognitive-affective representations of self and other and reproducing the same attachment classification he had before rapprochement. But now these affective representations are organized (or in the case of a borderline child, can never be organized) and accessible in verbal utterances, in re-enactments during play, or later on, in adulthood, through measurements such as the Reflective Functioning Scale (Fonagy, et al., 1998), Object Relations Interview (Blatt, et al., 1981), and Adult Attachment Interview (George, Kaplan and Main, 1985).

This reorganization process can also be viewed as the child's "retrospective study" of early relationships, whereby the child tries to organize earlier forms of sensorimotor representation into new forms of thought guided by language. When this "study" is completed at about the end of the rapprochement crisis, the child will most likely fall back on the distinctive features of relationships formed during the first year of his life. Assuming that the mother's way of being with her child did not change during rapprochement, the previous attachment organization and characteristic patterns of interaction will be newly organized in the form of verbal thoughts after the resolution of the rapprochement crisis (Tronick, in press). The child achieves new forms of representation, in the form of verbally mediated thoughts, which will govern the process of representing self, others, and self in relation to others afterwards. The resolution of the rapprochement crisis marks the beginning of this representational achievement; his representational and internalization processes are not completed at this time or immune to further modification or refinement. The rapprochement phase only defines the extent to which the child can rely on the mother as an organizing agent for his affective experiences. If the mother fails to attend to her role appropriately, the child will be burdened by a disproportionate share of the responsibility for organizing his affective experiences, even though he is not yet sufficiently equipped to do so. Under such circumstances, fantasy will play a major role in the child's capacity to represent affect and self and others. Clearly, the mother's emotional attunement to the needs of her child during rapprochement determines the child's successful completion of this developmental phase. According to Mahler, Pine, and Bergman (1975), "one cannot emphasize too strongly the importance of the optimal emotional availability of the mother during this subphase (rapprochement). It is the mother's love of her toddler and the acceptance of his ambivalence that enables the toddler to cathect his self-representation with neutralized energy" (p. 77).

As stated earlier, the child's intense need for the mother's availability during rapprochement resembles the child's need for the mother's presence in the first year of his life when she regulates the infant's anxiety associated with the experience of an internal or external fear. During rapprochement, however, the child's anxiety, associated with the need for proximity, is triggered by his emerging need for the mother to help him put the experience of both internal and external stimuli into words, into a theory of mind, and into accurate representations of self and others. During rapprochement, therefore, the need for the mother can be understood as "mental survival," crucial to adaptive functioning. The ability of the mother to respond to the child's new developmental needs is "tested" during rapprochement. If the mother fails to respond appropriately to these newly emerging needs, the child will no longer turn to her as a reliable resource. Mahler, Pine, and Bergman (1975) recognized the consequences associated with the mother's unavailability at this phase of development. They noted, for example, that if the mother is not available "this process drains so much of the child's available developmental energy that, as a result, not enough energy, not enough libido, and not enough constructive aggression are left for the evolution of the many ascending functions of the ego" (p. 80). Consequently, it is during the rapprochement phase that mentalization, as described by Fonagy and Target (2000), begins to take form.

The "good" mother, attuned to the child's newly emerging needs, can be viewed as the child's emotional narrator during rapprochement. At this stage, with the help of his mother, the child begins to narrate and, therefore, represent the complexity of the relationships that were formed in the first year of his life. One of the primary tasks during rapprochement is this reorganization of his more primitive level of emotional experience, which is in need of articulation, verbal expression, and narration. During rapprochement, verbally mediated thoughts become the primary level of organization; sensorimotor experiences that are not narrated during rapprochement remain linguistically uncoded in adulthood, and as with the child, demand narration. Although the importance of verbal interchanges during rapprochement was clearly observed by Mahler, Pine and Bergman (1975), the adult consequences of incomplete narration during rapprochement were not incorporated into their understanding of this developmental phase. They observed that "verbal communication becomes more and more necessary; gestural coercion on the part of the toddler or mutual preverbal empathy between mother and child will no longer suffice to attain the goal of satisfaction – that of well being" (1975, p. 79). However, they did not acknowledge that interference with the achievement of well being during rapprochement could result in adult interpersonal complications serious enough to require therapeutic intervention. In the case of unsuccessful resolution of the rapprochement crisis in childhood, an adult might specifically seek an analyst to narrate, from material presented by the analyzand, early experiences of object relations left inchoate or stagnant at the infantile level of organization.

The observed intensified vulnerability on the part of the child during rapprochement, originally thought by Mahler and her colleagues (1975) to be the result of the fear of losing his object of love, can in light of this fuller understanding be recognized as a broader need, a new motivation for relationship, where the mother serves as an organizing agent for the child's affective experience, allowing the child to reorganize previously internalized representations of self, other, and self in relation to others. Moreover, this stage also paves the way for symbolic activity to replace the primary sensorimotor regulatory systems. Sensorimotor representations have to be renegotiated through the mother during rapprochement, to be accounted for by her, and then to be narrated by her, to become suitable for the child's newly emerging representational structures where language becomes the primary psychological organizing mechanism. The early representations are thus re-internalized in a new form, giving rise to the child's ability for further analysis of feeling and experiences.

Not only do words come to be the organizing feature of representations at this stage but they also come to have a potential for affect regulation (Vygotsky, 1978; Wilson and Weinstein, 1990, 1992a, 1992b, 1996). Affect regulation previously achieved by non-verbal communication must be accomplished through language from rapprochement on. For example, when the mother says to her child "it's scary, but don't worry, I'm here right next to you," the words "don't worry" have the potential to regulate the anxious mood associated with a potentially fearful experience. This principle applies to positive emotional experiences as well; if the child approaches an attuned mother, happily sharing his experience of the world (e.g.., a toy or a new discovery) with her, the words "You are so excited; it makes you so happy" mark the child's emotional experience with appropriate signs and sense. During rapprochement, therefore, it is crucial for the mother to be emotionally available to the sharing experiences the child initiates since it is the nature and the content of particular affective-sharing experiences that make each exchange linguistically unique. The mother must not only be emotionally available to the child during rapprochement but she must also convey to the child that she has feelings associated with the ones that the child experiences when the child chooses to share his world with her. In other words, if a child puts a stuffed bear in his mother's lap at this phase, the child is not interested in the mother naming the object, as children can respond to objects' names as young as one year. He needs, instead, her emotional narration of the sharing experience and of the feeling attached to the object. In this way, the childhood developmental phase of rapprochement is parallel to the adult therapeutic process, as the therapist helps the client consciously organize his emotional experience in a relational context. We can think of the mother as a psychoanalyst during rapprochement, organizing and verbalizing as yet unspoken emotional experiences. In a therapeutic setting, an emotionally unavailable analyst will produce an ineffective interpretation for the analyzand. Similarly, a child will be unable to internalize his mother's narration if she is emotionally removed from her child's sharing experiences during rapprochement.

Conclusions

The seminal observations of Maher, Pine, and Bergman (1975) draw the attention to the importance of maternal emotional availability during rapprochement as a crucial factor in the move from early forms of sensorimotor representation to higher order representations and regulation processes. As Mahler and her colleagues noted:

> It is, however, the mother's continued emotional availability, we have found, that is essential if the child's autonomous ego is to attain optimal functioning capacity, while his reliance on the magic omnipotence recedes. If the mother is quietly available with a ready supply of object libido, if she shares the toddling adventurer's exploits, playfully reciprocates, and thus facilitates his salutary attempts at imitation and identification, then internalization of the relationship between mother and toddler is able to progress to the point where, in time, verbal communication takes over, even though vivid gestural behavior – that is, affectomotility – still predominants (p. 79).

Consequently, it appears that Bowlby's attachment theory may be incomplete since rapprochement appears to designate a new stage in the attachment process that is no less intense than that experienced by the child in the first year of his life. To define rapprochement as a need to reattach would be misleading because the child's style of attachment to the mother was already established during the first year of the child's life. In addition, the need for the mother during rapprochement is similar in many ways to the need experienced earlier, although the mother is redefined, and effectively rediscovered, as a source of emotional narration during the rapprochement phase. At this point in the child's development, reflective functioning (Fonagy, et al., 2002) is highlighted by the mother's capacity to think about her child's experience and ability to narrate it back to him. The capacity for verbal emotional regulation and interchange slowly replaces the pure physical touch and preverbal vocalizations, which were the primary tools previously available to the mother. This process can be described as the "power of words" to cure, comfort, or reassure, where the sign's meaning and sense come to inherit the power of regulation.

Rapprochement is clearly a purely attachment-defining phase but it is not one that is governed primarily by the anxiety of losing the object of love, as originally proposed by Mahler, Pine and Bergman (1975). In light of this revised understanding of rapprochement, the separation-individuation process needs to be viewed as a linear developmental continuum, rather than as a singular achievement of the rapprochement phase, which begins shortly after birth and stretches into early adulthood. Rooted both in mundane interactions and more complex emotional interchanges, the process of separation-individuation is propelled by sequences of understandings and misunderstandings, ruptures and repairs between the child and the persons or objects with which he interacts. (Lachmann and Beebe, 1991; Harris, 1992; Lachmann and Beebe, 1989; Stern, 1985; Tronick, 1989). From the child's motoric indications that he would like to disengage from dyadic activity (implying, "I don't like it") to his transition into verbal exchange (i.e., the mother feeds the toddler, saying "yummy banana," and the child utters a genuine reply, "yucky"), the child makes it known to his mother that he already thinks and operates independently of her. The more complex mirroring of affective experiences during the first year of the child's life as well as the emotional narration that takes place during rapprochement are both central to the child ability to recognize his own emotional experiences. Therefore, the child's heightened anxiety during rapprochement should be viewed, and treated, as an experience triggered not solely by the separation-individuation process but also by the child's need to seek proximity to the mother for the nurturing and the regulation of his new need to understand affect, self, and others with the help of words.

As a result, I strongly believe that the resolution of rapprochement carries strong implications for the internalization of representations and affect regulation processes from childhood into adulthood, as language becomes the primary organizing mechanism of affective experience. Moreover, this new understanding of rapprochement can lead to broader and more productive insights into the processes of relational psychoanalysis as well as the mechanisms underlying change.

REFERENCES

Aron, L. (1998). The clinical body and the reflexive mind. In L. Aron and F. S. Anderson (Eds.) *Relational perspectives on the body.* 3-37. Hillsdale, NJ: Analytic Press.

Auerbach, J.S. and Blatt, S.J. (2001). Self-reflexivity, intersubjectivity and therapeutic change. *Psychoanalytic Psychology.* 18, 427-450.

Auerbach, J.S., and Blatt, S.J. (2004). The concept of mind: A developmental analysis. In R. Lasky (Ed.) *Essay in honor of Bertram Freedman.* NY: Guilford.

Bach, S. (1994). *The Language of perversion and the language of love.* Northvale, NJ: Jason Aronson.

Beebe, B. (1988), The contribution of mother-infant mutual influence to the origins of self and object representations. *Psychoanalytic Psychology.* 5:305-337.

Beebe, B. and Lachmann, F. (1991), representational and selfobject transferences: A developmental perspective. *Progress in Self psychology,* Vol. 8. Hillsdale, NJ: The Analytic Press.

Beebe, B. andLachmann, F. M. (2002). *Infant research and adult treatment: Co-constructing interactions.* Hillsdale, NJ.

Beebe, B., Lachmann, F.M. and Jaffe, J. (1997). Mother-infant interaction structures and presymbolic self and object representations. *Psychoanalytic Dialogues,* 7, 133-182.

Behrends, R. S. and Blatt, S.J. (1985). Internalization and psychological development through the life cycle. *Psychoanalytic Study of the Child.* 40, 11-39.

Benjamin, J. (1985). *Like subjects, love objects: Essays on recognition and sexual difference.* New Haven, CT: Yale University Press.

Benjamin, J. (1988), *The Bounds of Love.* NY: Pantheon Press.

Bion, W.R. (1962). *Learning from experience.* London: Heinemann.

Blatt, S.J. (1995). Representational structures in psychopathology. In D. Cicchetti and S. Toch (Eds.) *Rochester Symposium on developmental Psychopathology. Vol. 6. Emotion, Cognition and Representation.* Rochester: University of Rochester Press.

Blatt, S.J. and Bers, S.A. (1993). The sense of self in depression: a psychodynamic perspective. In Z.V. Segal and S.J. Blatt (Eds), *Self representation and emotional disorders: Cognitive and psychodynamic perspective.* 171-210. NY: Guilford.

Blatt, S.J., Chevron, E.S., Quinlan, D.M., and Wein, S. (1981). *The assessment of qualitative and structural dimension of object representation.* Unpublished research manual, Department of Psychiatry, Yale University.

Bowlby, J. (1969). Attachment and Loss: Vol. 1. Attachment. New York: Basic Books.

Bruschweiler-Stern, N., Harrison, A.M., Lyons-Ruth, K., Morgan, A.C., Nahu, J.P., Sander, L.W., Stern, D.N. and Tronick, E. Z. (2002). Explicating the implicit: the local level and the microprocess of change in the analytic situation. *International Journal of Psychoanalysis.* 83,1051-62.

Cassidy, J. (1994). Emotion regulation: Influences of attachment relationships. In N.A. Fox (Ed) *The development of emotion regulation. Biological and behavioral considerations.* 228-249. University of Chicago Press.

Diamond, D., Blatt, S.J., Stayner, D., and Kaslow, N. (1991). *Self-other differentiation of object representations.* Unpublished research manual, Department of Psychiatry, Yale University.

Erikson, E. H. (1982). *The life cycle completed.* NY: Norton.

Fairbairn, W. R. D. (1952). *Psychoanalytic studies of the personality.* London: Routledge and Kegan Paul.

Fonagy, P. and Target, M. (1996). Playing with reality I: theory of mind and the normal development of psychic reality. *International Journal of Psychoanalysis.* 77, 217-233.

Fonagy, P. and Target, M. (1997). Attachment and reflective function: their role in self-organization. *Development and psychopathology.* 9, 679-700.

Fonagy, P. and Target, M. (2000). Playing with reality III: the persistence of dual psychic reality in borderline patients. *International Journal of Psychoanalysis.* 81, 853-873.

Fonagy, P., Target, M., Steele, H., and Steele, M. (1998). *Reflective-functioning manual, version 5, for application to AAI.* Unpublished research manual, Sub-Department of clinical health psychology, UCL.

Fonagy, P., Gergely, G., Jurist, E., and Target, M. (2002). *Affect regulation, metallization, and the development of the self.* NY: Other Press.

Fraiberg, S. (1969). Libidinal object constancy and mental representation. *Psychoanalytic Study of the Child.* 24, 9-47.

Freud, A. (1965). *The Psychoanalytic Study of the Child: XX.*

Freud, S. (1957). Civilization and its discontents. *Standard Edition, 21.* London: Hogarth Press.

George, C., Kaplan, N., and Main, M. (1985). *The Berkeley adult attachment interview.* Unpublished manuscript, Department of Psychology, UC Berkeley.

Harris, A. (1992). Dialogues as Transitional Space. In N. Sckolnick (Ed.) *Relational Perspectives in Psychoanalysis.* Hillsdale, NJ: Analytic Press.

Hofer, M. (1996). On the nature and consequences of early loss. *Psychosomatic Medicine. 58,* 570-581.

Johnson, D. B. (1983). Self-recognition in infants. *Infant Behavior and Development, 6,* 211–222.

Katan, A. (1961). Some thoughts about the role of verbalization in early childhood. *Psychoanalytic Study of the Child, 15,* 184-188.

Kohut, H. (1977). *The restoration of the self.* NY: International University Press.

Lachmann, F. M. (2001). Some contributions of empirical infant research to adult psychoanalysis: What have we learned? How can we apply it? *Psychoanalytic Dialogues.* 11, 167-185.

Lachmann, F. and Beebe, B. (1989), Oneness fantasies revisited. *Psychoanalytic Psychology,* 6:137-149.

Lewis, M., Brooks-Gunn, J., and Jaskir, J. (1985). Individual differences in early visual self-recognition. *Developmental Psychology, 21,* 1181–1187.

Lewis, M., Sullivan, M., Stanger, C., and Weiss, M. (1989). Self-development and self-conscious emotions. *Child Development, 60,* 146–156.

Lyons-Ruth, K. (2000). I sense that you sense that I sense . . .": Sander's recognition process and the specificity of relational moves in the psychotherapeutic setting. *Infant Mental Health Journal.* 21, 85-98.

Mahler, M., Pine, F.and Bergman, A. (1975), *The Psychological Birth of the Human Infant.* NY: Basic Books.

Main, M. (1995). Recent studies in attachment: Overview, with select implications for clinical work. In S. Goldberg, R. Muir and J. Kerr (Eds.) *Attachment theory: Social, developmental and clinical perspectives.* 407-474. Hillsadle, NJ: Analytic Press.

Mayes, L.C. and Cohen, D.J. (1996). Children's developing theory of mind. *Journal of the American Psychoanalytic Association, 44,* 117-142.

Ogdan, T. (1994). *Subject of analysis.* Northvale, NJ: Jason Aronson.

Piaget, J. (1945). *Play, dreams, and imitation in childhood.* NY: Norton.

Piaget, J. (1954). *The construction of reality in the child.* NY: Basic Books.

Piaget, J. (1970). *The construction of reality in the child.* NY: Basic Books.

Sander, L., (1980). New knowledge about the infant from current research: Implication for psychoanalysis. *Joarnal of the American Psychoanalytic Association,* 28, 181-198.

Sroufe, L.A. (1979). The coherence of individual development: Early care, attachment and subsequent developmental issues. *American Psychologist,* 34, 834-842.

Stern, D. (1983). *The Primary Relationship.* Cambridge, MA: Harvard University Press.

Tronick, E.Z. (1989). Emotional and emotional communication. *American Psychologist.* 44, 112-119.

Tronick, E. Z.(1998) Dyadically expanded states of consciousness and the process of therapeutic change. *Infant Mental Health Journal.* 19, 290-299.

Tronick, E. Z. (2002). A model of infant mood state and Sanderian affective waves. *Psychoanalytic Dialogues.* 12,73-99.

Vygotsky, L. S. (1966). Development of higher mental functions. In *Psychological Research in the USSR.* Moscow: Progress publishers.

Vygotsky, L. S. (1978). Tool and Symbol in children's development. In A. R. Luria and M. Cole (Eds.) *L.S. Vygotsky: Mind and Society.* Cambridge, MA: MIT Press.

Vygotsky, L. S. (1986). *Thought and Language.* Cambridge, MA: MIT Press.

Vygotsky, L. S. (1987). The problem of will and its development in childhood. In R. W. Rieber and A. S. Carton (Eds.) *The collected work of L. S. Vygotsky.* NY: Plenum Press.

Werner, H. (1957). *Comparative psychology of mental development.* NY: International University Press.

Werner, H. and Kaplan, B. (1963). *Symbol formation: An organismic-developmental approach to language and the expression of thought.* NY: Wiley.

Wilson, A. and Weinstein, L. (1990). Language, thought and interiorization – A Vygotskian and psychoanalytic perspective. *Contemporary Psychoanalysis.* 26, 24-39.

Wilson, A. and Weinstein, L. (1992a). An investigation into some implications of Vygotskian perspective on the origins of mind: psychoanalysis and Vygotskian psychology, part I. *Journal of the American Psychoanalytic Association.* 40, 349-379.

Wilson, A. and Weinstein, L. (1992b). Language and the psychoanalytic process: Psychoanalysis and Vygotskian psychology, part II. *Journal of the American Psychoanalytic Association.* 40, 725-759.

Wilson, A. and Weinstein, L. (1996). The transference and the zone of proximal development. *Journal of the American Psychoanalytic Association.* 44, 167-200.

Winnicott, D. W. (1956). Mirror role of mother and family in child development. In D.W. Winnicott (Ed.) *Playing and reality.* 111-118. London: Tavistock.

Winnicott, D.W. (1958), *Through Pediatrics to Psychoanalysis.* London: Hogarth Press.

Winnicott, D.W. (1971), *Playing and Reality.* London: Tavistock.

In: Parent-Child Relations: New Research
Editor: Dorothy M. Devore, pp. 45-63
ISBN 1-60021-167-4

Chapter 3

LONGITUDINAL STUDY OF POSTPARTUM DEPRESSION, MATERNAL-CHILD RELATIONSHIPS, AND CHILDREN'S BEHAVIOR TO 8 YEARS OF AGE

N. L. Letourneau, C. B. Fedick, J. D. Willms, C-L. Dennis, K. Hegadoren and M. J. Stewart
University of New Brunswick, Canadian Research Institute for Social Policy

ABSTRACT

This study describes the impact of maternal postpartum depression during the first two years of infant life on children's behavioural growth trajectories between two and eight years of age. Analysis of data from 3533 Canadian children reveals that children of mothers who experienced postpartum depression have higher levels of anxiety, hyperactivity and aggression than children of non-depressed mothers at age two. Over time, anxiety increases, while hyperactivity and aggression decrease at the same rate for children of depressed and non-depressed mothers. However, a constellation of other factors including parenting qualities of the mother-child relationship, social support, family structure, sex of the child, and socioeconomic variables also predict initial levels and rates of behavioural change.

Depression is a major public health problem that is twice as common in women as men between puberty and middle-age (Kessler, Berglund, Demler, and et al., 2003). Although the overall prevalence of depression is no greater in women after delivery than during pregnancy or other times during reproductive life, postpartum mood disorders represent the most frequent form of maternal morbidity following delivery (Stocky and Lynch, 2000). Included in these postpartum mood disorders is postpartum depression (PPD), a serious condition characterized by the disabling symptoms of dysphoria, emotional lability, sleep disturbance, confusion, significant anxiety, guilt, and suicidal ideation. Frequently, further exacerbating these symptoms, women experience low self-esteem, an inability to cope, feelings of incompetence, a loss of self, and social isolation (Beck, 1992; Mills, Finchilescu, and Lea, 1995; Righetti-Veltema, Conne-Perreard, Bousquet, and Manzano, 1998; Ritter et al., 2000).

PPD is a serious concern for many women (Affonso, De, Horowitz, and Mayberry, 2000). Longitudinal and epidemiological studies have yielded varying PPD prevalence rates ranging from 3% to more than 25% of women in the first year following delivery. A meta-analysis of 59 studies reported an overall prevalence of PPD of 13% (O'Hara and Swain, 1996). Extrapolating birth rate data from Statistics Canada, as many as 82,500 Canadian women experience PPD every year (Statistics Canada, 2001). The inception rate is greatest in the first 12 weeks postpartum (Cooper and Murray, 1998) with duration frequently dependent on severity (Cox, Murray, and Chapman, 1993) and time to onset of treatment (England, Ballard, and George, 1994). Residual depressive symptoms are common with 50% of mothers remaining clinically depressed at 6 months postpartum (Kessler et al., 2003; Kumar and Robson, 1984), and 25% of mothers with untreated PPD remaining clinically depressed past the first year (Holden, 1991). Women who have suffered from PPD are twice as likely to experience future episodes of depression over a 5-year period (Cooper and Murray, 1995).

The impact of depression on children can be profound (O'Hara, Schlechte, Lewis, and Varner, 1991). Research consistently suggests that PPD may lead to impaired maternal-infant interactions and negative perceptions of normal infant behavior (Murray and Cooper, 1996, 1997a, 1997b, 1997c, 1999; Murray, Cooper, Wilson, and Romaniuk, 2003; Murray, Fiori-Cowley, Hooper, and Cooper, 1996; Murray et al., 1999). In particular, depressed mothers are less likely to pick up on their infants' cues resulting in less positive feedback and a decreased likelihood of meeting their infants' needs (Beck, 1995; Field, 1994; Letourneau, 2001). In comparison to mothers with no history of mental health problems, mothers with PPD are more likely to: 1) be less sensitive and appropriate in their interactions with their children, and more negative in their play (Hipwell, Goossens, Melhuish, and Kumar, 2000; Murray et al., 1996; Righetti-Veltema, Bousquet, and Manzano, 2003); 2) speak more slowly and less often (Teasdale, Fogarty, and Williams, 1980); 3) be less emotionally expressive and responsive (Lewinsohn, Weinstein, and Alper, 1970; Libert and Lewinsohn, 1973); and 4) be less affectionate and more anxious (Righetti-Veltema et al., 2003; Stanley, Murray, and Stein, 2004). Moreover, Hipwell et al. (2000) found disturbances in mother-child interactions even in cases where few residual symptoms of PPD were detected at one year postpartum.

Importantly, these impaired maternal-infant interactions have been linked to diverse infant behavioral problems and poorer health outcomes. For example, infants of mothers with PPD are more likely to be abused or neglected (Buist, 1998), diagnosed with 'failure to thrive' (Drewett, Blair, Emmett, and Emond, 2004), and hospitalized for poor health (Casey et al., 2004). Two meta-analyses suggest that PPD has a significant effect on infants' cognitive and social development (Beck, 1998; Grace, Evindar, and Stewart, 2003). Studies examining infants 3- to 7-months old have demonstrated that in comparison to infants of non-depressed mothers, those with depressed mothers: 1) are more tense, less content, and deteriorate more quickly under the stress of developmental testing (Whiffen and Gotlib, 1993); 2) show fewer positive facial expressions, more negative expressions and protest behavior (Field, 1984); and 3) are more drowsy, fussy, withdrawn, disruptive, avoidant, and disengaged in maternal-infant interactions (Cohn and Tronick, 1987; Murray et al., 1996) and in toy play (Campbell, Cohn, and Myers, 1995).

Even where maternal depression had remitted, 19-month old infants of mothers who had PPD showed less affective sharing, concentration, and sociability to strangers, and a lower overall rate of interaction (Stein et al., 1991). Insecure (avoidant) attachment was observed in 12- and 18-month old infants of mothers who had PPD (Lyons-Ruth, Zoll, Connell, and Grunebaum, 1986; Murray, 1992). Furthermore, 18 to 19-month old infants of depressed mothers have been observed to be less responsive and interactive and to show decreased positive affect than control condition infants (Righetti-Veltema et al., 2003; 1991). Three- to 5-year old children of mothers who experienced PPD have been reported by both independent observers and maternal reports to be more difficult than children of other mothers (Murray et al., 1999; Sinclair, Murray, Stein, and Cooper, 1996). Recent research on the impact of maternal mental health on 12-year-old children's behavior confirms that parental mental health problems can compromise children's behavioral adjustment (Leinonen, Solantaus, and Punamaeki, 2003). Furthermore, boys of depressed mothers tend to display more externalizing behaviors including aggression and hyperactivity characterized by antisocial, active, and distractible behaviors (Leinonen et al., 2003; Sinclair et al., 1996). Girls of depressed mothers tend to display more internalizing behaviors such as anxiety and withdrawal (Leinonen et al., 2003). These results are consistent with research that suggests children of mothers who experienced PPD are two to five times more likely to develop long-term behavioral problems (Brennan et al., 2000; Elgar et al., 2003; Ghodsian, Zajicek, and Wolkind, 1984; Orvaschel, Walsh-Allis, and Ye, 1988; Wrate, Rooney, Thomas, and Cox, 1985).

Murray and Cooper (1999) suggest multiple mechanisms exist for the observed relationship between PPD and adverse child developmental outcomes. Direct effects result from the exposure of the developing infant to maternal depressive symptoms, with significant associations between the severity and duration of the maternal mood disorder and child outcomes. Indirect effects relate to the impact of PPD on maternal interactive behaviors (e.g. predictability, talkativeness, sensitivity and responsiveness) combined with the observation that infants, in general, are highly sensitive to such qualities in their maternal caregiving environment. This combination of factors is hypothesized to disrupt infant interactions and engagements with the mother, and as a consequence, impair infant health and developmental outcomes. However, social support may have a protective effect, reducing the impact of poor maternal-infant interactions (Barnard et al., 1985; Letourneau et al., 2001).

There are several pathways through which social support can affect maternal mental health (Berkman and Glass, 2000). Social support has been shown to have a positive effect on mental health in general (Cohen, Underwood, and Gottlieb, 2002; Dennis, 2003) with research suggesting that integration in a social network may produce positive psychological states and buffer responses to stress (Cohen et al., 2002; Lin, Ye, and Ensel, 1999). Depressed and non-depressed mothers differ with respect to positive social interactions, number of confidants (Chung and Yue, 1999), and perception of social isolation (Nielsen Forman et al., 2000). Moreover, mothers who perceive less social support present more depressive symptoms than mothers who perceive sufficient support (Brugha et al., 1998; Dankner, Goldberg, Fisch, and DCrum, 2000; Logsdon, Birkimer, and Usui, 2000; Ritter et al., 2000). The longitudinal impact of social support for mothers with PPD on children's behavior has not been examined.

The purpose of this study was to examine the impact of maternal PPD on children's vulnerability to behavioral problems. The mediating impacts of parenting, social support, and demographic variables [i.e. socioeconomic status (SES), maternal education, single parent status, child sex] in the first two years of infant life on growth trajectories of behavioral outcomes for children were also explored. Specifically, this study attempts to answer the question: Compared to mothers who are not depressed after childbirth, what is the impact of maternal depression on children's anxiety, hyperactivity, aggression and prosocial behaviors, and do factors such as parenting, social support, and demographic variables affect this impact? The first hypothesis predicts that children of mothers who experienced PPD in the first two years of their child's life will display higher levels of anxiety, hyperactivity and aggression and lower levels of prosocial behaviors than children of mothers who did not experience PPD. The second hypothesis predicts that parenting, social support, and demographic variables are not sufficient to attenuate the observed differences in infant behaviors between the two groups of mothers.

METHOD

Data from the National Longitudinal Survey of Children and Youth (NLSCY) was used in the current study. The survey was launched in 1994 by Statistics Canada to track the development, health, and well-being of a nationally-representative sample of children in Canada over time, with the original cohort continuing to be re-interviewed every two years. Four cycles of NLSCY data were available at the time of the current study: Cycle 1 (1994-95), Cycle 2 (1996-97), Cycle 3 (1998-99) and Cycle 4 (2000-01). The current study is based on children who were less than 24 months of age in Cycle 1 and participated in at least one subsequent cycle. Specifically, children between the ages of 0 and 24 months in Cycle 1 (1994-95) of the NLSCY were identified and followed in subsequent cycles, up to 96 months (8 years of age). Many of the predictor variables used in this study were designed to evaluate only children under the age of 24 months, while the outcome measures were designed to evaluate children 24 months of age and older. Therefore, information for the predictor variables was extracted from Cycle 1 data while information for the outcome measures was extracted from subsequent cycles.

The population of interest was children whose mothers reported being depressed within two years of the birth of the child; the sample for analysis included both depressed and non-depressed mothers for comparative purposes. Additional selection criteria required that the person providing responses to survey items, known as the person most knowledgeable (PMK), was the biological mother of the child. Sample size was maximized by including children surveyed in Cycle 1 (for predictor variable information) and at least one subsequent cycle of the NLSCY (Cycle 2, 3, or 4) (for valid outcome variable information). In total, 3533 children were included in the sample for analysis: 691 whose mothers reported being depressed within two years postpartum and 2842 children whose mothers did not. Table 1 details the cycle participation of the 3533 children selected from the NLSCY for this study.

Behavioral Outcomes

The behavioral outcome measures for this study were children's *anxiety*, *hyperactivity*, *aggression* and *prosocial behaviors*. These measures were derived from a series of items in the NLSCY, designed to assess aspects of behavior in children two years of age and older.

Examples of the items for anxiety include "How often would you say that your child is too fearful or anxious?" and "How often would you say that your child is worried?". For hyperactivity, examples include "How often would you say that your child is distractible or has trouble sticking to any activity?" and "How often would you say that your child can't sit still or is restless or hyperactive?". For the construct of aggression, examples of items include "How often would you say that your child gets into many fights?" and "How often would you say that your child kicks, bites or hits other children?". Finally, examples of prosocial behaviors items include "How often would you say that your child shows sympathy to someone who has made a mistake?" and "How often would you say that your child offers to help others with a difficult task?" (Statistics Canada, 1998). PMK responses to the items included 1 = Never or not true, 2 = Somewhat or sometimes true, and 3 = often or very true, with higher scores indicating an increased presence of the behavior in the child. Each behavioral outcome measure was computed as the mean of the item scores if the child had valid data on at least two of the construct items. If the child was missing data on all or all but one of the construct items, that behavioral outcome measure was treated as missing. Cronbach's alpha coefficients for the behavioural outcomes in Cycle 1 are as follows: anxiety – 0.59, hyperactivity – 0.80, aggression – 0.75 and prosocial behaviours – 0.85 (Statistics Canada, 1998)

Table 1. Number of children age 24 months or younger in Cycle 1 participating in two, three or four cycles of the NLSCY

In Cycle 1 and	Number of children (cases)
one of Cycle 2, 3 or 4 (total of two cycles)	263
two of Cycles 2, 3 or 4 (total of three cycles)	669
all of Cycles 2, 3 and 4 (total of four cycles)	2601

Predictors

Maternal Depression. Maternal depression was measured as a dichotomous variable based on 12 items from the National Institute of Mental Health's Centre for Epidemiological Studies Depression (CES-D) scale (Radloff, 1977). The dichotomous classification of depression used in this study is based on a method described by Somers and Willms (2002). The 12-item version of the CES-D (NLSCY Depression Scale) was rescaled to produce a cut-off proportional to that of the full, 20-item CES-D where scores range from 0 to 60 and a score of 16 represents a classification of depression. As such, the dichotomous cut-off for depression on the 12-item NLSCY Depression Scale, with scores ranging from 0 to 36, was set at 9. Mothers who scored 9 or above were coded 1 (depressed), and mothers who scored 8 or less were coded 0 (not depressed). The Cronbach's alpha of the 12-item scale was 0.82, slightly lower than the reliability of the full 20-item scale (0.85) (Somers and Willms, 2002).

Parenting. Parenting was examined on three dimensions including: (1) positive discipline, (2) warm and nurturing, and (3) consistent. Derived in a process similar to that described by Chao and Willms (2002), the Cronbach's alpha coefficients of these dimensions in Cycle 1 were calculated as 0.76, 0.80, and 0.66, respectively (Chao and Willms, 2002). Ten items comprise the scale for positive discipline (e.g. "How often do you have to discipline your child repeatedly for the same thing?" and "When your child breaks the rules or does things that he/she is not supposed to, how often do you calmly discuss the problem?"), six items comprised the dimension measuring warm and nurturing parenting (e.g. "How often do you praise your child saying something like 'Good for you!' or 'What a nice thing you did!' or 'That's good going!'?" and "How often do you and your child talk or play with each other, focusing attention on each other for 5 minutes or more, just for fun?"), and five items comprise the dimension of consistent parenting (e.g. "When you give your child a command, what proportion of the time so you make sure that he/she does it?" and "When your child breaks the rules or does things that he/she is not supposed to, how often do you ignore it, do nothing?") (Sommer, Whitman, Borkowski, and et al., 2000). Original item responses ranged from 1 to 5 with reverse coding of some questions; higher scores indicate more optimal parenting practices. These scores were converted to a 0 to 10 scale and the mean of items in each construct was calculated, provided at least one of the items in the group was valid. Theoretically, each construct ranges from 0 to 10; within the sample in our study, positive discipline ranges from 1.94 to 10, warm and nurturing ranges from 2.92 to 10, and consistent ranges from 1.00 to 10.

Social Support. A modified version of the Social Provisions Scale (Cutrona and Russell, 1987) was used to measure PMK perceptions of support from family, friends and others. The scale included six items, each of which contain four response categories including 0 = strongly disagree, 1 = disagree, 2 = agree, and 3 = strongly agree, so that the total scale score ranged between 0 and 18, with higher scores indicating more social support. Factor analysis on the individual aspects of social support (e.g. emotional support, instrumental support) indicated the presence of a single factor measuring global social support; as such, the individual aspects of social support were not specifically examined in the analysis. The reliability coefficient for social support in Cycle 1 was 0.82 (Statistics Canada, 1998).

Demographic Predictors. Demographic predictors known to affect children's behavioral outcomes, including maternal education, single parent status, SES, and sex of the child, were included in the analysis (Willms, 2002). Maternal education was measured as the total number of years of formal education of the mother. Single parent status was a dichotomous variable with those being raised by a single parent coded as 1 and those not being raised by a single parent coded as 0; likewise, sex of the child was measured by a dichotomous variable where females were coded 1 and males were coded 0. SES was derived from five NLSCY variables including PMK years of schooling, spouse years of schooling, PMK occupational status, spouse occupational status, and household income. The occupational variables used in the derivation of SES were modified versions of the scale developed by Pineo, Porter and McRoberts (1977) that groups occupations into 16 homogeneous categories and applies a logit transformation to express the 16 occupational categories on an interval scale. If no spouse was indicated, the primary caregiver's average over the three variables (years of schooling, occupation, and household income) was applied and imputed as the spouse's. The final SES composite was standardized to have a mean of 0 and a standard deviation of 1 for all families (Willms and Shields, 1996).

Interaction Terms. A set of interaction terms was calculated to examine the differential impact of predictor and demographic variables (positive discipline, warm and nurturing, consistent, social support, maternal education, SES, single parent status and sex of the child) in combination with maternal depression.

Analysis

Descriptive statistics were calculated to examine sample characteristics over time. Independent t-tests were conducted cross-sectionally to provide comparative data on sample characteristics. Hierarchical Linear Modeling (HLM) was used to model the data longitudinally, specifically to examine children's behavioral growth trajectories. HLM was used to address the non-independent nature of the data collected on the same children over multiple time points. Growth curve HLM takes into account the clustering of observations by estimating a single model that describes data at two levels: within-child and between-child (Raudenbush and Bryk, 2002). Within-child differences, specified in the Level-1 model, summarize an observed pattern of an outcome variable across measurement occasions into a functional relationship with time. A typical trajectory can be specified as follows:

$$Y_{it}= \beta_{0i} + \beta_{1i}X_{it}+\varepsilon_{it}$$

where Y_{it} represents an outcome score for the ith child at time t, X_{it} stands for each measurement occasion for the ith child, β_{0i} is the intercept of the underlying trajectory for the ith child, β_{1i} is the slope of the underlying trajectory of the ith child, and ε_{it} is the error term. Between-child differences are specified in the Level-2 model, where the effects of variables on β_{0i} and β_{1i} are calculated using:

$$\beta_{0i} = \gamma_{00i} Z_{1i}+ \gamma_{01i} Z_{2i} + \ldots r_{0i} \text{ and}$$
$$\beta_{1i} = \gamma_{10i} Z_{1i}+ \gamma_{11i} Z_{2i} + \ldots r_{0i}$$

where γ_{00}, γ_{01}, etc. are coefficients denoting the effects of selected predictor variables, Z. In this analysis, one-tailed testing was used as enough evidence exists in the literature to hypothesize directional effects on the outcome variables.

Longitudinal sampling weights are typically used to adjust for a complex multi-stage sample design and non-response of the original cohort over time. However, these weights do not take into account the design effect of the survey so that variance estimates are still underestimated (Pfefferman and Sverchkov, 2003). Moreover, it may be argued that if the specified model is correct, sampling will not induce bias in the unweighted estimators of the regression coefficients (Chambers and Skinner, 2003). Further, as the goal of the study was to examine relationships and not to generalize to the Canadian population, weights were not employed in the HLM procedures.

Two models were created and analyzed to explain the relationship between mother's depression and children's behavioral outcomes: Model 1 examined the differences in trajectories between children of depressed and non-depressed mothers on the measures of child behavior (*anxiety*, *hyperactivity*, *aggression* and *prosocial behaviors*), and Model 2 examined the differences in trajectories between children of depressed and non-depressed mothers on child behavior, taking into account the effects of other variables known to impact child behaviour (parenting constructs, social support, maternal education, single parent status, sex of the child, and SES*)* and interaction terms. Table 2 details each of the models.

Table 2. Details of HLM Models 1 and 2.

	Model 1	Model 2
Level-1 Equation	$Y = \beta_0 + \beta_1(\text{Age}) + \varepsilon$	$Y = \beta_0 + \beta_1(\text{Age}) + \varepsilon$
Level-2 Equations	$\beta_0 = \gamma_{00} + \gamma_{01}(\text{Depressed}) + \mu_0$	$\beta_0 = \gamma_{00} + \gamma_{01}(\text{Sex of Child}) + \gamma_{02}(\text{Depressed}) + \gamma_{03}(\text{Maternal Education}) + \gamma_{04}(\text{Single Parent Status}) + \gamma_{05}(\text{SES}) + \gamma_{06}(\text{Social Support}) + \gamma_{07}(\text{Positive Discipline}) + \gamma_{08}(\text{Warm and Nurturing}) + \gamma_{09}(\text{Consistent}) + \gamma_{010}(\text{Depressed}\cdot\text{Sex of Child}) + \gamma_{011}(\text{Depressed}\cdot\text{Maternal Education}) + \gamma_{012}(\text{Depressed}\cdot\text{Single Parent Status}) + \gamma_{013}(\text{Depressed}\cdot\text{SES}) + \gamma_{014}(\text{Depressed}\cdot\text{Social Support}) + \gamma_{015}(\text{Depressed}\cdot\text{Positive Discipline}) + \gamma_{016}(\text{Depressed}\cdot\text{Warm and Nurturing}) + \gamma_{017}(\text{Depressed}\cdot\text{Consistent}) + \mu_0$
	$\beta_1 = \gamma_{10} + \gamma_{11}(\text{Depressed}) + \mu_1$	$\beta_1 = \gamma_{10} + \gamma_{11}(\text{Sex of Child}) + \gamma_{12}(\text{Depressed}) + \gamma_{13}(\text{Maternal Education}) + \gamma_{14}(\text{Single Parent Status}) + \gamma_{15}(\text{SES}) + \gamma_{16}(\text{Social Support}) + \gamma_{17}(\text{Positive Discipline}) + \gamma_{18}(\text{Warm and Nurturing}) + \gamma_{19}(\text{Consistent}) + \gamma_{110}(\text{Depressed}\cdot\text{Sex of Child}) + \gamma_{111}(\text{Depressed}\cdot\text{Maternal Education}) + \gamma_{112}(\text{Depressed}\cdot\text{Single Parent Status}) + \gamma_{113}(\text{Depressed}\cdot\text{SES}) + \gamma_{114}(\text{Depressed}\cdot\text{Social Support}) + \gamma_{115}(\text{Depressed}\cdot\text{Positive Discipline}) + \gamma_{116}(\text{Depressed}\cdot\text{Warm and Nurturing}) + \gamma_{117}(\text{Depressed}\cdot\text{Consistent}) + \mu_1$

RESULTS

Table 3a compares children of depressed and non-depressed mothers' mean values on the first (earliest) valid value of predictor and demographic variables. In comparison to non-depressed mothers, those who were depressed: (1) had less education, (2) had decreased available social support, (3) headed more single parent households, and (4) had lower SES. They also exposed their children to less positive discipline, warm and nurturing parenting, and consistent parenting.

Comparisons between children of depressed and non-depressed mothers, using mean values on the four behavioral outcomes (*anxiety, hyperactivity, aggression* and *prosocial behaviors*) by NLSCY survey cycle, were conducted (Table 3b). Findings revealed that *anxiety* and *prosocial behaviors* increase while *hyperactivity* and *aggression* decrease over time for all children (regardless of their mother's depression history). Children of depressed mothers have higher mean values on *anxiety*, *hyperactivity,* and *aggression* in all cycles than children of non-depressed mothers. Independent samples t-tests revealed that children of depressed and non-depressed mothers significantly differ in every cycle on all outcome variables except *prosocial behaviors* (Table 3b).

Table 3a. Mean predictor and demographic statistics for children of depressed and non-depressed mothers

	Depressed	Non-depressed
N	691	2842
Maternal depression score (scale of 0-36 with ≥9 indicating depression)	13.5 (4.58)	3.02 (2.36)
Positive Discipline score	6.70 (1.34)	7.11 (1.15)
Warm and Nurturing score	7.84 (1.24)	8.08 (1.14)
Consistent score	6.95 (1.77)	7.35 (1.58)
Maternal education (years of formal schooling)	11.8 (2.03)	12.7 (2.08)
Percent of households that are headed by a single parent	24.6	9.2
Percent of children that are female	49.2	49.4
SES (number of standard deviations from the NLSCY average)	-0.457 (0.921)	-0.005 (0.956)
Social support (scale of 0 to 18)	13.8 (2.69)	14.9 (2.79)

Note: Standard deviations in brackets

Table 3b. Mean longitudinal outcomes statistics for independent t-tests of children of depressed and non-depressed mothers

Outcome variable	Cycle 2		Cycle 3		Cycle 4	
	Depressed	Non-depressed	Depressed	Non-depressed	Depressed	Non-depressed
Anxiety	1.28 (0.275)	1.20 (0.238)	1.32 (0.293)	1.25 (0.259)	1.38 (0.344)	1.31 (0.301)
Hyperactivity	1.74 (0.448)	1.62 (0.400)	1.74 (0.442)	1.58 (0.399)	1.72 (0.480)	1.58 (0.416)
Aggression	1.49 (0.478)	1.40 (0.428)	1.35 (0.390)	1.26 (0.311)	1.29 (0.380)	1.23 (0.308)
Prosocial Behavior	2.12 (0.544)	2.13 (0.524)	2.22 (0.407)	2.22 (0.385)	2.38 (0.406)	2.41 (0.363)

Notes:

[1]Standard deviations in brackets.

[2]Children of depressed and non-depressed mothers significantly differ at $p<.05$ for all outcomes except prosocial behavior.

HLM was used to examine the relationship between predictor and demographic variables and children's initial level (at age 2) and rate of change for each of the behavioral outcomes. Coefficients of each predictor or demographic variable were used to report the effect of the variable (within two years after the time of birth on the child) on child's levels of *anxiety*, *hyperactivity*, *aggression*, and *prosocial behaviors* from age 2 through 8.

Table 4 reports HLM results for Model 1 for each of the behavioral outcomes. The results suggest that children of depressed mothers have higher initial levels of *anxiety*, *hyperactivity*, and *aggression* than children of non-depressed mothers. Moreover, *anxiety* increases over time while *hyperactivity* and *aggression* decrease over time at the same rate for children of both depressed and non-depressed mothers. Figure 1 portrays the trajectories of *anxiety*, *hyperactivity*, *aggression*, and *prosocial behaviors* for children of depressed and non-depressed mothers from 2 through 8 years of age.

Table 4. Final estimation of fixed effects; HLM output for the trajectory of Anxiety, Hyperactivity, Aggression and Prosocial Behavior; Model 1

Fixed Effect	Anxiety	Hyperactivity	Aggression	Prosocial Behavior
Intercept (behavior at age 2), β_0				
Intrcpt2, γ_{00}	**1.17** (0.005)	**1.63** (0.009)	**1.42** (0.009)	**2.05** (0.001)
Depressed, γ_{01}	**0.077** (0.013)	**0.123** (0.021)	**0.104** (0.023)	-0.006 (0.026)
Slope (increase in behavior for one year of age), β_1				
Intrcpt2, γ_{10}	**0.027** (0.002)	**-0.010** (0.002)	**-0.041** (0.002)	**0.067** (0.003)
Depressed, γ_{11}	0.000 (0.004)	0.004 (0.006)	-0.008 (0.006)	-0.002 (0.006)

Notes:
[1]Standard errors in brackets.
[2]Coefficients in **bold** are significant at an alpha level of 0.05 (one-tailed).

HLM results for Model 2 for each of the behavioral outcomes are displayed in Table 5, which suggests the main effect of maternal depression on children's *anxiety*, *hyperactivity* and *aggression* at age 2 is negated when the selected predictor and demographic variables are included in the model. Positive discipline and consistent parenting lower the initial level of *anxiety* in 2-year-old children, while being in a single parent household raises the initial level of *anxiety*. Significant interactions between depression and maternal education, single parent status and SES indicate that, for depressed mothers, higher maternal education increases initial levels of *anxiety* in their children, while being a single parent or having higher SES decreased initial levels of *anxiety*. In addition, including the selected predictor and demographic variables reverses the trajectory of *anxiety* so that it decreases over time; positive discipline lessens this decrease, but only for non-depressed mothers.

Positive discipline, and to a lesser extent, warm and nurturing parenting and SES all decrease initial levels of *hyperactivity* in children and female children have lower initial levels of *hyperactivity* than males. *Hyperactivity* decreases with age, more so for female children and both positive discipline and being from a single parent family lessen this decrease over time.

Initial levels of *aggression* are lower for children who experience positive discipline and, to a lesser extent, warm and nurturing parenting, and females of depressed mothers seem to have lower initial levels of *aggression* than males. *Aggression* decreases with age, but for females of depressed mothers, this decrease is lessened. Positive discipline also seems to lessen this decrease for all children.

Finally, *prosocial behaviors* are initially higher for female children, those exposed to warm and nurturing, and consistent parenting, and those from single parent families. Social support also appears to increase initial levels of *prosocial behaviors*. Overall, *prosocial behaviors* increase with age, and this increase is lessened by consistent parenting, increased maternal education, and single parent status. This relationship may be explained by the fact that children with higher initial levels of prosocial behavior have less gains to make overall, compared to their less prosocial counterparts.

Table 5. Final estimation of fixed effects; HLM output for the trajectory of Anxiety, Hyperactivity, Aggression and Prosocial Behavior; Model 2

Fixed Effect	Anxiety	Hyperactivity	Aggression	Prosocial Behavior
Intercept (behavior at age 2), β_0				
Intrcpt2, γ_{00}	**1.69** (0.077)	**2.80** (0.107)	**2.66** (0.125)	**0.887** (0.152)
Depressed, γ_{02}	-0.251 (0.177)	-0.022 (0.271)	0.288 (0.290)	-0.527 (0.335)
Positive Discipline, γ_{07}	**-0.064** (0.005)	**-0.149** (0.008)	**-0.134** (0.009)	0.008 (0.010)
Warm and Nurturing, γ_{08}	0.003 (0.005)	-0.010 (0.008)	**-0.032** (0.008)	**0.063** (0.010)
Consistent, γ_{09}	**-0.011** (0.003)	**-0.013** (0.005)	-0.005 (0.006)	**0.042** (0.007)
Social Support, γ_{06}	-0.001 (0.002)	0.001 (0.003)	0.001 (0.003)	**0.009** (0.004)
Maternal Education, γ_{03}	0.000 (0.004)	0.006 (0.006)	0.002 (0.006)	0.006 (0.008)
Single Parent Status, γ_{04}	**0.036** (0.021)	0.011 (0.030)	-0.002 (0.036)	**0.124** (0.037)
SES, γ_{05}	0.000 (0.009)	**-0.053** (0.013)	-0.017 (0.015)	0.011 (0.019)
Sex of Child, γ_{01}	0.016 (0.010)	**-0.056** (0.016)	-0.024 (0.017)	**0.146** (0.022)
Depressed·Sex of Child, γ_{010}			**-0.106** (0.041)	
Depressed·Maternal Education, γ_{011}	**0.021** (0.010)			
Depressed·Single Parent Status, γ_{012}	**-0.074** (0.040)			
Depressed·SES, γ_{013}	**-0.058** (0.024)			
Slope (increase in behavior for one year of age), β_1				
Intrcpt2, γ_{10}	**-0.067** (0.024)	**-0.109** (0.030)	**-0.216** (0.031)	**0.172** (0.037)
Depressed, γ_{12}	0.052 (0.057)	0.001 (0.078)	-0.044 (0.070)	0.116 (0.076)
Positive Discipline, γ_{17}	**0.009** (0.002)	**0.019** (0.002)	**0.018** (0.002)	0.002 (0.002)
Warm and Nurturing, γ_{18}	-0.001 (0.002)	-0.002 (0.002)	0.002 (0.002)	-0.003 (0.002)
Consistent, γ_{19}	0.002 (0.001)	0.001 (0.001)	0.001 (0.001)	**-0.006** (0.002)
Social Support, γ_{16}	0.001 (0.001)	-0.000 (0.001)	0.001 (0.001)	-0.000 (0.001)
Maternal Education, γ_{13}	0.001 (0.001)	-0.001 (0.002)	0.001 (0.002)	**-0.004** (0.002)
Single Parent Status, γ_{14}	-0.003 (0.006)	**0.015** (0.009)	0.006 (0.009)	**-0.023** (0.010)
SES, γ_{15}	-0.003 (0.003)	-0.001 (0.004)	-0.001 (0.003)	0.001 (0.005)
Sex of Child, γ_{11}	-0.003 (0.003)	**-0.018** (0.004)	**-0.011** (0.004)	-0.008 (0.005)
Depressed·Sex of Child, γ_{010}			**0.022** (0.010)	
Depressed·Positive Discipline, γ_{115}	**-0.007** (0.004)			

Notes:

[1]Standard errors in brackets.

[2]Coefficients in **bold** are significant at an alpha level of 0.05 (one-tailed).

[3]Of the tested interaction terms, only significant terms are listed.

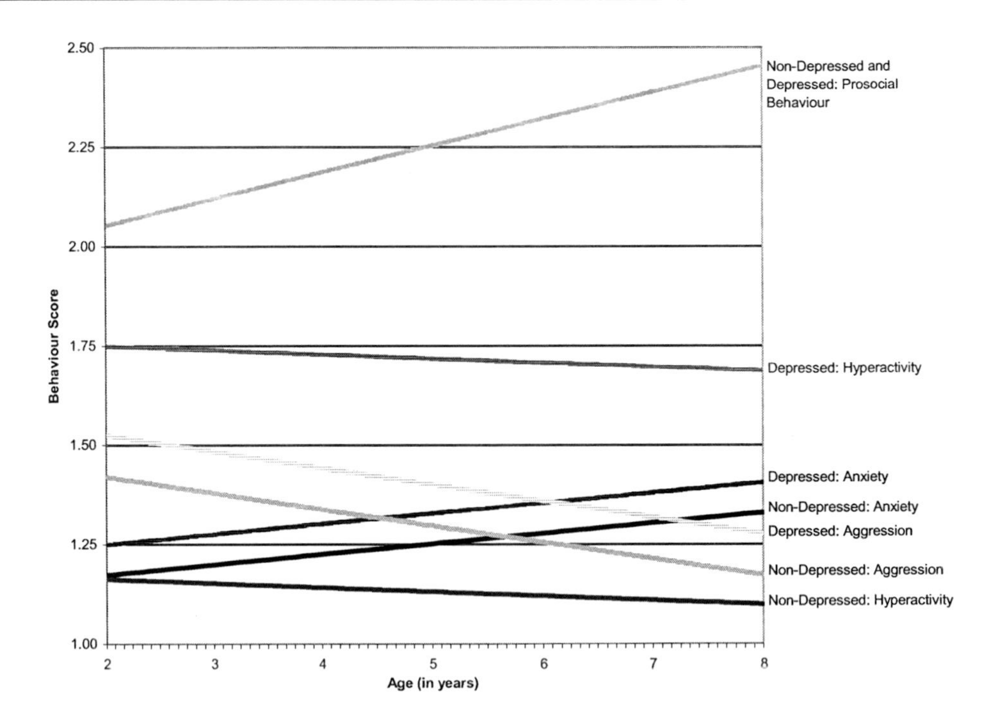

Figure 1. Behavioral outcome trajectories of children of depressed and non-depressed mothers, from the age of 2 to 8 (Source: NLSCY, 1994-2001)

DISCUSSION

Exposure to maternal depression in infancy appears to affect children's behavior at two years of age and these effects may persist to eight years of age and beyond. However, features of the mother-child relationship reduce children's anxiety, hyperactivity, aggression, and improve prosocial behaviors.

Model 1 findings suggest that the effects of depression on children's behavior are evident as early as two years of age. This coincides with Stein et al.'s (1991) observation that effects of maternal depression in toddlers persisted well after their mothers' depression had remitted. These findings provide support for the hypothesis that children of mothers who experience depression in the first two years postpartum would display higher levels of anxiety, hyperactivity, and aggression and lower levels of prosocial behaviors than children of mothers who did not experience such depression. However, when additional predictor and demographic variables were added in Model 2, the main effects of maternal depression on children's behavior at age two disappeared and our second hypothesis was not supported. The constant pattern in the analyses revealed that parenting style, whether positive, consistent, or warm and nurturing, reduced anxiety, hyperactivity, aggression, and increased prosocial behaviors. This builds on recent observations of Murray and Cooper (1999) that suggest an indirect impact of PPD on child behavior via maternal interactive behaviors (e.g. predictability, talkativeness, sensitivity and responsiveness).

Single parenthood increased both anxiety and prosocial behaviors at age two. This finding suggests that the stresses associated with single parenthood not only influence maternal mood but can also impact the affective condition of children as well. In relation to increased prosocial behaviors, it may be that children reared in single parent homes have more caregivers and/or are exposed to more children in care, and therefore develop social skills earlier than children in two-parent homes. In contrast, for depressed mothers, single parenthood decreased anxiety in children at age two. These mothers may have been more readily identified by health professionals as high-risk and they may have received supportive interventions to assist them with parenting (e.g. home visiting) (Olds and et al., 1998; Olds and Kitzman, 1990). Social support has been shown to have a positive effect on mental health (Cohen et al., 2002; Dennis, 2003) and might promote positive maternal-infant interaction and optimal development (Barnard et al., 1985; Letourneau et al., 2001). Moreover, it has been suggested that social support provided to mothers may assist them in their ability to parent well (Barnard et al., 1985; Booth, Barnard, Mitchell, and Spieker, 1987; Booth, Mitchell, Barnard, and Spieker, 1989; Letourneau, 2001).

Depressed mothers with more education had children with higher initial levels of anxiety at age two. This finding contrasts with other recent research suggesting that children of mothers with less education experience more behavioral challenges (Galboda-Liyanage, Prince, and Scott, 2003). Additional research to explore this possible relationship is warranted. Consistent with other research (Benzies, 2001; Galboda-Liyanage et al., 2003), being from a higher socioeconomic background decreased initial levels of hyperactivity in children.

Hyperactivity decreased with age for all children; however, adding additional stresses such as being in a single parent home lessened the rate of decrease over time. This finding is supported by research suggesting that family stresses account for some of the variance in externalizing child behavior problems such as hyperactivity (Prevatt, 2003). Consistent with recent research (Tremblay et al., 2005), aggression also decreased with age and positive discipline seemed to reduce the rate of decrease for all children. On the surface, this finding appears to contradict the main finding that parenting style reduces anxiety, hyperactivity and aggression and improves prosocial behaviors. Perhaps mothers of children with increased displays of aggression utilize more positive parenting discipline strategies over time to cope with their children's aggression. However, this finding contradicts recent findings that negative parental control (Braet, 2004), more coercive parenting (Friedman, 2004), and disciplinary aggression (Woodward, Taylor, and Dowdney, 1998) predict externalizing behavior such as aggression in children.

Consistent with the literature (Leinonen et al., 2003), a sex effect was noted in the trajectories of behavioral outcomes. Females appear to be less vulnerable to hyperactivity and aggression than males and more prosocial, regardless of maternal mental health at age two and over time. Social support appears to increase initial levels of prosocial behaviors. As noted above, perhaps children of single mothers are more prosocial because they are exposed to more forms of social support (e.g. child care help, family support). Prosocial behaviors increase with age, and this increase is minimized by consistent parenting, higher maternal education, and single parent status. As is the case for children of single mothers, the rate of change may be less for children that have a higher initial value of prosocial behaviors at age two.

In conclusion, a significant gap between children of depressed and non-depressed mothers was observed in measures of children's anxiety, hyperactivity and aggression. Moreover, this gap is apparent at age 2 and is maintained to age 8. This finding is explained by a constellation of factors including social support, parenting, family structure, sex of the child, and socioeconomic variables. These findings may be limited by the reliance on maternal report and possible confounding due to maternal depression. In particular, mothers who are depressed may rate their children more negatively than mothers who are not depressed. However, these findings provide direction for interventions aimed at reducing the impact of depression on children's behavioral development via support for parenting.

References

Affonso, D. D., De, A. K., Horowitz, J. A., and Mayberry, L. J. (2000). An international study exploring levels of postpartum depressive symptomatology. *Journal of Psychosomatic Research, 49*(3), 207-216.

Barnard, K. E., Hammond, M., Mitchell, S. K., Booth, C. L., Spietz, A., Snyder, C., et al. (1985). Caring for high-risk infants and their families. In M. Green (Ed.), *The psychosocial aspect of the family* (pp. 245 - 266). Lexington, MA: Lexington Books.

Beck, C. T. (1992). The lived experience of postpartum depression: A phenomenological study. *Nursing Research, 41*(3), 166-170.

Beck, C. T. (1995). The effects of postpartum depression on maternal-infant interaction: a meta-analysis. *Nursing Research, 44*(5), 298-304.

Beck, C. T. (1998). The effects of postpartum depression on child development: A meta-analysis. *Archives of Psychiatric Nursing, 12*(1), 12-20.

Benzies, K. M. (2001). *Relationship of early family environment to child behavioural development at age 7 years.* U Alberta, Canada.

Berkman, L., and Glass, T. (2000). Social integration, social networks, social support, and health. In L. Berkman and I. Kawachi (Eds.), *Social Epidemiology* (pp. 137-173). New York: Oxford University Press.

Booth, C. L., Barnard, K. E., Mitchell, S. K., and Spieker, S. J. (1987). Successful intervention with multi-problem mothers: Effects on the mother-infant relationship. *Infant Mental Health Journal, 8*(3), 288 - 306.

Booth, C. L., Mitchell, S. K., Barnard, K. E., and Spieker, S. J. (1989). Development of maternal social skills in multiproblem families: Effects on the mother-child relationship. *Developmental Psychology, 25*(3), 403 - 412.

Braet, C. (2004). Child personality and parental behavior as moderators of problem behavior. *Developmental Psychology, 40*(6), 1028-1055.

Brennan, P. A., Hammen, C., Andersen, M. J., Bor, W., Najman, J. M., and Williams, G. M. (2000). Chronicity, severity, and timing of maternal depressive symptoms: Relationships with child outcomes at age 5. *Developmental Psychology, 36*(6), 759-766.

Brugha, T. S., Sharp, H. M., Cooper, S. A., Weisender, C., Britto, D., Shinkwin, R., et al. (1998). The Leicester 500 Project. Social support and the development of postnatal depressive symptoms, a prospective cohort survey. *Psychological Medicine, 28*(1), 63-79.

Buist, A. (1998). Childhood abuse, postpartum depression and parenting difficulties: A literature review of associations. *Australian and New Zealand Journal of Psychiatry, 32*(3), 370-378.

Campbell, S., Cohn, J., and Myers, T. (1995). Depression in first-time mothers: Mother-infant interaction and depression chronicity. *Developmental Psychology, 31*(349-357).

Casey, P., Goolsby, S., Berkowitz, C., Frank, D., Cook, J., and et al. (2004). Maternal depression, changing public assistance, food security, and child health status. *Pediatrics, 113*(2), 298-304.

Chambers, R., and Skinner, C. (Eds.). (2003). *Analysis of Survey Data*. Southampton, UK: John Wiley and Sons.

Chao, R. K., and Willms, J. D. (2002). The effects of parenting practices on children's outcomes. In J. D. Willms (Ed.), *Vulnerable Children: Findings from Canada's National Longitudinal Survey of Children and Youth* (pp. 149-165). Edmonton: University of Alberta Press.

Chung, P., and Yue, X. (1999). Postpartum depression and social support: A comparative study in Hong Kong. *Psychologia, 42*(2), 111-121.

Cohen, S., Underwood, L., and Gottlieb, B. (Eds.). (2002). *Social support measurement and intervention: A guide for health and social scientists*. New York: Oxford University Press.

Cohn, J. F., and Tronick, E. Z. (1987). Mother-infant face-to-face interaction: The sequence of dyadic states at 3, 6, and 9 months. *Developmental Psychology, 23*(1), 68 - 77.

Cooper, P. J., and Murray, L. (1995). Course and recurrence of postnatal depression. Evidence for the specificity of the diagnostic concept. *British Journal of Psychiatry, 166*(2), 191-195.

Cooper, P. J., and Murray, L. (1998). Postnatal depression. *British Medical Journal, 316*(7148), 1884-1886.

Cox, J. L., Murray, D., and Chapman, G. (1993). A controlled study of the onset, duration and prevalence of postnatal depression. *British Journal of Psychiatry, 163*, 27-31.

Cutrona, C., and Russell, D. (1987). The provisions of social relationships and adaptation to stress. In W. Jones and D. P. (eds.) (Eds.), *Advances in Personal Relationships* (Vol. 1, pp. 37-67). Greenwich, CT: JAI Press.

Dankner, R., Goldberg, R. P., Fisch, R. Z., and DCrum, R. M. (2000). Cultural elements of portpartum depression: A study of 327Jewish Jerusalem women. *Journal of Reproductive Medicine, 45*(2), 97-104.

Dennis, C. (2003). Peer support within a health care context: a concept analysis. *International Journal of Nursing Studies, 40*(3), 321-332.

Drewett, R., Blair, P., Emmett, P., and Emond, A. (2004). Failure to thrive in the term and preterm infants of mothers depressed in the postnatal period: a population-based birth cohort study. *Journal of Child Psychology and Psychiatry and Allied Disciplines, 45*(2), 359-366.

Elgar, F., Curtis, L., McGrath, P., Waschbusch, D., and Stewart, S. (2003). Antecedent-consequence conditions in maternal mood and child adjustment: A four-year cross-lagged study. *Journal of Clinical Child and Adolescent Psychiatry, 32*(3), 362-374.

England, Ballard, and George. (1994). Chronicity in postnatal depression. *European Journal of Psychiatry, 8*(2), 93-96.

Field, T. (1984). Early interactions between infants and their postpartum depression mothers. *Infant Behavior and Development, 7*(4), 517 - 522.

Field, T. (1994). The effects of mother's physical and emotional unavailability on emotion regulation. *Monographs for the Society of Research in Child Development, 59*(2-3), 208-227.

Friedman, J. e. a. (2004). The relation between parental coping styles and parent-child interactions before and after treatment for children with ADHD adn Oppositional Behavior. *Journal of Clinical Child and Adolescent Psychology, 33*(1), 158-168.

Galboda-Liyanage, K. C., Prince, M. J., and Scott, S. (2003). Mother-child joint activity and behaviour problems of pre-school children. *Journal of Child Psychology and Psychiatry and Allied Disciplines, 44*(7), 1037-1048.

Ghodsian, M., Zajicek, E., and Wolkind, S. (1984). A longitudinal study of maternal depression and child behavior problems. *Journal of Child Psychology and Psychiatry, 25*, 91-109.

Grace, S. L., Evindar, A., and Stewart, D. E. (2003). The effect of postpartum depression on child cognitive development and behavior: a review and critical analysis of the literature. *Archives of Women's Mental Health, 6*(4), 263-274.

Hipwell, A. E., Goossens, F. A., Melhuish, E. C., and Kumar, R. (2000). Severe maternal psychopathology and infant-mother attachment. *Developmental Psychopathology, 12*(2), 157-175.

Holden, J. M. (1991). Postnatal depression: its nature, effects, and identification using the Edinburgh Postnatal Depression scale. *Birth, 18*(4), 211-221.

Kessler, R. C., Berglund, P., Demler, O., and et al. (2003). The epidemiology of major depressive disorder: Results from the National Comorbidity Survey Replication (NCS-R). *Journal of the American Medical Association, 289*(23), 3095-3105.

Kumar, R., and Robson, K. M. (1984). A prospective study of emotional disorders in childbearing women. *British Journal of Psychiatry, 144*, 35-47.

Leinonen, J. A., Solantaus, T. S., and Punamaeki, R.-L. (2003). Parental mental health and children's adjustment: The quality of marital interaction and parenting as mediating factors. *Journal of Child Psychology and Psychiatry and Allied Disciplines, 44*(2), 227-241.

Letourneau, N. (2001). Improving adolescent parent-infant interactions: a pilot study. *Journal of Pediatric Nursing, 16*(1), 53-62.

Letourneau, N., Drummond, J., Fleming, D., Kysela, G., McDonald, L., and Stewart, M. (2001). Supporting parents: Can intervention improve parent-child relationships? *Journal of Family Nursing, 7*(2), 159-187.

Lewinsohn, P., Weinstein, M., and Alper, T. (1970). A behavioral approach to the group treatment of depressed persons: Methodological contribution. *Journal of Clinical Psychology, 26*, 525-532.

Libert, J., and Lewinsohn, P. (1973). The concept of social skill with special reference to the behavior of depressed persons. *Journal of Consulting and Clinical Psychology, 40*, 304-312.

Lin, N., Ye, X., and Ensel, W. M. (1999). Social support and depressed mood: a structural analysis. *Journal of Health and Social Behavior, 40*(4), 344-359.

Logsdon, M. C., Birkimer, J. C., and Usui, W. M. (2000). The link of social support and postpartum depressive symptoms in African-American women with low incomes. *MCN, American Journal of Maternal Child Nursing, 25*(5), 262-266.

Lyons-Ruth, K., Zoll, D., Connell, D., and Grunebaum, H. U. (1986). The depressed mother and her one-year-old infant: Environment, interaction, attachment, and infant development. In E. Z. Tronick and T. Field (Eds.), *Maternal Depression and Infant Disturbance* (eds ed., Vol. 34, pp. 61 - 82). San Fransisco: Josey-Bass.

Mills, E. P., Finchilescu, G., and Lea, S. J. (1995). Postnatal depression - An examination of psychosocial factors. *South African Medical Journal, 85*(2), 99-105.

Murray, L. (1992). The impact of postnatal depression on infant development. *Journal fo Child Psychology and Psychiatry and Allied Disciplines, 33*(3), 543-561.

Murray, L., and Cooper, P. (1996). The impact of postpartum depression on child development. *International Review of Psychiatry, 8*(1), 55-63.

Murray, L., and Cooper, P. (1997a). Effects of postnatal depression on infant development. *Archives of Disease of Childhood, 77*, 97-101.

Murray, L., and Cooper, P. (1997b). Postpartum depression and child development. *Psychological Medicine, 27*(2), 253-260.

Murray, L., and Cooper, P. (1997c). The role of infant and maternal factors in postpartum depression, mother-infant interactions, and infant outcome. In L. Murray and P. J. Cooper (Eds.), *Postpartum depression and child development.* (pp. 111-135): Guilford Press.

Murray, L., and Cooper, P. (Eds.). (1999). *Postpartum Depression and Child Development*: Guilford Press.

Murray, L., Cooper, P. J., Wilson, A., and Romaniuk, H. (2003). Controlled trial of the short- and long-term effect of psychological treatment of post-partum depression. 2. Impact on the mother--child relationship and child outcome. *British Journal of Psychiatry, 182*(5), 420-427.

Murray, L., Fiori-Cowley, A., Hooper, R., and Cooper, P. (1996). The impact of postnatal depression and associated adversity on early mother-infant interactions and later infant outcomes. *Child Development, 67*(5), 2512-2526.

Murray, L., Sinclair, D., Cooper, P., Ducournau, P., and Turner, P. (1999). The socioemotional development of 5-year-old children of postnatally depressed mothers. *Journal of Child Psychology and Psychiatry and Allied Disciplines, 40*(8), 1259-1271.

Nielsen Forman, D., Videbech, P., Hedegaard, M., Dalby Salvig, J., and Secher, N. J. (2000). Postpartum depression: identification of women at risk. [see comments.]. *British Journal of Obstetrics and Gynaecology, 107*(10), 1210-1217.

O'Hara, M., and Swain, A. (1996). Rates and risk of postpartum depression - a meta-analysis. *International Review of Psychiatry, 8*, 37-54.

O'Hara, M. W., Schlechte, J. A., Lewis, D. A., and Varner, M. W. (1991). Controlled prospective study of postpartum mood disorders: psychological, environmental, and hormonal variables. *Journal of Abnormal Psychology, 100*(1), 63-73.

Olds, D. L., and et al. (1998). Long-term effects of a nurse home visitation on children's criminal and antisocial behaviour: 15 year follow-up of a randomized controlled trial. *Journal of the American Medical Association, 280*(14), 1238-1244.

Olds, D. L., and Kitzman, H. (1990). Can home visitation improve the health of women and children at environmental risk? *Pediatrics, 86*(1), 108 - 116.

Orvaschel, H., Walsh-Allis, G., and Ye, W. J. (1988). Psychopathology in children of parents with recurrent depression. *Journal of Abnormal Child Psychology, 16*(1), 17-28.

Pfefferman, D., and Sverchkov, M. (2003). Fitting generalized linear models under informative sampling. In R. Chambers and C. Skinner (Eds.), *Analysis of Survey Data* (pp. 175-195). Southampton, UK: John Wiley and Sons.

Pineo, P. C., Porter, J., and McRoberts, H. A. (1977). The 1971 Census and the socioeconomic classification of occupations. *Canadian Review of Sociology and Anthropology, 14*, 91-102.

Prevatt, F. F. (2003). The contribution of parenting practices in a risk and resiliency model of children's adjustment. *British Journal of Developmental Psychology, 21*(4), 469-480.

Radloff, L. S. (1977). The CES-D Scale: A self-report depression scale for research in the general population. *Applied Psychological Measurement, 1*(3), 385-401.

Raudenbush, S., and Bryk, A. (2002). *Hierarchical linear models: Applications and data analysis methods.* (2nd ed.). Thousand Oaks, CA: Sage.

Righetti-Veltema, M., Bousquet, A., and Manzano, J. (2003). Impact of postpartum depressive symptoms on mother and her 18-month-old infant. *European Child and Adolescent Psychiatry, 12*(2), 75-83.

Righetti-Veltema, M., Conne-Perreard, E., Bousquet, A., and Manzano, J. (1998). Risk factors and predictive signs of postpartum depression. *Journal of Affective Disorders, 49*(3), 167-180.

Ritter, C., Hobfoll, S. E., Lavin, J., Cameron, R. P., and Hulsizer, M. R. (2000). Stress, psychosocial resources, and depressive symptomatology during pregnancy in low-income, inner-city women. *Health Psychology, 19*(6), 576-585.

Sinclair, D., Murray, L., Stein, A., and Cooper, P. (1996). Teacher reports of adjustment to school of postnatally depressed and well mothers' children.

Somers, M.-A., and Willms, J. D. (2002). Maternal Depression and Childhood Vulnerability. In J. D. Willms (Ed.), *Vulnerable Children: Findings from Canada's National Longitudinal Survey of Children and Youth.* Edmonton: University of Alberta Press and Human Resources Development Canada.

Sommer, K., Whitman, T., Borkowski, J., and et al. (2000). Prenatal and maternal predictors of cognitive and emotional delays in children of adolescent mothers. *Adolescence, 35*, 87-112.

Stanley, C., Murray, L., and Stein, A. (2004). The effect of postnatal depression on mother-infant interaction, infant response to the Still-face perturbation, and performance on an Instrumental Learning task. *Development and Psychopathology, 16*(1), 1-18.

Statistics Canada. (1998). *National Longitudinal Survey of Children: Data Dictionary for Cycle 1.* Ottawa, ON: Statistics Canada and Human Resources Development Canada.

Statistics Canada. (2001). *Births.* Ottawa, Canada: Statistics Canada.

Stein, A., Gath, D. H., Bucher, J., Bond, A., Day, A., and Cooper, P. J. (1991). The relationship between post-natal depression and mother-child interaction. *British Journal of Psychiatry, 158*, 46-52.

Stocky, A., and Lynch, J. (2000). Acute psychiatric disturbance in pregnancy and the puerperium. *Baillieres Best Practices Res Clin Obstet Gynaecol, 14*(1), 73087.

Teasdale, J., Fogarty, S., and Williams, J. (1980). Speech rate as a measure of short term variation in depression. *British Journal of Clinical Psychology, 19*(271-278).

Tremblay, R. E., Nagin, D. S., Seguin, J. R., Zoccolillo, M., Zelazo, P. D., Boivin, M., et al. (2005). Physical aggression during early childhood: Trajectories and predictors. *Canadian Child and Adolescent Psychiatry Review, 14*(1), 3-9.

Whiffen, V. E., and Gotlib, I. H. (1993). Comparison of postpartum and nonpostpartum depression: clinical presentation, psychiatric history, and psychosocial functioning. *Journal of Consulting and Clinical Psychology, 61*(3), 485-494.

Willms, J. D., and Shields, M. (1996). *A measure of socioeconomic status for the National Longitudinal Study of Children*: Report prepared for the Canadian National Longitudinal Study of Children.

Woodward, L., Taylor, E., and Dowdney, L. (1998). Parenting style was associated with hyperactivity in school aged boys. *Journal of Child Psychology and Psychiatry, 39*, 161-169.

Wrate, R., Rooney, A., Thomas, P., and Cox, J. (1985). Postnatal depression and child development: A three-year follow-up study. *British Journal of Psychiatry, 146*, 622-627.

In: Parent-Child Relations: New Research
Editor: Dorothy M. Devore, pp. 65-82
ISBN 1-60021-167-4

Chapter 4

PARENT-ADOLESCENT CONFLICTS AND ADOLESCENT ADJUSTMENTS IN HMONG IMMIGRANT FAMILIES IN THE UNITED STATES*

Zha Blong Xiong[1], Kathryn D. Rettig and Arunya Tuicomepee
General College, Department of Family Social Science, Department of Educational Psychology
University of Minnesota

ABSTRACT

The purposes of this study were to investigate the frequency, intensity, and subjects of arguments that Hmong second-generation adolescents have with their immigrant parents, and to explore whether the relationships of these conflicts and acculturation have any effect on the adolescent adjustment, as measured by self-esteem, depression, delinquent behaviors, and school performance. One hundred eighty-one adolescents (105 males, 76 females) of Hmong descent, ages 12 – 24 years (M = 15.82, SD = 2.00) participated in the study. The results indicate that 74% of the adolescents reported at least one conflict with their parents and an average of 4.47 (SD = 4.78) conflicts over the past month. The most frequently mentioned conflict issues with fathers and mothers were helping around the house, getting low grades, talking back to parents, watching television, and telephone calls. Conflicts with mothers, but not fathers, were significantly related to adolescents' reports of depression and delinquent behavior. Some educational approaches are

* The work reported here was supported by the University of Minnesota's Office of the Vice President for Research and Dean of the Graduate School Grants-in-Aid Award, the President's Faculty Multicultural Research Award, and the University of Minnesota Faculty Summer Research Fellowship Award. The continuous financial support of the General College is gratefully acknowledged. We also acknowledge agencies and community groups in Minnesota that collaborated with this research project: Boys Totem Town Correctional Facility, Lauj Youth Society, Hmong American Mutual Assistance Association, Hmong American Partnership, Patrick Henry High School, and other smaller community-based groups. We also want to express our most sincere thanks to the graduate and undergraduate students and the McNair Scholar Program students for their assistance in helping collect data. Finally, we would like to thank Drs. Michael Cleveland and Robert delMas for reading earlier versions of this manuscript.
[1] Address correspondence to: Zha Blong Xiong, 140 Appleby Hall, 128 Pleasant Street S.E., Minneapolis, Minnesota, 55455. E-mail: xiong008@umn.edu.

discussed when professionals intervene parent-adolescent conflicts in Hmong immigrant families.

One of the most enduring themes in adolescent research is the parent-adolescent relationship. Steinberg (2001) noted in his presidential address to the Society for Research on Adolescence (SRA) that the study of family relationships as they relate to adolescence, and specifically, the parent-adolescent relationship, constituted a significant body of research during the 1990's. Much of the literature on parent-adolescent relationships, however, has been devoted to large ethnic groups (Arnett, 1999; Fuligni, 1998; Laursen and Collins, 1994). Very few studies have paid attention to smaller ethnic groups in the United States, such as the Hmong.

The Hmong are a sub-Asian group who lived in the mountainous regions of Laos[2] after the conclusion of the Indochinese War. During the war, the Hmong were recruited by the United States Army to serve in a "special force" of guerilla fighters to prevent the penetration of North Vietnamese to Laos and South Vietnam and to rescue fallen American pilots (Quincy, 1995). However, after the war in 1975, thousands of Hmong left the country for fear of retribution for supporting the United States. They settled in various Western countries, including the United Sates, Canada, France, French Guyana, Australia, and Germany (Hamilton-Merritt, 1993).

There are an estimated number of 186,310 Hmong-descended persons living in the United States, and approximately 78% of them lived in California (36%), Minnesota (23%), and Wisconsin (19%) (U.S. Census Bureau, 2000). Though small in number, Hmong immigrants in the United States are the 4th largest population in the world, followed by China, Vietnam, and Laos. Minnesota, where the data for the present study were collected, is home to the second largest Hmong population in the United States (43,000) and the Minneapolis-Saint Paul Metropolitan area has the largest Hmong population of any metropolitan area in the country. The number is expected to rise dramatically over the next few decades since more than half of the Hmong population (56%) is under the age of 19 years, with a median age of 16.1, compared to 35.3 for U. S. population (Thao and Pfeifer, 2004).

This rapid growth of the second Hmong generation[3] poses many challenges to Hmong parents and to parent-adolescent relationships, particularly conflicts between the two generations. Most immigrant studies have suggested that parent-adolescent conflicts in immigrant families tended to occur as a result of the acculturation gap between the two generations (Farver, Narang, and Bhadha, 2002; Fuligni, 1998; Nguyen and Williams, 1989; Rick and Forward, 1992; Rosenthal, Ranieri, and Klimidis, 1996). Specifically, immigrant children acculturated to the mainstream culture faster than their parents (Nguyen and Williams, 1989; Zhou and Bankston, 1998). As a result, immigrant parents lagged behind, thus leading to role reversals and misunderstandings in parent-adolescent relationships (Detzner, Xiong, and Eliason, 1999; Xiong, Detzner, and Rettig, 2001).

Research studies have documented some of the factors that contributed to parent-adolescent conflicts in immigrant families (Farver et al., 2002; Fuligni, 1998; Nguyen and Williams, 1989; Portes and Rumbaut, 2001), but some limitations in these studies remain. First, most parent-adolescent conflict studies have focused on Mexican, Chinese, and

---

[2] Laos is a land-locked country located south of China, east of Vietnam, west of Thailand, and north of Cambodia.

[3] Second generation includes children who were brought to the United States before 7 years old and those who were born in the United States (Zhou and Bankston, 1998).

Vietnamese immigrants, instead of Hmong (Fuligni, 1998; Roosa, Deng, Ryu, Barrell, Tein, Johnes, Lopes, and Crowder, 2005; Zhou and Bankston, 1998). Only a few studies have included Hmong in their samples (Portes and Rumbaut, 2001; Lee, 2001; Rick and Forward, 1992).

The studies that did include Hmong participants were further limited by their small sample sizes ($n < 100$). Focusing on the Hmong is important, since Hmong adolescents have been found to experience more adjustment problems than other Southeast Asian groups (Rumbaut, 1995). Some research suggested that Hmong youth are at greater risk for parent-adolescent conflicts (Portes and Rumbaut, 2001), school difficulties (Lee, 2001), and social adjustment problems (Ngo, 2002). None of the above-mentioned studies used an issue-based assessment that determined the subjects of arguments adolescents had with their parents, identified who was having what argument with whom, or explored how these conflicts were related to the Hmong adolescents' psychological adjustment and academic performance.

The purposes of the current study were to examine the frequency, intensity, and subjects of arguments between Hmong adolescents and their immigrant parents and to determine whether parent-adolescent conflicts and acculturation were related to adolescent adjustment, as measured by self-esteem, depression, delinquent behaviors, and self-reported grade point average.

Literature Review

Parent-Adolescent Relationships

Parent-adolescent relationships in North America are characterized by significant changes as a result of biological maturation and developing cognitive complexity (Laursen and Collins, 1994; Smetana, 1989; Steinberg, 1990). During this developmental stage, adolescents become more critical of parental regulations of their personal choices and they are expected to distance from parents and to establish a stronger relationship with peers (Elliott and Feldman, 1990; Smetana). As a result of these changes, some arguments and continuing conflicts are to be expected (Laursen, Coy, and Collins, 1998).

Previous studies have reported that most of the parent-adolescent arguments involved everyday activities in the home, rather than major conflicts resulting from extraordinary circumstances (Arnett, 1999; Steinberg, 2001). Allison (2000) studied a group of eighth graders in Ohio using the *Issues Checklist* (Prinz, Foster, Kent, and O'Leary, 1979; Robin and Foster, 1989) and found that most parent-adolescent arguments involved everyday issues in the family, such as helping around the home (85%), keeping the house neat (82%), and cleaning the bedroom (80%). Similarly, Smetana and Gaines (1999) used the same measure (Prinz et al., 1979) to examine middle-class African-American families and found similar patterns where helping around house (77 %), neatness or cleanliness (67 %), and cleaning the bedroom (66%) were among the top three issues argued between parents and adolescents.

Hmong adolescents in their country of origin did not distance from the family. Instead, they were expected to take on more responsibilities as they aged and to obey their parents without questions even during adolescence (Chan, 1986). Any questioning or "talking back" was considered disobedient (Detzner et al., 1999). Recent studies with adolescents have shown a shift in the dynamics of parent-child relationships in Hmong families due to immigration and acculturation (Lee, 2001; Xiong, Eliason, Detzner, and Cleveland, 2005). Adolescents who became more acculturated overlooked their parents' values and modes of behavior, and they adopted values and modes of behavior in their daily interactions with siblings and peers (Feldman and Rosenthal, 1990; Zhou and Bankston, 1998). Thus, the shift of ecologies, values, and modes of behavior seemed to play critical roles in changing parent-adolescent relationships (Rick and Forward, 1992; Xiong and Detzner, 2005).

Some studies have found that Hmong adolescents were at greater risk of encountering parent-adolescent conflicts (Portes and Rumbaut, 2001; Ngo, 2002), particularly adolescent girls (DuongTran, Lee, and Khoi, 1996). However, most of these studies did not address what issues adolescent boys and girls were more likely to have with their fathers and mothers, and whether these issues affected adolescent adjustment.

Gender, Age, Acculturation, and Parent-Adolescent Conflicts

Gender and age of adolescents have been shown to affect the degree to which adolescents interact with their parents (Galambos and Almeida, 1992; Steinberg, 1981, 1988). Girls, compared to boys, were more likely to disagree with their parents, particularly mothers (Fuligni, 1998). Early adolescents (10- to 12- years-old), compared to mid adolescents (13- to 16- years-old) and late adolescents (17- to 22- years- old), experienced more frequent conflicts with their parents (Laursen et al., 1998), and mid adolescents, compared to early and late adolescents, tended to experience more intense conflicts with their parents (Laursen et al.,1998). Conversely, Fuligni (1998) studied immigrant adolescents in grades 6 to 12 in California and found that 10th graders (mid adolescents), compared to 6th and 8th graders (early adolescents), reported more frequent conflicts with their parents. To date, limited studies have investigated whether age and gender affect the variation of parent-adolescent conflicts in Hmong immigrant families.

The role of acculturation in immigrant parent-adolescent conflicts has been well documented in the literature (Moon, Wolfer, and Robinson, 2001; Nguyen and Williams, 1989; Rick and Forward, 1992; Rosenthal et al., 1996). However, the results have been mixed. Some studies reported that participants who scored lower, compared to those who scored higher on the acculturation scale, scored higher on the conflict scale (Rosenthal et al.; Sodowsky, Lai, and Plake, 1991). Other studies suggested that the second-generation adolescents, who are highly acculturated, compared to the first-generation adolescents, encountered more conflicts with their immigrant parents (Fuligni, 1998; Handal, Le-Stiebel, Dicarlo, and Gutzwiller, 1999). Portes and Rumbaut (2001), however, found no evidence to support the relationships between acculturation and parent-adolescent conflicts in a large study with several immigrant groups living in Florida and California. They reported that Hmong and Cambodian, compared to other immigrant groups, reported more conflicts.

Effects of Parent-Adolescent Conflicts on Adolescent Adjustment

Research has consistently shown that adolescents who came from conflicted families performed poorly in school (Rumbaut, 1996; Sivan, Kosh, Baier, and Adiga, 1999), experienced greater depression (Whitbeck et al., 1992), had lower self-esteem (Barber, Chadwick, and Oerter, 1992), and engaged in more delinquent acts (Mason, Cauce, Gonzales, and Hiraga 1996; Go, 1998, Roosa et al., 2005). Portes and Rumbaut (2001), for example, found a significant relationship between levels of family conflict and adolescents' school performance, as measured by grade point average.

A study of Steinberg, Dornbusch, and Brown (1992) indicated that parents across Asian, Hispanic, and Caucasian ethnic groups were the most salient influence on students' long-term educational plans. In addition, students whose parents supported achievement performed better than those who received no support from parents. Research has further indicated that caring, supportive parents acted as buffers against the outside world and assisted young people in achieving their goals, including academic achievement (Blum et al., 2000).

The relationship between parent-adolescent conflicts and adolescents' psychological adjustment has also been documented in the literature (Mason et al., 1994; Roosa et al., 2005). Roosa's group (2005) studied 189 inner-city, low-income Anglo and Mexican American families and found that parent-adolescent conflicts were significantly associated with youth delinquent and other externalizing behaviors. Whitbeck et al. (1992) found a significant link between parental influence and adolescent depressed mood with a non-immigrant population and Barber et al. (1992) studied the association between parent-adolescent relationship and youth self-esteem and found that a negative parent-adolescent relationship (or conflict) was significantly related to self-esteem.

Empirical evidence shows that adolescent's delinquent acts can be traced back to the family, particularly to parent-adolescent conflicts (Portes and Rumbaut, 2001; Shek, 1998; Shek and Ma, 2001; Zhou and Bankston, 1998). For example, Go (1998) conducted a study with 206 Southeast Asian youth from 12 to 16 years of age and found a positive correlation between family conflict and youth delinquency. Sivan et al. (1999) studied delinquency in immigrant families and concluded that the absence of bonds with parents due to conflicted relationships served as a reason for adolescents to depend on gangs as a replacement for the family. The current study adds to the literature by seeking information from adolescents about parent-adolescent conflicts and acculturation in Hmong immigrant families in order to explore relationships of these variables to four indicators of adolescent adjustment, including depression, self-esteem, delinquent behaviors, and self-reported grade point average.

METHOD

Procedure and Sample

Participants were recruited from non-profit organizations, schools, churches, and community centers that served youth in a metropolitan area of Minnesota. Staff members from the community agencies assisted in announcing the study and distributing information to adolescents and parents. All individuals were offered $10 for participating. Interested adolescents provided their contact information, which allowed the research team to contact them in order to explain the purposes, risks, and benefits of the study. Participants who agreed to participate needed to submit a parental consent form and also sign an assent form prior to receiving the questionnaire. The questionnaires were self-administered in homes or in the cooperating agencies and could be completed in 30-60 minutes, depending on reading ability.

The resulting sample included 181 adolescents of Hmong descent from Minnesota (105 males, 76 females), ages 12 – 24 years (M = 15.82, SD = 2.00) and grades 6th – 12th (M = 8.87, SD = 2.85). Ninety percent of the respondents belonged to the second-generation (Zhou and Bankston, 1998). All of their parents were foreign-born. Despite being immigrants, 96% of the parents had lived in the United States for more than 10 years (M = 18, SD = 6), and the majority of them were employed (60%) and owned their own homes (78%).

Measures

The independent variables in the study were age, gender, parent-adolescent conflicts, and acculturation. The four dependent variables were self-esteem, depression, delinquent behaviors, and grade point average.

Parent-adolescent conflicts. The conflicts were assessed based on a modified version of the Issues Checklist (Prinz, Foster, Kent, and O'Leary, 1979; Robin and Foster, 1989). The Checklist originally consisted of 44 potential topics of conflict in households with adolescents. For the current study, the Issues Checklist was first translated to the Hmong language by two Hmong human service professionals. It was then pilot tested with a group of Hmong parents and adolescents, resulting in 28 items that were culturally relevant. The relevant items were then placed on the questionnaire administered to the adolescents.

Each adolescent was asked to recall disagreements with his/her father and mother simultaneously over the past four weeks. For each identified disagreement, the adolescent was asked to rate the intensity of the discussion or argument on a five-point range (1 = *very calm,* 3 = *neutral/mixed,* 5 = *very angry*). The modified Hmong Issues Checklist yields two scores for each respondent. The first score is based on the frequency of conflicts, as indicated by the total number of issues endorsed. The second score is the intensity of conflicts indicated by the mean intensity rating score. Low scores in each case indicate less frequent and less intense conflicts, and high scores reflect more frequent and more intense conflicts in the relationship. Internal consistency reliabilities for both subscales are presented in Table 1.

Acculturation. The indicator of acculturation was a single-item: "How much have you adopted American ways of doing things?" The respondents used a 4-point rating (1 = *not at all*, 2 = *a little*, 3 = *much,* and 4 = *very much, just like an American*). This single-item indicator of acculturation performed well in discriminating between non acculturated and acculturated immigrant adolescents in a previous study (Ranieri, Klimidis, and Rosenthal, 1994).

Self-esteem. The Rosenberg Global Self-Esteem Scale (Rosenberg, 1965), adapted from Portes and Rumbaut (2001), was used to measure self-esteem of adolescents. Each respondent was asked to rate the ten items as 1 (*disagree a lot*), 2 (*disagree*), 3 (*agree*), and 4 (*agree a lot*). Sample items included "I feel that I am a person of worth, at least on an equal basis with others" and "I feel that I have a number of good qualities." Higher scores indicate higher self-esteem. The ten-item index had reasonable internal consistency reliability (alpha = .83) for immigrant populations in a previous study (Portes and Rumbaut, 2001), and the internal consistency reliability for the current study was also acceptable (Table 1).

Table 1. Means, Standard Deviations, and Internal Reliabilities of All Variables (n = 58)

Variable and Sampled Questions/Items	Possible Range of Scores	Mean	SD	Coefficient Alpha
Father-Adolescent Conflict (Frequency)	1-22	4.13	4.82	.90
Have you and your parents argued about the following issues during the last 4 weeks?				
Mother-Adolescent Conflict (Frequency)	1-22	4.82	4.74	.88
Have you and your parents argued about the following issues during the last 4 weeks?				
Father-Adolescent Conflict (Intensity)	1-110	11.10	15.85	.91
If you have, how intense was the argument?				
Mother-Adolescent Conflict (Intensity)	1-110	13.36	16.43	.90
If you have, how intense was the argument?				
Acculturation	1-4	2.74	.71	--
To what extent have you adopted American ways of doing things?				
Self-esteem	1-32	16.32	5.02	.64
I take a positive attitude toward myself				
I feel that I am a person of worth, at least on an equal basis with others.				
I feel that I have a number of good qualities				
Depression	1.20	7.80	3.34	.86
In the past week I felt sad				
I could not get "going."				
My appetite was poor				
Delinquent Behaviors	1-10	1.91	2.53	.86
Have you ever been placed in detention or jail?				
Have you ever attacked someone with a weapon or try to seriously hurt them?				
School Performance (GPA)	1-5	3.52	1.69	--
Which is closest to your grade point average (GPA)?				

Note. The dashes represent a single-item measure. To obtain a full report of the longer scales, contact the first author

Depression. Depression was measured with four items from the Center for Epidemiologic Studies Depression Scale (CES-D; Radloff, 1977), which was adapted from Portes and Rumbaut (2001). Adolescents were asked how often during the past week they "felt sad," "could not get going," "did not feel like eating," and "felt depressed." Each item was rated from 1 (*rarely or less than once a week*) to 4 (*most of the time or 5 to 7 days a week*). The internal consistency reliability coefficient for the four-item index for immigrant population was .76 (Portes and Rumbaut), and the internal consistency reliability coefficient for the four-item index for the current study was acceptable (Table 1).

Delinquent Behaviors. A ten-item index indicated whether the respondents were involved in any delinquent acts over the past six months. Respondents were asked to provide a "yes" or "no" response if they had run away from home, cut classes, stolen something worth more than $5, beaten up someone, or been placed on probation for something they had done (Conger and Elder, 1994; Elliott, Huizinga, and Ageton, 1985). The internal consistency reliability of the delinquent behavior index of ten items was acceptable (Table 1).

Grade point average (GPA). Performance in school was indicated by the adolescents' self-reports. This strategy was due to data privacy laws that prevented access to school records. Respondents were asked: "Which is closest to your grade point average (GPA)?" Eleven grade categories were listed as possible responses. The eleven letter grades checked were converted into a numeric grade: A = 4, B = 3, C = 2, D = 1 and F = 0.

RESULTS

Parent- Adolescent Conflicts as Reported by Adolescents

Percentages of adolescents reporting conflicts with parents. The results showed that about 74% of the adolescents reported at least one conflict with their parents over the past month. Of the 28 issues listed on the Issues Checklist, adolescents reported an average of four issues (M =4.47, SD = 4.78) on which they had conflicts with parents over the past month. The number of reported conflicts ranged from zero to 22 with a median of 4.0 with mothers and 2.0 with the fathers.

Conflict issues. The five most frequently mentioned conflicts with fathers included helping around the house (31%), getting low grades (28%), talking back to parents (26%), watching television (25%), and telephone calls (22%). For conflicts with mothers, the most frequently cited were helping around the house (44%), talking back to parents (32%), not coming home on time (30%), watching television (27%), and how neat clothing looks (26%).

Intensity of conflicts. The most intense conflicts reported by adolescents with their parents were not the same as the most frequently mentioned conflicts. The results showed that the top five intense conflicts with fathers were doing drugs (M = 3.56, SD = 1.40), acting like gangsters (M = 3.45, SD = 1.61), drinking beer or other liquor (M = 3.32, SD = 1.41), not going to school (M = 3.26, SD = 1.40), and not wanting to get a job (M =3.12, SD = 1.27). Similarly, the five most intense conflicts with mothers were doing drugs (M = 3.45, SD = 1.50), not going to school (M = 3.36, SD = 1.37), talking back to parents (M = 3.28, SD = 1.26), drinking beer or other liquor (M = 3.26, SD = 1.46), and not coming home on time (M = 3.14, SD = 1.23).

Chi-square analysis and independent t-tests (Table 2) were used to compare boys' and girls' ten most frequently mentioned and intense parent-adolescent conflict issues. Running multiple comparisons posed a risk of inflating Type I error due to the accumulation of error rate per comparison (Howell, 1997). Therefore, the risk was controlled for by dividing the acceptable significance level (α = .05) by the number of comparisons (Tabachnick and Fidell, 2001). Tabachnick and Fidell (2001) suggested using the following formula to calculate the significance level when including multiple comparisons in the analysis: $\alpha = 1\text{-}(1\text{-}\ \alpha')\ c$ where *c* is the number of comparisons. Results of the chi-square analysis found no significant differences between boys and girls except for conflicts with mothers concerning telephone calls. For example, there were more girls (35.9%), compared to boys (16.8%), endorsing conflict over telephone calls with their mothers ($p<.004$). On the other hand, Table 2 shows that there were more boys rating intense conflicts with their father (mean = 3.73) compared to girls (mean = 3.11).

Table 2. Average Intensity of the Top Ten Parent-Adolescent Conflict Issues by Gender

Topic of Conflict	Boys (n = 102)		Girls (n = 79)			
	Mean	SD	Mean	SD	t (df)	p value
Conflict with Father						
Doing drugs	3.29	1.53	4.00	1.05	-1.29 (25)	.21
Acting like gangsters	3.73	1.68	3.11	1.54	-2.10 (23)	.05*
Not going to school	3.09	1.41	3.58	1.38	-0.98 (32)	.33
Not wanting to get a job	3.18	1.40	3.00	1.09	0.27 (15)	.79
Taking back to parents	3.04	1.11	3.05	1.21	-0.01 (43)	.10
Dyeing hair	3.31	1.65	2.58	1.24	1.23 (23)	.23
Not coming home on time	2.67	1.37	3.24	1.20	-1.30 (33)	.20
Going on dates	2.71	1.50	3.00	1.48	-0.40 (16)	.70
Getting low grades in school	2.82	1.28	2.89	1.20	-0.20 (45)	.84
Conflict with Mother						
Doing drugs	3.06	1.59	4.09	1.14	-1.88 (27)	.07
Not going to school	3.16	1.41	3.71	1.27	-1.22 (37)	.23
Taking back to parents	3.15	1.06	3.39	1.41	-0.75 (58)	.46
Drinking beer or other liquor	2.94	1.35	3.89	1.54	-1.64 (25)	.11
Not coming home on time	2.86	1.30	3.41	1.24	-1.65 (56)	.10
Not wanting to get a job	2.91	1.45	3.00	1.33	-0.15 (19)	.88
Going on dates	2.50	1.65	3.18	1.59	-1.05 (25)	.30
Getting low grades in school	2.77	1.28	3.15	1.23	-1.02 (44)	.31
Acting like gangsters	2.81	1.64	3.10	1.45	-0.45 (24)	.65
Dyeing hair	3.21	1.67	2.56	1.29	1.26 (30)	.22

Note. Intensity scores vary from 1 (*very calm*) to 5 (*very angry*). * p<.005

Effects of Adolescents' Gender, Acculturation, and Age on Parent-Adolescent Conflicts

A 2 x2 x 2 analysis of variance (ANOVA) was performed to explore the impact of gender (boys vs. girls), acculturation (low vs. high acculturation level), and age (mid- vs. late-adolescence) have on father-adolescent conflict and mother-adolescent conflict separately. The analyses found no significant main effects for father-adolescent conflicts (all p values < .13). However, there was a significant interaction between gender and acculturation level for father-adolescent conflict (F = 4.672, p< .032). In other words, girls who scored lower on the acculturation item were more likely to mention more conflicts with their fathers, compared to both boys and girls who scored higher on acculturation and boys who scored lower on the acculturation item. On the other hand, the mother model (Table 3) showed there was a significant main effect for gender (F= 5.23, p< .02), but no significant interactions among the three variables included. Regardless of acculturation and age, girls were more likely to report more conflicts with their mothers than boys.

Table 3. Reported Mother-Adolescent Conflicts as a Function of Adolescents' Gender, Acculturation, and Age

Source	SS	df	MS	F	Sig
Main Effects					
Gender	116.33	1	116.33	5.23	.02*
Acculturation	18.45	1	18.45	.83	.36
Age	44.80	1	44.80	2.01	.16
Interaction					
Gender x Acculturation	76.11	1	76.11	3.42	.07
Gender x Age	12.16	1	12.16	.55	.46
Acculturation x Age	65.74	1	65.74	2.96	.09
Gender x Acculturation x Age	24.79	1	24.79	1.12	.29
Residual	3758.94	169	22.24		
Total	7952.00	177			

* P<.05

Parent-Adolescent Conflicts and Adolescent Adjustment

A one-way between-groups multivariate analysis of variance (MANOVA) was performed to determine if conflict with parents was associated with the four dependent variables. Due to the high correlation between the frequency and intensity scores ($r = .93 - .95$), only the frequency of conflict score was used in separate analyses for the fathers and mothers. This variable was recoded to represent three groups. The "conflict-free" group represented adolescents who reported no conflict with their parents over the past month. The "low-conflict" group represented those who reported one to five conflicts with their parents; and the "high-conflict" group represented those who reported six or more conflicts with their parents. The four dependent variables were delinquent behaviors, self-esteem, depression, and grade point average. Correlations among all the variables are displayed in Table 4. As seen in the table, frequency of conflicts was significantly correlated with adolescent reports of depression while age was significantly correlated with self-reported delinquency.

The result of the MANOVA showed no significant effect for the father model (data not shown) on the dependent variables ($\Lambda = .93$; $p < .19$). Overall, the model accounted for only 4% of the variance in the dependent variables. Conversely, there was a significant effect for the mother model ($\Lambda = .82$; $p < .00$), accounting for 10% of the variance in the dependent variables (Table 5). A post hoc comparison using the Scheffé procedure to protect against inflated Type I error due to multiple tests (Tabachnick and Fidell, 2001) found significant group effects for the delinquent behavior index and the depression scale. Specifically, the conflict-free adolescent group, compared to the low-conflict and high-conflict adolescent groups, was less likely to engage in delinquent behaviors (both ps $< .01$). Furthermore, they also reported less depressed compared to the high conflict group. However, their score was not statistically significant different from those who reported low conflict with parents. None of the three groups' scores on self-esteem and school performance were statistically different from one another.

CONCLUSION

The discussion first summarizes the results concerning the frequency of conflicts and adolescents reporting conflicts, followed by the topics of those arguments, and the intensity of the conflicts as perceived by adolescents. The findings indicate that parent-adolescent conflicts in Hmong immigrant families are less prevalent than the literature has suggested. Adolescents reported few conflicts (M = 4.47, SD = 4.78) over the past month. The percentage of Hmong adolescents indicating issues over which they had conflict with parents is significant lower (44%) when comparing the issues of conflict endorsed by Caucasian American and African-American adolescents in other studies (Allison, 2000; Smetana and Gaines, 1999). This finding contradicts results from previous studies which suggested that conflicts between Hmong parents and adolescents were frequent (Ngo, 2002; Portes and Rumbaut, 2001), perhaps due to how conflict was measured.

Consistent with other studies (Allison, 2000; Arnett, 1999; Smetana and Gaines, 1999; Steinberg, 2001), most mundane conflicts between Hmong parents and adolescents also involved daily issues. The intense conflicts, however, were major problems, such as drugs, gangs, schools, and jobs. This finding seems to contradict previous studies based on samples of Caucasian and middle class African-American adolescents (Allison, 2000; Smetana and Gaines, 1999). In addition, the intensity of conflict, as measured by the mean for the present sample, is also significantly higher compared to other studies. Our sample was recruited from youth programs in poor neighborhoods in a region that has a high concentration of immigrants (Thao and Pfeifer, 2004) and high rates of immigrant juvenile delinquency (Minnesota Planning, n.d.). Studies have shown that parents, particularly Hmong, who live in this type of harsh environment are more vigilant and controlled in their interactions with children (Xiong et al., 2001; Zhou and Bankston, 1998).

It is possible that parents' sensitivities and reactions to this risky environment, as manifested by adolescents' behaviors and types of friends, lead to more scolding, controlling, and harsher discipline which further created more of the intensity of conflicts involving drugs, gangs, and school problems (Xiong et al., 2001).

We also found that boys reported more intense arguments with their fathers about their "acting like gangsters behaviors," compare to girls. Girls, on the other hand, fought more frequently with their mothers, particularly about phone privileges, compared to boys. This is expected since fathers in traditional families tended to responsible for the disciplining the sons and mothers were supposed to train and scold the daughters (Donnelly, 1994; Lee, Xiong, and Yuen, in press). Given what is known about Hmong family dynamics, it is not surprising to find these gender-specific conflicts. What is surprising, however, was the similarity of reports between boys and girls for both of their parents across different conflict issues.

Table 4. Correlations Among Parent-Adolescent Conflicts and Related Variables

		2	3	4	5	7	8	9	10	11
									-.069	.211**
1	F-AIC-Freq	.898**	.949**	.816**	-.044	-.008	-.073	.123		
2	M-AIC-Freq	--	.861**	.933**	-.075	.012	-.047	.127	-.069	.286**
3	F-AIC-Intensity		--	.892**	-.077	-.046	-.103	.082	-.089	.246**
4	M-AIC-Intensity			--	-.069	-.010	-.053	.088	-.107	.338**
5	Age				--	-.043	-.051	.292**	0.25	-.056
7	Acculturation					--	.064	-.010	.034	-.085
8	GPA						--	-.179**	.103	-.052
9	Delinquent Behavior							--	-.101	.262**
10	Self-esteem								--	-.131
11	Depression									--

Note: n varies from 157 to 181. * p<.05. ** p<.01

Table 5. Comparisons of Mother-Adolescent Conflicts on GPA, Delinquent Acts, Self Esteem, and Depression

Variable	Conflict-Free vs LO-Conflict (n=38)	(n=68)		Conflict-Free vs HI-Conflict (n=38)	(n=67)		LO-Conflict vs HI-Conflict (n=68)	(n=67)	
	Mean(SD)	Mean(SD)	P value	Mean(SD)	Mean(SD)	P value	Mean(SD)	Mean(SD)	P value
GPA	3.42(1.82)	3.74(1.57)	653	3.42(1.82)	3.45(1.69)	.997	3.74(1.57)	3.45(1.69)	.610
Delinquent Behavior	0.55(1.01)	2.18(2.81)	.004*	0.55(1.01)	2.25(2.43)	.002*	2.18(2.81)	2.25(2.43)	.982
Self Esteem	15.90(3.72)	15.99(6.15)	.996	15.90(3.72)	16.99(4.34)	.566	15.99(6.15)	16.99(4.34)	.514
Depression	6.55(2.21)	7.49(3.38)	.340	6.55(2.21)	8.73(3.28)	.003*	7.49(3.38)	8.73(3.28)	.071

Note: * p ≤.05

We believe this invariant report between boys and girls suggests that both parents have become more flexible in their parenting practices and perhaps are more comfortable of reprimanding both girls and boys. This interpretation seems to be consistent with another study that included Southeast Asian fathers in the sample. This study found that fathers in the United States have moved away from a distant relationship to a more involved and close relationship with their adolescent children in order to be effective parents (Xiong and Detzner, 2005). Perhaps, by putting emphasis on relationship building versus gender- specific training, both parents are at risk for having disagreements with both their sons and daughters.

Acculturation has been found to affect parent-adolescent conflict in some studies (Fuligni, 1998; Rosenthal et al. 1996), but the current study, like the one conducted by Portes and Rumbaut (2001), found no differences between the less acculturated and more acculturated adolescents. We suspect that the reliance on a single indicator of acculturation, coupled with the homogeneous sample, where 90.1% of the adolescents were born in the United States or had lived in the country for more than 10 years may account for this finding. These limitations may also play a role in non-significant correlations between parent-adolescent conflicts and acculturation levels. Future studies need to include a more comprehensive acculturation scale that measures multiple dimensions of acculturation in order to determine the relationship between parent-adolescent conflict and acculturation for the second-generation Hmong adolescents.

Consistent with other studies which suggest that children who grew up in conflicted family are more at risk to become depressed and engage in delinquent acts (Go, 1998; Portes and Rumbaut, 2001; Sivan et al., 1999), the present study found that adolescents who reported some conflicts with their parents also report more delinquent acts. Adolescents who reported six or more conflicts with their parents were more likely to report depression. Depression and delinquent behavior are significantly correlated ($r = .26$, $p = .01$). These findings are significant since Hmong immigrant families have many children in closer age proximity (Rumbaut, 1995; Rumbaut and Weeks, 1986; Thao and Pfeifer, 2004). If one child does not have a nurturing environment, chances are this environment will impact the other siblings as well. Studies on sibling delinquency show that a child has a greater probability of becoming delinquent if his or her older sibling is already experienced (Conger and Conger (1994).

It is vital for service providers and educators to help Hmong parents and adolescents learn additional skills to manage these conflicts without the deleterious consequences of depression and delinquency. We suggest a combination of education (e.g., parenting program) and counseling to empower parents to learn bicultural communication and problem solving skills to effectively communicate with their adolescents. For example, program such as the *Helping Youth Succeed* (Detzner, Xiong, and Eliason, 1999) should be adopted to work with Hmong families to intervene these problems early. Helping Youth Succeed is a parent education program that is designed to build bicultural skills for Southeast Asian immigrant parents (namely Cambodian, Hmong, Lao, and Vietnamese) to address and minimize conflicts between parents and their adolescent children.

In conclusion, we believe that the study on parent-adolescent conflicts with Hmong immigrant populations in the United States needs future attention. The current study highlights some dimensions of parent-adolescent conflicts and the deleterious effects that conflicts have on adolescent adjustments, but the study has several limitations. First, the respondents were recruited from a convenience sample from the upper Mid-western state, and therefore the results cannot be generalized to Hmong across the Untied States and other Western countries. Second, due to the cross-sectional design of the study, it is not possible to determine the direction of the relationships. For instance, whether parent-adolescent conflict causes the adolescent's delinquency and depression or vise-versa is unknown. Third, the single-item measure of acculturation places limits on interpretations of the results. Although some panel studies using non-Southeast Asian immigrant families agree with the relationship of parent-adolescent conflicts and adolescent adjustments (Patterson, Reid, and Dishion, 1992; Simons, Robertson, and Downs, 1989), a similar path must be established for this group of new Americans in order to effectively intervene with adolescent gangs and delinquency in this community.

REFERENCES

Allison, B. N. (2000). Parent-adolescent in early adolescence: Precursor to adolescent adjustment and behavior problems. *Journal of Family and Consumer Sciences, 92(5),* 53-56.

Arnett, J. J. (1999). Adolescent storm and stress, reconsidered. *American Psychologist, 54(5),* 317-326.

Barber, B. K., Chadwick, B. A., and Oerter, R. (1992). Parental behaviors and adolescent self-esteem in the United States and Germany. *Journal of Marriage and the Family, 54,* 128-141.

Blum, R.W., Beuhring, T., Shew, M. L, Bearinger, L. H., Sieving, R. E., Resnick, M. D. (2000). The effects of race, ethnicity, income, and family structure on adolescent risk behaviors. *American Journal of Public Health, 90,* 1879-1884.

Chan, S. (1986). Parents of exceptional children. In M. K Kitano and P. C. Chinn (Eds.), *Exceptional Asian children and youth.* Washington, DC: ERIC (Exceptional Child Education Report).

Conger, K. J., and Conger, R. D. (1994). Differential parenting and change in sibling differences in delinquency. *Journal of Family Psychology, 8* (3), 287-302.

Conger, R. D., and Elder, G. H., Jr. (1994). *Families in troubled times: Adapting to change in rural America.* New York: Aldine de Gruyter.

Detzner, D. F., Xiong, Z. B., and Eliason, P. (1999). *Helping youth succeed: Bicultural parenting for Southeast Asian families.* St. Paul, MN: Regents of the University of Minnesota.

Donnelly, N. (1994). *Changing lives of refugee Hmong women.* Seattle: University of Washington Press.

DuongTran, Q., Lee, S. and Khoi, S. (1996). Ethnic and gender differences in parental expectations and life stress. *Child and Adolescent Social Work Journal, 13*(6), 515-526.

Elliott, G. R., and Feldman, S. S. (1990). Capturing the adolescent experience. In S. S. Feldman and G. R. Elliott (Eds.), *At the threshold: The developing adolescent* (pp.1-13). Cambridge, MA: Harvard University Press.

Elliott, D. S., Huizinga, D., and Ageton, S. S. (1985). *Explaining delinquency and drug use.* Beverly Hills, CA: Sage.

Farver, J. A. M., Narang, S. K., and Bhadha, B. R. (2002). East meets West: Ethnic identity, acculturation, and conflict in Asian Indian families. *Journal of Family Psychology, 16(3),* 338-350.

Feldman, S. S., and Rosenthal, D. A. (1990). The acculturation of autonomy expectations in Chinese schoolers residing in two western nations. *International Journal of Psychology, 25,* 259-281.

Fuligni, A. (1998). Authority, autonomy, and parent-adolescent conflict and cohesion: A study of adolescents from Mexican, Chinese, Filipino, and European backgrounds. *Developmental Psychology, 34 (4)*, 782-792.

Galambos, N. L., and Almeida, D. M. (1992). Does parent-adolescent conflict increase in early adolescent? *Journal of Marriage and the Family, 54*, 737-747.

Go, C. G. (1998). *The relationship of acculturation, parent and peer relations to delinquency and depression: An exploratory study of adaptation among Southeast Asian youth.* Unpublished dissertation, University of California at Davis, California.

Hamilton-Merritt, J. (1993). *Tragic mountains: The Hmong, the Americans, and the secret wars for Laos.* Indianapolis, Indiana: Indiana University Press.

Handal, P. J., Le-Stiebel, N., Dicarlo, M., and Gutzwilles, J. (1999). Perceived family environment and adjustment in American-born and immigrant Asian adolescents. *Psychological Reports, 85,* 1244-1249.

Herz, L. and Gullone, E. (1999). The relationship between self-esteem and parenting style: A cross-cultural comparison of Australian and Vietnamese Australian adolescents. *Journal of Cross-Cultural Psychology 30*(6): 742-761.

Howell, D. C. (1997). *Statistical methods for psychology* (4th ed.). Albany, NY: Wadsworth Publishing Company.

Hyman, I., Vu, N., and Beiser, M. (2000). Post-migration stresses among Southeast Asian refugee youth in Canada: A research note. *Journal of Comparative Family Studies, 31*(2), 281-293.

Laursen, B. and Collins, W. A. (1994). Interpersonal conflict during adolescence. *Psychological Bulletin*, 115, 197-209.

Laursen, B., Coy, K., and Collins, W. A. (1998). Reconsidering changes in parent-child conflict across adolescence: A meta-analysis. *Child Development*, 69, 817-832.

Lee, S. J. (2001). More than "model minorities" or "delinquents": A look at Hmong American high school students. *Harvard Educational Review, 71, 505-528.*

Lee, C. S., Xiong, Z. B., and Yuen, F. (in press). Explaining early marriage in Hmong immigrant community. In H. Holgate, R. Evans, and R. Yuen. (Eds.), *Teen pregnancy and parenthood: Global perspectives, issues, and interventions.* London: Taylor and Francis.

Mason, G., Cauce, A, Gonzales, N, and Hiraga, Y. (1996). Neither too sweet nor too sour: Problem peers, maternal control, and problem behavior in African American adolescents. *Child Development, 67*, 2115-2130.

Minnesota Planning (n.d). Criminal Justice Statistics Center. Retrieved September 9, 2002, from http://www.MnPlan.State.MN.US/cj/index.html

Moon, S. S., Wolfer, T. A., and Robinson, M. M. (2001). Culturally-based Korean American family conflict and how churches can help: An exploratory survey. *Social Work and Christianity*, *28*, 106-123.

Ngo, B. (2002). Contesting "Culture": The perspective of Hmong American female students on early marriage. *Anthropology and Education Quarterly, 33*(2), 163-199.

Nguyen, N. A., and Williams, H. L. (1989). Transition from East to West: Vietnamese adolescents and their parents. *Journal of the American Academy of Child and Adolescent Psychiatry, 28,* 505-515.

Patterson, G. R., Reid, J. B., and Dishion, T. J. (1992). *Antisocial boys.* Eugene, OR: Castalia.

Portes, A. and Rumbaut, R. G. (2001). *Legacies: The story of the immigrant second generation.* New York: Russell Sage Foundation.

Prinz, R. J., Foster, S., Kent, R. N., and O'Leary, D. (1979). Multivariate assessment of conflict in distressed and nondistressed mother-adolescent dyads. *Journal of Applied Behavior Analysis*, 12, 691-700.

Radloff, L. (1977). The CES-D scale: A self-report depression scale for research in the general population. *Applied Psychological Measure, 1*, 385-401.

Quincy, K. (1995). *Hmong, history of a people*. Cheney, WA: Eastern Washington University Press.

Ranieri, N. F., Klimidis, S., and Rosenthal, D. A. (1994). Validity of a single-item index of acculturation in Vietnamese immigrant youth. *Psychological Reports*, *74*, 735-738.

Rick, K., and Forward, J. (1992). Acculturation and perceived intergenerational differences among Hmong youth. *Journal of Cross-Cultural Psychology, 23(1),* 85-94.

Robin, A. L., and Foster, S. L. (1989). *Negotiating parent-adolescent conflict: A behavioral-family systems approach.* New York, NY: The Guilford Press.

Roosa, M. W., Deng, S., Ryu, E., Burrell, G.L., Tein, J.Y, Jones, S., Lopez, V., and Crowder, S. (2005). Family and child characteristics linking neighborhood context and child externalizing behavior. *Journal of Marriage and Family, 67*, 515-529.

Rosenberg, M. (1965). *Society and the adolescent self-image.* Princeton, NJ: Princeton University Press.

Rosenthal, D., Ranieri, N., and Klimidis, S. (1996). Vietnamese adolescents in Australia: Relationships between perceptions of self and parental values, intergenerational conflict, and gender dissatisfaction. *International Journal of Psychology, 31*, 81-91.

Rumbaut, R. G. (1995). Vietnamese, Laotian, and Cambodian Americans. In P. G. Min (Ed.), *Asian Americans: Contemporary trends and issues* (pp. 232-270). Thousand Oaks, CA: Sage.

Rumbaut, R. G. (1996). The crucible within: Ethnic identity, self-esteem, and segmented assimilation among children of immigrants. In A. Portes (ed.), *The new second generation* (pp. 748-794). New York: Russell Sage Foundation Press.

Rumbaut, R. G. and Weeks, J. R. (1986). Fertility and adaptation: Indochinese refugees in the United States. *International Migration Review, 20(2),* 428-466.

Shek, D. T. L. (1998). A longitudinal study of the relations between parent-adolescent conflict and adolescent psychological well-being. *The Journal of Genetic Psychology, 159(1)*, 53-67.

Shek, D. T. L., and Ma, H. K. (2001). Parent-adolescent conflict and adolescent antisocial and prosocial behavior: A longitudinal study in a Chinese context. *Adolescence, 36(143)*, 545-555.

Simons, R., Robertson, J., and Downs, W. (1989). The nature of the association between parental rejection and delinquent behavior. *Journal of Youth and Adolescence*, 18 (3), 297-310.

Sivan, A. B., Kosh, L., Baier, C., and Adiga, M. (1999). Refugee youth at risk: A quest for rational policy. *Children's Services: Social Policy, Research, and Practice*, 2(3), 139-158.

Smetana, G. J. (1988). Adolescents' and parents' conceptions of parental authority. *Child Development*, 59(2), 321-335.

Smetana, G. J. (1989). Adolescents' and parents' reasoning about actual family conflict. *Child Development,* 60, 1052-1067.

Smetana, J. G., and Gaines, C. (1999). Adolescent-parent conflict in middle class African American families. *Child Development*, 70, 1447-1463.

Sodowsky, G. R., Lai, E. W. M., and Plake, B. S. (1991). Moderating effects of sociocultural variables on acculturation attitudes of Hispanics and Asian Americans. *Journal of Counseling and Development, 70*, 194-204.

Steinberg, L. (1981). Transformations in family relations at puberty. *Developmental Psychology, 17*, 833-840.

Steinberg, L. (1988). Reciprocal relation between parent-child distance and pubertal maturation. *Developmental Psychology, 24*, 122-128.

Steinberg, L. (1990). Interdependency in the family: Autonomy, conflict, and harmony in the parent-adolescent relationship. In S. S. Feldman and G. R. Elliot (Eds.), *At the threshold: The developing adolescent* (pp. 255-276). Cambridge, MA: Harvard University Press.

Steinberg, L. (2001). We know some things: Parent-adolescent relationships in retrospect and prospect. *Journal of Research on Adolescence, 11*, 1-19.

Steinberg, L., Dornbusch, S.M., and Brown, B. B. (1992). Ethnic differences in adolescent achievement: An ecological perspective. *American Psychologist, 47,* 723-729.

Suárez-Orozco, C., and Suárez-Orozco, M. M. (2001). *Children of immigration.* Cambridge, MA: Harvard University Press.

Tabachnick, B. G., and Fidell, L. S. (2001). *Using multivariate statistics* (4th ed.). Needham Heights, MA: Allyn and Bacon.

Thao, and M. Pfeifer (Eds.) (2004). *Hmong National Development 2000 Census Report.* Washington D.C.: Hmong National Development, Inc.

U.S. Bureau of the Census (2000). *Trends in Hmong population distribution across the regions of the United States.* St. Paul, MN: Hmong Culture Center.

Whitbeck, L.B., Hoyt, D.R., Simons, R.L., Conger, R.D., Elder, G.H., Lorenz, F.O., and Huck, S. (1992). Intergenerational continuity of parental rejection and depressed affect. *Journal of Personality and Social Psychology, 63*, 1036-1045.

Xiong, Z. B., and Detzner, D. F. (2005). Southeast Asian fathers' experiences with adolescents: Challenges and change. *Hmong Study Journal,* 6, 1-23.

Xiong, Z. B., Detzner, D. F., and Rettig, K. D. (2001). Southeast Asian immigrant parenting practices and perceptions of parent-adolescent conflicts. *Journal of Teaching Marriage and Family: Innovations in Family Science Education, 1*(1), *27-45.*

Xiong, Z. B., Eliason, P., Detzner, D. F., and Cleveland, M. J. (2005). Southeast Asian immigrants' perceptions of good adolescents and good parents. *Journal of Psychology, 139(2)*, 159-175.

Zhou, M., and Bankston, C. L., III. (1998). *Growing up American: How Vietnamese children adapt to life in the United States.* New York: Russell Sage.

In: Parent-Child Relations: New Research
Editor: Dorothy M. Devore, pp. 83-99
ISBN 1-60021-167-4

Chapter 5

The Parent-Young Child Relationship: Dealing with and Surviving Toddlerhood

Kimberly Renk*[*], *Jenny Klein*, *Arazais Oliveros and Cliff McKinney
University of Central Florida

Abstract

This chapter will examine the interactions that occur between parents and their young children as they navigate through one of the most difficult stages of development. In particular, this chapter will review the normative developments that occur for young children during toddlerhood, such as rapid cognitive development, the development of a sense of self, and the first signs of growing autonomy. Certainly, a common consequence of young children reaching these developmental milestones is that they will demonstrate frequently testing of the limits placed upon them by their mothers and fathers (Campbell, 1990) and a certain level of negativity (Keenan and Wakschlag, 2000). Next, the types of discipline that parents use with their young children in response to these behaviors will be described and critiqued. Unfortunately, mothers and fathers frequently report problems and uncertainties in disciplining their young children (Campbell, 1990; Jenkins, Bax, and Hart, 1980). This fact is concerning, in that children below the age of 4-years tend to be most vulnerable to poor quality parenting (Loeber, 1990). Finally, the possibilities of parent-young child interactions going off-course at this stage and young children demonstrating the beginning signs of a disruptive behavior disorder will be examined. To summarize and put this information into context, suggestions regarding the promotion of a healthy parent-young child relationship and positive adaptation for young children will be offered.

Toddlerhood is one of the most difficult stages of development faced by parents and their young children. Toddlers achieve many unique developmental milestones at their young age,

[*] Correspondence to: Kimberly Renk, Ph.D., University of Central Florida, Department of Psychology, P.O. Box 161390, Orlando, FL 32816. E-mail: krenk@pegasus.cc.ucf.edu

including rapid cognitive development, the development of a sense of self, and the first signs of growing autonomy (Campbell, 1990). Given these developments, transitions also must occur in the relationship that parents have with their young children. Unfortunately, the parent-young child relationship is tested frequently. For example, a common consequence of young children reaching the above mentioned developmental milestones is that they will test frequently the limits placed upon them by their mothers and fathers (Campbell, 1990) and will exhibit a certain level of negativity (Keenan and Wakschlag, 2000). These characteristics, although normative, may promote negative interactions between parents and their young children, particularly if parents are not expecting such characteristics to color their interactions or if parents are unaware that such characteristics are normative.

Nonetheless, mothers and fathers frequently report problems and uncertainties in disciplining their young children (Campbell, 1990; Jenkins, Bax, and Hart, 1980). This fact is concerning, in that children younger than 4-years of age tend to be most vulnerable to poor quality parenting (Loeber, 1990). Should difficulties in discipline or poor quality parenting persist, the possibilities of parent-young child interactions going off-course during toddlerhood and of young children beginning to demonstrate disruptive behaviors may become more likely. To try to better understand the parent-young child relationship, this chapter will explore the normative developmental milestones that young children reach during toddlerhood, the types of discipline that are used by parents of young children, and the beginning signs of disruptive behavior disorders. To summarize and put this information into context, suggestions regarding the promotion of a healthy parent-young child relationship and positive adaptation for young children will be offered.

Developmental Milestones During Toddlerhood

As young children progress through toddlerhood, they tackle many unique milestones. The achievement of these milestones, particularly in relationship to young children's interactions with their parents or other primary caregivers, is vitally important to achievements that will be mastered in later developmental stages. Early interactions between young children and their parents set the groundwork for the development of behavioral patterns and the synchrony that will occur between young children's behavior and their environment. As young children develop, their parents must adapt over time to their children's changing physical, cognitive, and emotional needs. These adaptations begin in infancy and continue through toddlerhood into childhood (Sroufe, 1996).

Prior to toddlerhood, there are several developments in the parent-infant relationship that serve as precursors to the relationship that develops between toddlers and their parents. Drawing from decades of previous developmental research and theory (e.g., Ainsworth, Blehar, Waters, and Wall, 1978; Bowlby, 1973), Sroufe (1996) suggested that, during the time period of development between birth and approximately 3-months of age, parents learn about the unique characteristics of their infants and can support the development of smooth routines that will meet the infants' need for physiological regulation (e.g., feeding, sleeping). Between 3- and 6-months of age, parents should guide infants' regulation of tension and frustration. Parents hopefully will recognize their infants' signals and provide sensitive, cooperative interactions using acts of stimulation (e.g., gentle voice tones, pausing, nodding head, changing facial expressions). Parents must be careful to refrain from overstimulating their infants and to assist their infants in remaining organized and affectively positive when presented with new stimuli or situations (Sroufe, 1996). Given these developments, caregivers can begin setting the stage during infancy for positive developments during toddlerhood.

Sroufe (1996) also described the period between 6- and 12-months of age as a time when the parent-infant relationship further develops. At this time, a secure attachment relationship can become established as a result of parents' increased emotional availability. Parental care that is reliable, warm, and responsive is particularly important during this stage (Sroufe, 1996). After infants reach 12-months of age, the following six-month period is marked by behaviors geared toward environmental exploration and mastery of skills, with parents serving as a secure base for their budding toddlers. Once toddlers have acquired a basic skill set, including mobility and communication, 18- to 30-month-old toddlers begin to strive for autonomy (i.e., individuation) from their caregivers by utilizing the firm support that their caregivers provide. Toddlers attempt to organize their actions toward achieving particular goals (e.g., completing a discrete task), and parents should provide feedback and support for such efforts (Sroufe, 1996).

The development of such goal-directed behavior is a central component of several theories of developmental psychology (e.g., Bandura, 1997; Erikson, 1968). The ethological approach to understanding such goal-directed behavior as it relates to toddlers' autonomy seeking has been accepted most widely, however. The first dyadic theory of attachment, Object-Relations Theory (Bowlby, 1973), suggested that young children's sensitive periods and learning capacity biologically predispose them and their parents to become synchronized into what Bowlby referred to as an attachment behavioral system (Miller, 2002). Children and their parents develop mental representations of each other and their relationship based on their behavioral interactions. These internal working models help children to interpret and react to novel situations (Bowlby, 1973; Miller, 2002). Additionally, Attachment Theory (Ainsworth et al., 1978) suggested that the attachment bond formed between parents and their young children provides a means for children to securely and effectively achieve their goals. The infant who develops a secure attachment style (i.e., as compared to insecure-avoidant, insecure-resistant, or disorganized) will likely become more emotionally independent and able to navigate successfully in an autonomous fashion within varying contexts (Miller, 2002; Sroufe, 1996). In contrast, a disrupted parent-child bond may inhibit the development of autonomy, feelings of self-efficacy, and competence.

Several other developing processes underlie toddlers' goal-directed behavior, including cognitive representational abilities, focused attention, affect and action regulation, and self-focused evaluation (Jennings, 2004). These processes interact with the environmental demands and relational factors present in interactions between young children and other individuals, especially their primary caregivers. Jennings (2004) investigated the rapid development of organization in toddlers' goal-directed behavior between the ages of 15- and 35-months. Results of this study indicated that older toddlers were more successful than younger toddlers in their ability to maintain images of distal goals over time, to use those goals to organize their behavior, and to complete tasks. Additionally, older toddlers demonstrated more self-awareness and positive affect and required fewer adult prompts, indicating higher attainment of effective autonomous behavior (Jennings, 2004). Thus, as young children progress through toddlerhood, they will be able to better regulate their own behaviors.

As toddlers make attempts to achieve their own goals, an ever-evolving component of the parent-young child relationship is the interaction between parents' struggle to maintain behavioral control over their young children and young children's development of their goal-directed and autonomous behavior. As toddlers progress toward the development of cognitive and emotional awareness, they continue to rely upon parental support while making attempts to achieve self-reliance and self-sufficiency. The increased capacity to organize goal-directed behaviors during this time allows toddlers to make behavioral choices, including their demonstration of resistance to parental directives and control. In general, parents vary in their strategies of negotiation and control over the behavior of their young children, and parents' resolution of control issues is central to the maintenance of a successful parent-child relationship (Donovan, Leavitt, and Walsh, 2000). Thus, parents' ability to positively traverse toddlers' testing of the limits will benefit the parent-child relationship over time.

To examine the pitfalls of this journey further, Crockenberg and Litman (1990) described the relationship between different sets of parental control behaviors and varying levels of autonomous behaviors in toddlers. For example, low power-assertion parental strategies (e.g., suggestions, persuasions, explanations) and moderately clear directives regarding expectations were associated with toddler compliance and self-assertion. In contrast, high parental power-assertions in the form of negative control (e.g., threats, criticism, physical interventions, negative affect) were associated with toddler defiance. Donovan and colleagues (2000) provided further support for the finding that parenting strategies that are highly intrusive and high in power-assertion are associated with toddler defiance. These investigations suggested that parenting strategies utilizing inductive reasoning and low power-assertion may be more effective in managing toddler noncompliance.

It is assumed commonly that a certain level of resistance toward parental authority signifies progression toward gaining autonomy; however, this resistance presents a great challenge to parents. In fact, temper tantrums, noncompliance, and aggression can be expected during the toddler years (Keenan, Shaw, Delliquadri, Giovannelli, and Walsh, 1998). As mentioned previously, toddlers are developing their own autonomy, experimenting with and learning about their environment, and testing limits that parents place on them (Campbell, 1998). When a toddler's desire for autonomy collides with limits and rules, an increase in negativity and oppositionality may occur (Campbell, 1990; Keenan and Wakschlag, 2000). This pattern of behavior then can result in noncompliance, which characterizes patterns of normal development and is considered to be an adaptive form of autonomous behavior that facilitates the toddler's understanding of appropriate expectations and limits put forth by adults (Crockenberg and Litman, 1990; Kaler and Kopp, 1990).

Kuczynski, Kochanska, Radke-Yarrow, and Girnius-Brown (1987) proposed that noncompliance may serve some adaptive functions as well, such as assertion of autonomy within the parent-young child relationship and the development and appropriate expression of social skills. Kuczynski and colleagues (1987) demonstrated that, from a developmental perspective, children adopt more skillful expressions of resistance as they grow older. For example, in a group of toddlers aged 15- to 44-months examined by Kuczynski and colleagues (1987), passive noncompliance and direct defiance were found to decrease with age, whereas more sophisticated forms of noncompliance (e.g., negotiation) increased in later toddlerhood. Further, Kuczynski and Kochanska (1990) found that the use of direct defiance decreased in frequency between toddlerhood and early preschool age, whereas more skillful methods of resistance (e.g., simple refusals and negotiation) increased over time.

Additionally, noncompliant behavior can be viewed as a method used by young children to persuade their parents to modify or discontinue their direction or requests. Parents' behavior, in turn, also changes over time, as demonstrated by parents' more frequent use of verbally based persuasive strategies (e.g., bargaining and explanations) and less nonverbal strategies (e.g., distraction) to elicit desired behavior (Kuczynski et al., 1987). Thus, children's noncompliance (and parents' related behavior) appears to co-occur with the development of autonomous functioning and interpersonal competence.

Other achievements assist young children in their journey through toddlerhood and in managing their compliance to parents' requests. Children's representational thinking (Piaget, 1952), moral reasoning (Kagan, 1984), and social relatedness with peers (Howes and Matheson, 1992) all increase young children's understanding of social norms. In particular, young children's ability to symbolically represent chains of actions and their consequences develops during the second year and is a prerequisite to internalized compliance (Kagan, 1984; Piaget, 1952). Consistent with the timing of these achievements, Gralinski and Kopp (1993) have documented an age-related progression from externally controlled or situational compliance (active enforcement by mother which prompts obedience under parental monitoring without evidence that the toddler has internalized these expectations; Kochanska and Aksan, 1995) to internally mediated compliance. In particular, committed compliance, in which young children demonstrate an internally motivated acceptance of parental expectations (Kochanska and Aksan, 1995), is more likely as toddlers develop greater emotional regulation ability, meaning they have lower emotional lability and higher frustration tolerance (Feldman and Klein, 2003).

Both parent and child variables have been implicated in the development of committed compliance (Feldman and Klein, 2003; Kochanska, 1995, 1997; Larzelere and Merenda, 1994). For example, parents who experience anxiety have been shown to interfere more often in their children's problem solving (Whaley, Pinto, and Sigman, 1999). Additionally, parents' perceptions of their child's temperament also may affect their interactions, as some studies have demonstrated that parents' who view their young children as difficult tend to be more controlling and directive, providing less support for their young children's autonomy and fewer opportunities for independent skills practice (Fagot and Gauvain, 1997; Gauvain and Fagot, 1995). Recent research conducted by Neitzel and Stright (2004) supported this initial finding. In addition, maternal education modified the relationship between perceived difficult temperament and restricted autonomy granting. Thus, parents who perceived their child as being difficult but who had sufficient education were more likely to regulate problem solving task difficulty, encourage their young children's efforts, and support their young children's active role (Neitzel and Stright, 2004).

Discipline and Toddlers

As mentioned previously, parents' strategies for managing the behaviors of their toddlers may be related closely to the level of noncompliance exhibited by their toddlers. When parents are feeling that their management strategies are not effective, they may resort to disciplining their young children for their difficult or noncompliant behaviors. The term discipline stems from the Latin word *disciplinare*, meaning *to teach* (Merriam-Webster,

1995). Although discipline is often equated erroneously with the concept of punishment, punishment reflects only one element of discipline. Described more fully, discipline is a multifaceted approach that includes modeling, attitudes, rewards, and punishment, all of which are used to teach and reinforce socially acceptable behavior (American Academy of Pediatrics, 1998).

Unfortunately, mothers and fathers frequently report problems and uncertainties in disciplining their young children (Campbell, 1990; Jenkins et al., 1980). For example, parents of 2.5- to 3.5-year olds often express concerns about disciplinary problems, such as how and when to set limits (Campbell, 1990). Further, research has suggested that 23 percent of parents with 3-year olds are unsure of how to discipline their children (Jenkins et al., 1980). Overall, children between the ages of birth and 4-years of age may be most susceptible to poor parenting and discipline practices (Loeber, 1990). Given that a large proportion of parents may be uncertain about how to parent their toddler during such a critical period of development and that different types of discipline may be more or less effective, it may be important for parents of toddlers to receive information about optimal forms of discipline.

Certainly, when parents attempt to manage the behavior of their young children or use disciplinary methods, they are attempting to make the behavior of their young children consistent with their expectations for the situation. Thus, the short-term goal of discipline is compliance; however, the long-term goal of discipline is internalization of social norms (i.e., consistent with the idea of committed compliance mentioned earlier; Kochanska and Aksan, 1995). Infants' maturing behavioral inhibition and mutuality in the mother-infant dyad are antecedents to young children's compliance, with evidence of self-regulation emerging around 2-years of age (Kopp, 1982). In fact, mother-infant synchrony during the first months of life provides children with experience in the give-and-take exchange of social relationships and forms the basis for socialization (Feldman and Klein, 2003). The period of toddlerhood has been underscored as the context for the internalization of social norms (Kochanska, 1995).

Discipline may be viewed within the context of the general style of parenting used by parents. The most widely used taxonomy of parenting style is based on the level of warmth and control used by parents in their interactions with their young children (Baumrind, 1967, 1993). Based on these two dimensions, four styles of parenting have been described. *Authoritative* parents are both highly demanding, in terms of limit setting and monitoring (i.e., behavioral control) of children's behavior, and highly responsive (i.e., accepting and nurturing; Baumrind, 1967, 1993). Authoritative parents emphasize clear boundaries, respect their children's autonomy, and use dialogue rather than power assertion. Further, authoritative parenting has been related to higher levels of prosocial behavior and lower levels of internalizing and externalizing problem behaviors (Baumrind, 1993; Slicker, 1998). The *authoritarian* parenting style consists of high behavioral control and low responsiveness. Parents with an *indulgent* parenting style are high in acceptance but low in behavioral control. Low behavioral control and low responsiveness characterize the *unengaged* parenting style (Baumrind, 1967, 1993). Overall, the authoritative parenting style has shown the most beneficial effects for children and adolescents. Thus, a combination of warmth and control appears to provide the most benefits to young children.

Although an authoritative style appears to be beneficial to children, parents also are more likely to be effective when discipline is based on expectations for children's behavior that are appropriate for the age and, more importantly, the developmental stage of the child (Howard,

1996). This match is particularly significant during the toddler years, when the major developments described previously are occurring for young children. In this regard, various disciplinary responses have been described in the literature (e.g., Banks, 2002; Barkley, 1997; Forehand and McMahon, 1981), providing useful recommendations for effective discipline of young children. For instance, it has been proposed that disciplinary limits, while remaining consistent, also should allow for young children to make choices among acceptable alternatives. This kind of negotiation may be important as young children's involvement in the discipline process increases compliance (Banks, 2002; Barkley, 1997). Although numerous techniques have been described to manage young children's behavior, the evidence has not been conclusive regarding the effectiveness of alternative responses in delaying the next occurrence of their misbehavior (Larzelere and Merenda, 1994). Those techniques that have been examined will be described briefly below.

Banks (2002) suggested that positive reinforcement and redirecting can be utilized effectively during infancy and toddlerhood. Further, one of the most powerful forms of positive reinforcement is parental attention. Positive reinforcement can include any parental behavior that young children like and seek to evoke, such as smiling, affection, words of praise, and giving the child desired privileges or material rewards (Barkley, 1997). When parental attention is provided in response to young children's desirable behaviors, these behaviors often increase in frequency. Unfortunately, young children's misbehavior often evokes parental attention as well, resulting in the parent unwittingly reinforcing such misbehavior instead (Patterson, 1982). Further, despite parents' best attempts to reinforce positive behaviors, young children will naturally exhibit behaviors that are undesirable, especially as they develop feelings of autonomy and experiment with motor abilities (e.g., locomotor skills) while their understanding of danger is minimal (Gesell and Amatruda, 1947). Young children can usually be redirected from misbehaving by directing their attention to a different stimulus or behavior, taking advantage of the lower attention span and higher curiosity that is normal for this developmental stage (Banks, 2002; Gesell and Amatruda, 1947).

Responding to misbehavior with extinction takes into account the reinforcing power of parental attention, such that parents ignore a non-dangerous misbehavior (e.g., whining, tantrums) rather than reinforce it. This procedure causes young children's misbehavior to occur less frequently (Banks, 2002; Barkley, 1997; Forehand and McMahon, 1981). In fact, extinction techniques have demonstrated effectiveness during toddlerhood (Banks, 2002). Time-out, the most common form of extinction, involves taking the young child from the problem situation to a safe but boring corner or room. Then, the parent ignores the young child for a predetermined time (e.g., one minute per year of life) without interaction until after a specified amount of time has passed and/or only after the child has been calm and quiet for 15 seconds (Barkley, 1997; Forehand and Long, 2002). The most common reason for parents reporting that this technique is ineffective is parents' inability to ignore young children's complaints during the time-out (Barkley, 1997). Time-out is most effective when young children receive attention and praise for good behavior (time-*in*) so that they are aware of a sharp contrast and because a warm parent-young child relationship motivates young children to exhibit socialized behavior (Kochanska, 1997). Further, other research has suggested that appropriate use of time-out procedures may reduce the occurrence of disruptive behaviors when other methods, such as physical control and demands, are not successful (Pailthorpe and Ralph, 1998).

Using verbal instructions or explanations in disciplinary responses has been shown to have variable effectiveness with young children due to their early stage of development in verbal reasoning (Banks, 2002; Dunn, 1987). In fact, a longitudinal study of mothers' verbal requests and rules directed at young children ranging in age from 13- to 48-months documented that young children show greater compliance with rules involving safety and other's possessions (e.g., sharing). This result may have been related to the fact that mothers tend to verbalize these simple rules for young children from an earlier age (i.e., around 13-months old; Gralinsky and Kopp, 1993). Mothers' rule networks became progressively more complex over time. By the time toddlers were about 3.5-years old, mothers' rules were most often about safety, interpersonal behavior, and self-care, and mothers increasingly elaborated rules about family and social norms (e.g., helping with chores). The marked increase in the number, types (e.g., safety, self-care, respect), and complexity of prohibitions and requests that mothers communicate coincided with increases in young children's age and linguistic abilities. This finding suggested that mothers may hold intuitive knowledge of their young children's needs (Gralinski and Kopp, 1993).

Other discipline techniques have been found to be ineffective with young children. For example, grounding and withholding privileges have not demonstrated any effectiveness during either infancy or toddlerhood (Banks, 2002). Research also has suggested that young children are less likely to comply with parental commands and prohibitions compared to parental suggestions, especially when young children experience physical control and negative interactions (Lytton and Zwirner, 1975; Olson, Bates, and Sandy, 2000). Of more concern, among primarily Caucasian, low education, low income mothers, corporal punishment was a frequent response to behaviors that are actually typical and age-appropriate for toddlers, such as saying no or not wanting to eat during mealtime (Culp, Culp, Dengler, and Maisano, 1999). Further, research has indicated that minority children in low-income settings are at a particularly high risk for disruptive behavior problems (Deater-Deckard, Dodge, Bates, and Pettit, 1998) and that their mothers are especially in need of guidance regarding discipline practices effective in reducing negative child behavior (Lequerica and Hermosa, 1995). Thus, those parents who are faced with environmental stressors also may be most in need of guidance for managing their young children's problematic behaviors.

Overall, the socialization process is facilitated for young children when parents' response to their misbehavior is implemented immediately. In this way, young children learn the cause-and-effect relationship between behavior and consequences (Banks, 2002). This immediacy also can help to prevent the escalation of misbehavior (Patterson, 1982). In fact, parents may unwittingly engage in coercion training, a cycle of parent and child behavior that reinforces the use of coercion by both parties. In this process, the parent issues a directive, the young child counterattacks (e.g., whining, shouting), and the parent backs off, reinforcing negatively the young child's use of coercion to avoid compliance. At the fourth step, the young child yields, reinforcing the parent's backing off. This chain of mutual reinforcement makes it increasingly likely that a pattern of coercive exchange will take place again, with potential escalation of parental discipline and child aggression (Forehand and Long, 2002; Patterson, 1982). Responding immediately with a logical or natural consequence to misbehavior facilitates the socialization of young children (Banks, 2002).

THE DEVELOPMENT OF DISRUPTIVE BEHAVIOR IN YOUNG CHILDREN

Generally, behaviors that are viewed as problematic (e.g., noncompliance, tantrums, aggression) are common during the toddler years. Further, they may be adaptive as they signal that young children are experiencing age-appropriate transitions and autonomy struggles. Given these types of behaviors, the preschool period may be a critically important time when significant behavior problems can emerge (Keenan and Wakschlag, 2000). When faced with young children's noncompliant behaviors, parents must set appropriate limits and provide support so that their young children can explore and master their environment (Campbell, 1997). As toddlers develop, they require more control but also more freedom to test their autonomy and differentiate themselves from others (Campbell, 1997). As young children accomplish the tasks of this developmental time period, however, they may begin to balance their own autonomy with the expectations that others have for their cooperation (Crockenberg and Litman, 1990). These needs place parents in a precarious position. Parents must achieve a balance between setting firm limits and doing so in a clear, warm, and supportive manner (Campbell, 1997). Overall, parents must not suppress the developmentally normative, adaptive noncompliance that reflects individuation.

In an effort to achieve this balance, parents must distinguish appropriate noncompliance from inappropriate noncompliance that occurs in the context of angry defiance (Crockenberg and Litman, 1990). Many parents find this distinction to be at least somewhat difficult. As a result, parents may benefit from education about appropriate and inappropriate behaviors and patterns of development. To facilitate the identification of appropriate versus inappropriate noncompliance, examining the intent of young children's noncompliant behavior may be helpful. For example, nonclinical aggressive behavior is characterized by instrumental or goal-driven behavior, whereas more problematic aggressive behavior is characterized by hostile or person-oriented behaviors with the intent to cause harm (Feshbach and Feshbach, 1972). Most young children, particularly with the setting of appropriate limits, learn to inhibit their aggression over time (Tremblay, 2000). Dysregulated aggression, however, may signal potential difficulties (Keenan and Shaw, 1994; Rubin, Burgess, Dwyer, and Hastings, 2003). In contrast, self-assertion may be viewed as a positive developmental achievement and as an indicator of early social competence (Campbell, 1997), particularly if these developmental tasks are accomplished without escalating conflict (Crockenberg and Litman, 1990).

Further, there are many parental factors that may be related to elevated levels of disruptive behaviors in young children, including parenting stress, low behavioral responsiveness, parental negativity, and the use of harsh discipline (Rubin et al., 2003; Shaw, Keenan, and Vondra, 1994; Wakschlag and Keenan, 2001). Specifically, authoritative parenting, described previously as parenting characterized by warmth and firm but reasonable control (Baumrind, 1967), has been associated with child compliance, whereas inconsistent, negative, arbitrary, or uninvolved parenting behaviors have been associated with child noncompliance (Kuczynski et al., 1987). Additionally, higher levels of negative maternal control and lower levels of parental warmth have been related to noncompliant behavior in young children (Campbell, Pierce, March, and Ewing, 1991; Campbell, Pierce, Moore, Marakovitz, and Newby, 1996; Olson et al., 2000; Rubin et al., 2003). Overall, poor parenting practices and discipline, as well as negative interactions between parents and their young children, have been shown to be strong predictors of later disruptive behavior problems (Loeber and Dishion, 1983; Shaw et al., 1994).

It should be noted, however, that the relationship between parenting behavior and children's behavior is bidirectional. Although negative maternal control has been shown to predict children's noncompliance or aggression, difficult children also may elicit more inconsistent behavior from their parents (Shaw et al., 1994). For example, mothers of preschoolers who exhibited problematic behaviors engaged in more confrontation, and children were less likely to comply with the requests of their mothers. When mothers' requests were followed by child noncompliance, mothers were less likely to follow through to gain compliance (Gardner, 1989). In general, children with problematic behaviors have a history of higher rates of negative interaction and of lower rates of harmonious interaction (Gardner, 1987). Some researchers, however, have emphasized that coercive interactions between young children and their parents are necessary in a long-term pattern of antisocial behavior that is related to other problems, such as in school or in other relationships (e.g., Patterson, 1982). Other research has supported this supposition. For example, toddlers who had families exhibiting persistent conflict in parent-child interactions as well as other adversity experiences exhibited higher levels of externalizing behavior problems at the age of 18-months when compared to toddlers from nontroubled families (Belsky, Woodworth, and Crnic, 1996).

Other characteristics of young children also may be related to the development of disruptive behaviors. For example, previous disruptive behaviors often predict later difficulties with disruptive behavior disorders (Loeber and Dishion, 1983; Shaw et al., 1994). Behavioral disinhibition also may be related to disruptive behaviors in toddlers (Hirshfeld-Becker et al., 2002). Specifically, children with behavioral disinhibition are more likely than other children to display disruptive behaviors, suggesting that behavioral disinhibition may be a temperamental precursor to disruptive behavior problems (Hirshfeld-Becker et al., 2002). Other research (Hipwell et al., 2002) has suggested that, at least for girls, age and living in a disadvantaged neighborhood are correlated positively with disruptive behaviors. Another factor related to disruptive behaviors is the parent's perception of the toddler's emotional responsiveness. For example, toddlers who are perceived as emotionally unresponsive to their parents are more likely to develop externalizing behaviors, suggesting that negative parental cognitions may be associated with conduct problems (Olson et al., 2000).

When a constellation of behavior problems tends to co-occur in young children, one may become concerned that a clinically significant problem is present (Campbell, 1995). In particular, clinically significant problems are likely to be frequent and severe, to be evident across domains of functioning and across situations, and to be expressed with a variety of different individuals (Campbell, 1990). In such cases, a diagnosis from the *Diagnostic and Statistical Manual of Mental Disorders (Fourth Edition-Text Revision; DSM;* American Psychiatric Association (APA), 2000), such as Oppositional Defiant Disorder or Conduct Disorder, may be warranted.

Oppositional Defiant Disorder (ODD) consists of a pattern of behavior that is characterized as negative, hostile, and defiant (APA, 2000). To receive an ODD diagnosis, children must display consistently problematic behaviors, such as losing their temper, arguing with adults, defying or refusing to comply with requests made by adults, annoying other individuals deliberately, blaming others for his or her mistakes, being annoyed easily by others, being angry and resentful, and being spiteful and vindictive, over the course of at least a six-month period (APA, 2000). To receive this diagnosis, children must exhibit these behaviors more frequently than would be anticipated in individuals of a comparable age and developmental level (APA, 2000). As the DSM recognizes the commonness of transient oppositional behaviors in preschool children and emphasizes that caution should be used in applying this diagnosis in this age group (APA, 2000), making a distinction between normative and clinically significant behaviors may be more difficult for young children (Keenan and Wakschlag, 2002). Thus, to make a diagnosis of ODD, the behaviors listed as part of ODD should interfere with normal developmental functioning as well (Keenan and Wakschlag, 2002).

A proportion of children diagnosed with ODD will eventually receive a diagnosis of Conduct Disorder (CD; Loeber and Hay, 1997). CD is characterized as a pattern of behavior in which children violate the basic right of other individuals as well as major age-appropriate societal norms or rules, such as exhibiting aggression toward people and animals, destruction of property, deceitfulness or theft, and serious violations of rules (APA, 2000). To meet diagnostic criteria for CD, a child has to exhibit three or more specific criteria over the course of a twelve-month period, with at least one of the specific criteria being present in the past six months. In addition to the DSM diagnostic criteria for CD mentioned above, Keenan and Wakschlag (2002) consider the proposition that a child must knowingly violate rules and, thus, must have knowledge of the rules and the intent to break them to meet CD criteria. As a result, it may be important to consider young children's understanding of rules and their ability to control their own behavior before utilizing this diagnosis with this population (Keenan and Wakschalg, 2002). Although many young children do have the ability to understand rules, many needed skills are in the process of emerging during this developmental period. For example, preschool-age children are in the process of developing the ability to inhibit their behavior (Kochanska, Murray, and Coy, 1997), to engage in deception about rule violations (Lewis, Stanger, and Sullivan, 1989), and to generate alternatives to problems (Reznick Corley, and Robinson, 1997). Thus, it may be more difficult to diagnose CD in young children.

RECOMMENDATIONS

In an effort to prevent disruptive behaviors from occurring in the first place and to ameliorate such problems once they have been identified, several parenting and environmental changes can be put in place for young children. For many parents, the first step must be recognizing that a certain level of noncompliance and defiance from young children is normative during the toddler years. As such, parents should not take such behaviors personally or hold expectations for their young children that are unreasonable or too difficult for them to follow. Further, once these behaviors become severe and begin to co-occur frequently (e.g., Campbell, 1990, 1995), parents should begin to investigate the possibility that they and their young children may need assistance from a mental health professional. In either case, parents should begin to examine their parenting behaviors and consider alternative discipline strategies.

In so many ways, parents serve as models for their children. As a result, parents must model appropriate ways of interacting with other individuals and of dealing with their own anger. By doing so, parents can provide their young children with visible alternatives for coping with their own frustrations (Murphy, 2004). Parents should recognize that they are not perfect. Given this fact, they must be willing to admit and apologize for the mistakes that they do make (Murphy, 2004). Such a gesture will further model appropriate behavior to young children regarding the manner in which they can deal with their own misbehaviors or mistakes. Further, parents should find a way to remain emotionally available, even during the course of their young children's tantrums, so that young children will not feel left alone with their frustrations (Lieberman, 1993). Finally, parents should follow through when they say that they are going to do something, as young children will take you at your word (Murphy, 2004). Although these suggestions may seem commonsensical or simple, they can be highly beneficial to the relationship that continues to develop between parents and their young children.

As parents continue on their journey with their young children, they should recognize that achieving compliance from their young children sometimes will be difficult. Over the long term, appropriate levels of parental warmth, support, control, and discipline may facilitate the toddler's development of compliance (Campbell, 1990). In the short term, however, parents may incorporate ignoring of certain minor misbehaviors so as to not reinforce them (Forehand and Long, 2002). When parents must give directions to their young children in an effort to shape their misbehavior, parents may wish to incorporate likeable alternatives as part of their requests, use a tone of voice that communicates that the request is important and meaningful, provide their young children with an explanation that they (i.e., the parents) are in charge of this particular decision, use humor, and then take action with further discipline if it is necessary (Lieberman, 1993). More importantly, parents should pay attention to the positive behaviors exhibited by their young children whenever possible (Barkley, 1997; Christophersen and Mortweet, 2003). As mentioned previously, such attention will reinforce these behaviors and increase their occurrence in the future (Banks, 2002; Barkley, 1997). Positive feedback should be incorporated before parents devise any discipline plan for their young children (Christophersen and Mortweet, 2003).

If discipline is required for the misbehavior of young children, parents should remain as unemotional and matter-of-fact as possible (Christophersen and Mortweet, 2003) during the course of using their discipline of choice. One thing that may prevent parents from becoming too emotional is to administer the chosen discipline method before the interaction between themselves and their young children have had a chance to escalate and before they have become too upset (e.g., Patterson, 1982). If parents allow themselves to become upset, it is more likely that an argument will ensue (Christophersen and Mortweet, 2003) and that some level of coercion will be incorporated into the interactions that occur between parents and their young children (Patterson, 1982). Of the discipline techniques discussed previously, positive reinforcement for appropriate behavior, redirection, and time-out have had the most evidence of effectiveness with young children (Banks, 2002). Time-out can be particularly effective when it removes young children from the environment that provides them with positive reinforcement. Time-out provides young children with the opportunity to learn that their misbehavior will result in a negative consequence, that they would rather be involved in the activities of their usual environment, and that they do not get to enjoy positive interactions with others during time-out (Christophersen and Mortweet, 2003). Thus, time-out can prove effective with young children when used appropriately.

Finally, parents should come to appreciate young children for who they are - individuals who are striving to understand their own individuality, to master their own abilities, and to achieve autonomy (e.g., Campbell, 1998). Unfortunately, temper tantrums, noncompliance, and aggression come hand-in-hand with these other accomplishments during the toddler years (Keenan et al., 1998). If parents can come to recognize these misbehaviors as tools of learning, rather than perceive them to be personal attacks on their authority over their young children, parents can come to effectively utilize their relationships with their young children as a means of furthering their young children's achievement of individuality and confidence.

REFERENCES

Ainsworth, M. D., Blehar, M. C., Waters, E., and Wall, S. (1978). *Patterns of attachment.* Hillsdale, NJ: Erlbaum.

American Academy of Pediatrics. (1998). Committee on psychosocial aspects of child and family health: Guidance for effective discipline. *Pediatrics, 101*, 723-728.

American Psychiatric Association (APA). (2000). *Diagnostic and statistical manual of mental disorders (Fourth edition-Text revision).* Washington, DC: Author.

Bandura, A. (1997). *Self-efficacy: The exercise of control.* New York: Freeman.

Banks, J. B. (2002). Childhood discipline: Challenges for clinicians and parents. *American Family Physician, 66*, 1447-1452.

Barkley, R. A. (1997). *Defiant children: A clinician's manual for parent training.* New York: Guilford.

Baumrind, D. (1967). Child care practices anteceding three patters of preschool behavior. *Genetic Psychology Monographs, 75*, 43-88.

Baumrind, D. (1993). The average expectable environment is not good enough: A response to Scarr. *Child Development, 64,* 1299-1317.

Belsky, J., Woodworth, S., and Crnic, K. (1996). Trouble in the second year: Three questions about family interaction. *Child Development, 67,* 556-578.

Bowlby, J. (1973). *Attachment and loss: Vol. 2. Separation.* New York: Basic Books.

Campbell, S. B. (1990). *Behavior problems in preschool children: Clinical and developmental issues.* New York: Guilford Press.

Campbell, S. B. (1995). Behavior problems in preschool children: A review of recent research. *Journal of Child Psychology and Psychiatry, 36,* 113-149.

Campbell, S. B. (1997). Behavior problems in preschool children: Developmental and family issues. In T. H. Ollendick and R. J. Prinz, *Advances in Clinical Psychology, Vol. 19.* New York: Plenum Press.

Campbell, S. B. (1998). Developmental perspectives. In T. H. Ollendick and M. Hersen (Eds.), *Handbook of child psychopathology (Third edition).* New York: Plenum Press.

Campbell, S. B., Pierce, E. W., March, C. L., and Ewing, L. J. (1991). Noncompliant behavior, overactivity, and family stress as predictors of negative maternal control with preschool children. *Development and Psychopathology, 3,* 175-190.

Campbell, S. B., Pierce, E. W., Moore, G., Marakovitz, S., and Newby, K. (1996). Boys' externalizing problems at elementary school age: Pathways from early behavior problems, maternal control, and family stress. *Development and Psychopathology, 8,* 701-719.

Christophersen, E. R., and Mortweet, S. L. (2003). *Parenting that works: Building skills that last a lifetime.* Washington, DC: American Psychological Association.

Crockenberg, S., and Litman, C. (1990). Autonomy as competence in 2-year-olds: Maternal correlates of child defiance, compliance and self-assertion. *Developmental Psychology, 26,* 961-971.

Culp, R. E., Culp, A. M., Dengler, B., and Maisano, P. C. (1999). First-time young mothers living in rural communities use corporal punishment with their toddlers. *Journal of Community Psychology, 27,* 503-509.

Deater-Deckard, K., Dodge, K. A., Bates, J. E., and Pettit, G. S. (1998). Multiple risk factors in the development of externalizing behavior problems: Group and individual differences. *Development and Psychopathology, 10,* 469-494.

Donovan, W. L., Leavitt, L. A., and Walsh, R. O. (2000). Maternal illusory control predicts socialization strategies and toddler compliance. *Developmental Psychology, 36,* 402-411.

Dunn, J. (1987). The beginnings of moral understanding: Development in the second year. In J. Kagan and S. Lang (Eds.), *The emergence of morality in young children* (pp. 91-112). Chicago: University of Chicago Press.

Erikson, E. H. (1968). *Identity: Youth and crisis.* New York: Norton.

Fagot, B. I., and Gauvain, M. (1997). Mother-child problem-solving: Continuity through the early childhood years. *Developmental Psychology, 33,* 480-488.

Feldman, R., and Klein, P. S. (2003). Toddlers' self-regulated compliance to mothers, caregivers, and fathers: Implications for theories of socialization. *Developmental Psychology, 39,* 680-692.

Feshbach, N., and Feshbach, S. (1972). Children's aggression. In W. W. Hartup (Ed.), *The young child: Reviews of research (Vol. 2,* pp. 284-302). Washington, DC: National Association for the Education of Young Children.

Forehand, R., and Long, N. (2002). *Parenting the strong-willed child.* New York: Contemporary Books.

Forehand, R. L., and McMahon, R. J. (1981). *Helping the noncompliant child: A clinician's guide to parent training.* New York: Guilford.

Gardner, F. E. (1987). Positive interactions between mothers and conduct-problem children: Is there training for harmony as well as fighting? *Journal of Abnormal Child Psychology, 15,* 283-293.

Gardner, F. E. (1989). Inconsistent parenting: Is there evidence for a link with children's conduct problems? *Journal of Abnormal Child Psychology, 17,* 223-233.

Gauvain, M., and Fagot, B. I. (1995). Child temperament as a mediator of mother-toddler problem-solving. *Social Development, 4,* 257-276.

Gesell, G., and Amatruda, C. S. (1947). *Developmental diagnosis: Normal and abnormal child development, clinical methods and pediatric applications* (2nd rev. ed.). New York: Harper and Row.

Gralinski, J. H., and Kopp, C. B. (1993). Everyday rules for behavior: Mothers' requests to young children. *Developmental Psychology, 29,* 573-584.

Hipwell, A. E., Loeber, R., Stouthamer-Loeber, M., Keenan, K., White, H. R., and Krone-Man, L. (2002). Characteristics of girls with early onset disruptive and antisocial behaviour. *Criminal Behaviour and Mental Health, 12,* 99-118.

Hirshfeld-Becker, D. R., Biederman, J., Faraone, S. V., Violette, H., Wrightsman, J., and Rosenbaum, J. F. (2002). Temperamental correlates of disruptive behavior disorders in young children: Preliminary findings. *Biological Psychiatry, 51,* 563-574.

Howard, B. J. (1996). Advising parents on discipline: What works. *Pediatrics, 98,* 809-815.

Howes, C., and Matheson, C. (1992). Sequences in the development of competent play with peers: Social and social pretend play. *Developmental Psychology, 27,* 961-974.

Jenkins, S., Bax, M., and Hart, H. (1980). Behaviour problems in pre-school children. *Journal of Child Psychology and Psychiatry, 21,* 5-18.

Jennings, K. D. (2004). Development of goal-directed behaviour and related self-processes in toddlers. *International Journal of Behavioral Development, 28,* 319-327.

Kagan, J. (1984). *The nature of the child.* New York: Basic Books.

Kaler, S. R., and Kopp, C. B. (1990). Compliance and comprehension in very young toddlers. *Child Development, 61,* 1997-2003.

Keenan, K., and Shaw, D. (1994). The development of aggression in toddlers: A study of low-income families. *Journal of Abnormal Child Psychology, 22,* 53-77.

Keenan, K., Shaw, D., Delliquadri, E., Giovannelli, J., and Walsh, B. (1998). Evidence for the continuity of early problem behaviors: Application of a developmental model. *Journal of Abnormal Child Psychology, 26,* 441-454.

Keenan, K., and Wakschlag, L. S. (2000). More than the terrible twos: The nature and severity of behavior problems in clinic-referred preschool children. *Journal of Abnormal Child Psychology, 28,* 33-46.

Keenan, K., and Wakschlag, L. S. (2002). Can a valid diagnosis of disruptive behavior disorder be made in preschool children? *American Journal of Psychiatry, 159,* 351-358.

Kochanska, G. (1995). Children's temperament, mothers' discipline and security of attachment: Multiple pathways to emerging internalization. *Child Development, 66,* 597-615.

Kochanska, G. (1997). Multiple pathways to conscience for children with different temperaments: From toddlerhood to age 5. *Developmental Psychology, 33,* 228-240.

Kochanska, G., and Aksan, N. (1995). Mother-child mutually positive affect, the quality of child compliance to requests and prohibitions, and maternal control as correlates of early internalization. *Child Development, 66,* 236-254.

Kochanska, G., Murray, K. T., and Coy, K. C. (1997). Inhibitory control as a contributor to conscience in childhood: From toddler to early school age. *Child Development, 68,* 263-277.

Kopp, C. B. (1982). Antecedents of self-regulations: A developmental perspective. *Developmental Psychology, 18,* 199-214.

Kuczynski, L., and Kochanska, G. (1990). Development of children's noncompliance strategies from toddlerhood to age 5. *Developmental Psychology, 26,* 398-408.

Kuczynski, L., Kochanska, G., Radke-Yarrow, M., and Girnius-Brown, O. (1987). A developmental interpretation of young children's noncompliance. *Developmental Psychology, 23,* 799-806.

Larzelere, R. E., and Merenda, J. A. (1994). The effectiveness of parental discipline for toddler misbehavior at different levels of child distress. *Family Relations, 43,* 480-488.

Lequerica, M., and Hermosa, B. (1995). Maternal reports of behavior problems in preschool hispanic children: An exploration study in preventive pediatrics. *Journal of the National Medical Association, 87,* 861-868.

Lewis, M., Stanger, C., and Sullivan, M. W. (1989). Deception in 3-year-olds. *Developmental Psychology, 25,* 439-443.

Lieberman, A. F. (1993). *The emotional life of the toddler.* New York: The Free Press.

Loeber, R. (1990). Development and risk factors of juvenile antisocial behavior and delinquency. *Clinical Psychology Review, 10,* 1-41.

Loeber, R., and Dishion, T. J. (1983). Early predictors of male delinquency: A review. *Psychological Bulletin, 94,* 68-99.

Loeber, R., and Hay, D. (1997). Key issues in the development of aggression and violence from childhood to early adulthood. *Annual Review of Psychology, 48,* 371-410.

Lytton, H., and Zwirner, W. (1975). Compliance and its controlling stimuli observed in a natural setting. *Developmental Psychology, 11,* 769-779.

Merriam-Webster's Desk Dictionary. (1995). Springfield, Mass.: Merriam Webster, Inc.

Miller, P. H. (2002). *Theories of developmental psychology (4th ed.).* New York: Worth Publishers.

Murphy, J. (2004). *The secret life of toddlers: A parent's guide to the wonderful, terrible, fascinating behavior of children ages 1 to 3.* New York: A Pedigree Book.

Neitzel, C., and Stright, A. D. (2004). Parenting behaviours during child problem solving: The roles of child temperament, mother education and personality, and the problem-solving context. *International Journal of Behavioral Development, 28*, 166-179.

Olson, S. L., Bates, J. E., and Sandy, J. M. (2000). Early developmental precursors of externalizing behavior in middle childhood and adolescence. *Journal of Abnormal Child Psychology, 28,* 119-133.

Pailthorpe, W. K., and Ralph, A. (1998). Time-out as a means of shaping whole-task completion as a precursor to establishing rule-following behaviour with a severely noncompliant preschool child. *Behaviour Change, 15,* 50-61.

Patterson, G. R. (1982). *Coercive family process.* Eugene, OR: Castalia.

Piaget, J. (1952). *The origins of intelligence in children.* New York: International Universities Press.

Reznick, J. S., Corley, R., and Robinson, J. (1997). A longitudinal twin study of intelligence in the second year. *Monographs in Social Research in Child Development, 62,* 1-157.

Rubin, K. H., Burgess, K. B., Dwyer, K. M., and Hastings, P. D. (2003). Predicting preschoolers' externalizing behaviors from toddler temperament, conflict, and maternal negativity. *Developmental Psychology, 39,* 164-176.

Shaw, D. S., Keenan, K., and Vondra, J. I. (1994). Developmental precursors of externalizing behavior. *Developmental Psychology, 30,* 355-364.

Slicker, E. K. (1998). Relationship of parenting style to behavior adjustment in graduating high school seniors. *Journal of Youth and Adolescence, 27,* 345-372.

Sroufe, L. A. (1996). *Emotional development: The organization of emotional life in the early years.* New York: Cambridge University Press.

Tremblay, R. E. (2000). The development of aggressive behavior during childhood: What have we learned in the past century? *International Journal of Behavior Development, 24,* 129-141.

Wakschlag, L. S., and Keenan, K. (2001). Clinical significance and correlates of disruptive behavior in environmentally at-risk preschoolers. *Journal of Clinical Child Psychology, 30,* 262-275.

Whaley, S. E., Pinto, A., and Sigman, M. (1999). Characterizing interactions between anxious mothers and their children. *Journal of Consulting and Clinical Psychology, 67*, 826-836.

In: Parent-Child Relations: New Research
Editor: Dorothy M. Devore, pp. 101-120
ISBN 1-60021-167-4

Chapter 6

TWO TO TANGO: EVIDENCE FOR A SYSTEMS VIEW OF PARENTING IN THE TODDLER PERIOD

Nancy S. Weinfield[*]
University of Virginia, Charlottesville, VA 22904

ABSTRACT

Although parents who live in the same household parent their children concurrently, research often approaches parenting as if mothers' and fathers' behavior were independent rather than interdependent. Yet in practice parents do seem to coordinate their parenting, organizing parenting activities to reinforce shared beliefs and to avoid redundant tasks. The nature and success of such arrangements, however, has not been extensively studied. During the sometimes-turbulent toddler period successful joint parenting efforts should result in interparental agreement on whether their child's behavior is normal or problematic, as this is the starting point for family decisions about socialization and discipline. This chapter reviews theory and research about parenting configurations that individual and systemic theories predict should promote agreement about child behavior. New data are presented that explored different configurations of parenting styles, and which of these parenting configurations best predicted consensus about child behavior. Participants were parents from 51 families with 30-month-old children. Primary and secondary caregivers reported on their toddlers' behavior problems and on their own parenting activities. Results indicated that parents agreed moderately on both parenting and child behavior. Specific configurations of parenting styles did predict agreement on child behavior problems. Parents with similar but non-optimal parenting styles showed the lowest levels of agreement about their children. The highest levels of agreement about child behavior were predicted by parenting configurations that provided balanced parenting coverage, even if their individual parenting styles seemed dissimilar. This relation could not be accounted for by marital consensus more generally.

[*] Author Contact Information: Nancy S. Weinfield, PhD. Department of Psychology, University of Virginia, P.O. Box 400400. Charlottesville, VA 22904. Phone: 434-924-0601; fax: 434-982-4766; email: nweinfield@virginia.edu

INTRODUCTION

Patricia Minuchin, a psychologist and family systems expert, astutely observed that "psychological researchers created the single-parent family long before it was a characteristic of American society," (Minuchin, 1985, p.296). Although parents who live in the same household parent their children concurrently, research often approaches parenting in two-parent families as if mothers' and fathers' behavior were independent rather than interdependent. The family is an organized unit, and the behavior of a single individual cannot be fully and richly understood in isolation from the context of other family members (Cox and Paley, 1997). Consequently, studying parenting by just one parent is likely an incomplete view of the family. Outside the realm of our research models parents do seem to coordinate their parenting, organizing parenting activities to reinforce shared beliefs and to avoid redundant tasks. The nature and success of such arrangements, however, has not been extensively studied. The sometimes turbulent toddler period may be one of the crucial tests of these parenting arrangements, as socialization comes to the forefront of parenting issues. Successful joint parenting efforts should, at their most basic, result in interparental agreement on whether their toddler's behavior is normal or problematic, as this is the starting point for family decisions about socialization and discipline. This chapter reviews theory and research about coparenting, proposing and exploring a systems view of parenting during the toddler period. New data are also presented, investigating the combinations of parenting behaviors that result in compatible parenting teams during this challenging period of children's development.

CONCEPTUALIZING AND STUDYING COPARENTING

Systems theory, when applied to families, conceptualizes the family as an organized, dynamic set of interdependent relationships and processes (Minuchin, 1988). Systems in general tend to be self-stabilizing, such that they operate in ways that keep themselves functioning (Minuchin, 1985) even if the behaviors that keep them functioning are maladaptive from an outside perspective (Boszormenyi-Nagy and Spark, 1984). Thus individual behaviors we see in families might seem illogical or even dysfunctional when considered in isolation, but in the context of the rest of the family they serve a predictable purpose. Parents are a functioning subsystem of the family, and from a family systems perspective individual parenting behaviors may only cohere when seen as a unified effort of two parents rather than as two independently functioning contributors.

When research has addressed parenting by both parents in families, often the methodology is examining whether each parent reports similar beliefs about parenting (Block, Block, and Morrison, 1981; Deal, Halverson, and Wampler, 1989; Gjerde, 1988), or whether one parent indicates that there is interparental disagreement about parenting (Jouriles et al., 1991). Agreement about parenting beliefs, rather than the nature of those beliefs, is the focus of such research. Shared beliefs about parenting, of course, may be essential to an effective parenting partnership, as beliefs are a prerequisite and corequisite of choices in parenting. Beliefs and behaviors, however, may be different as even among parents with shared beliefs actual parenting duties may be split in uneven or even contrasting ways.

There is some literature on coparenting behaviors, and often such behavior is assessed through observations of mother and fathers engaging in parenting behaviors during a single, triadic observation (Belsky, Putnam, and Crnic, 1996; Fivaz-Depeursinge, Frascarolo, and Corboz-Warnery, 1996; Gable, Belsky, and Crnic, 1992; Gable, Crnic, and Belsky, 1994). These procedures capture systemic parenting behavior in a way that neither measures of shared beliefs nor single reports of discord could. These approaches, however, often implicitly assume that the behavior parents show when they are parenting their children in the same moment mirrors what happens when they parent separately.

In one study of observed triadic interaction, Gable et al. (1994) defined coparenting as events where parents reinforce or contradict each others' parenting behaviors during an observation of the family. Mothers and fathers were deemed to be engaging in supportive coparenting if they reiterated or otherwise supported the other parent's initial parenting behaviors. Such operationalizations do take the step of defining coparenting in ways that do not require redundancy of behavior in the situation. Nonetheless, this type of supportive coparenting does not take quality of parenting into account. Parents who reinforce each other's punitive orientations would be deemed as supportive a coparenting alliance as parents who coordinate a more optimal parenting approach.

Marital couples divide labor within the family, developing even more clear divisions of labor once they become parents (Cowan, Cowan, Heming, and Miller, 1991). Like other things in the marital relationship, division of labor may dictate that parents engage in seemingly different parenting behaviors to achieve a coherent approach to parenting. Division of labor, as a purely practical consideration, also suggests that a more common scenario is for each parent to have arenas of responsibility with regard to parenting. Additionally, shared responsibilities that exist are unlikely to be carried out simultaneously. A pattern where both parents consistently engage in simultaneous parenting activities would be inefficient, and likely too disruptive to the lives of families with young children.

Division of labor is evident even in families where parenting duties are not claimed by one parent primarily. Qualitative research by Dienhart (2001) describes couples who engage in tag-team parenting where both parents share duties equally, yet still alternate primary responsibility. Even in this type of family configuration where mothers and fathers identified no hierarchy in caregiver status, parents within the same family described different parenting behaviors. Parents indicated that they carried out even similar parenting activities differently due to differences in individual style, despite sharing core beliefs. So although these couples might be interchangeable in taking responsibility for parenting activities, each parent would carry out the activity in a more individual way. Parents also reported dividing up many duties based on individual preference or skill, so that some activities were dealt with primarily by one parent or the other even if both were available to split the duty. Within these families parents recognized that they sometimes parented differently, but they felt little need to match each other's styles, instead suggesting that within family variation in how parenting is done is natural and normal.

THE STRUCTURE OF EFFECTIVE PARTNERSHIPS

Despite an emerging understanding of the diversity of parenting partnerships, we know little about how effective partnerships are structured. Baumrind (1966, 1967) described three main styles of individual parenting: authoritative, authoritarian, and permissive. Authoritative parenting, characterized by warmth and democratic interactions as well as firm control and expectations for maturity, was the optimal parenting style in her study of preschool children's parents. Authoritative parents also seemed to exercise the most flexibility in dealing with the balance between necessary structure and their children's autonomy strivings. Authoritarian parenting, characterized by strict control, little warmth, and little child input, and permissive parenting, characterized by some warmth but lax control and few expectations for maturity, were the less optimal and less flexible parenting styles. But when parents are engaging in a division of labor must both parents be authoritative for the partnership to be effective? Given divisions of labor, might different parenting styles combined within one family system also result in a coherent, effective partnership? It is plausible that within a systems perspective parenting partnerships can, and perhaps should, be conceptualized as a nonindependent pairing of parenting styles.

Because both mothers and fathers are engaging in parenting behavior in the context of the family, parents may be described as a functioning subsystem of the family and the effectiveness of that subsystem may depend on the cohesiveness of the dyad's parenting behaviors. Such cohesiveness has been conceptualized in two major ways: (a) Similarity of parenting behavior or attitudes, or (b) Complementarity of the contributions of both parents to the parenting subsystem.

The Similarity Hypothesis

Similarity of parenting behavior has been a common way of examining cohesiveness of the parenting subsystem. Literature on parenting has suggested that similarity in parenting attitudes predicts absolute levels of child outcomes, with greater similarity predicting more optimal child outcomes. Agreement on parenting has predicted maternal reports of child behavior problems (Deal et al., 1989), and positive psychosocial functioning in boys (Block et al., 1981). Additionally, maternal reports of interparental disagreement about parenting predicted boys' behavior problems, with reports of less agreement predicting more behavior problems (Jouriles et al., 1991).

This literature suggests that similarity in parenting may be key for cohesiveness in the parenting system. Such research, however, has generally focused on parenting beliefs rather than behaviors, and it remains an empirical question whether similar *behaviors* also relate to child outcomes. The similarity hypothesis, then, would predict that dyads that share similar parenting styles would demonstrate better agreement about child behavior problems than would dyads that differ in parenting styles.

The Complementarity Hypothesis

Division of labor within parenting partnerships may result in parents who differ in behavior even in the presence of similar core beliefs. Some complementary combinations of different parenting styles may therefore be effective expressions of a shared vision for parenting split in duties across two people. For example, one parent may take primary responsibility for comfort and nurturance, whereas the other parent is primarily a playmate or disciplinarian. Together, the combination of parenting behaviors could still form a coherent and effective parenting system. It may be difficult to create a cohesive system, however, when neither parent adheres to a more flexible authoritative strategy in response to toddler autonomy; at least one parent who adheres to an authoritative strategy should be necessary to balance the system. Nonetheless, authoritative styles might also combine effectively with authoritarian or permissive styles, with the non-authoritarian parent taking a complementary role in discipline or play activities. Thus adherence to similar parenting styles may not always be indicative of a cohesive system, and some patterns of difference may be more compatible than others (Bateson, 1972; Minuchin, 1985). Minuchin (1985) noted that in her research and clinical work parents within the same family often seemed to differ in their socialization strategies, yet complement each other well. The complementarity hypothesis suggests that differences in parenting may be adaptive, particularly if when juxtaposed the different styles produce a coherent whole.

Despite the fact that different parenting styles might fit together coherently, systems-oriented research approaches suggest that we should not average across parenting, or see each parent as an individually functioning unit contributing independently to an outcome (Cox and Paley, 1997). Although averaging similar parenting results is a reiteration of already present styles, averaging discrepant parenting behaviors loses the texture of the full range of parenting behaviors and creates a counterfactual middle ground. Instead, systems approaches dictate that we should look for ways in which individuals fit together into pairings that encompass the full range of parenting behavior.

Correlates of Effective Partnerships

Agreement on parenting has sometimes been addressed in the literature as if it were a component of marital relationship quality (Cox and Paley, 1997; Gable et al., 1992; Gjerde, 1988). From this perspective, agreement on parenting may be considered a simple extension of agreement in the marital relationship. If differences in parenting behavior are a potential source of interparental conflict, as previous literature might suggest, it would be important to establish what makes some patterns complementary rather than just contrasting, and consequently to differentiate complementary but functional parenting from more detrimental marital disagreements.

One approach to studying effective parenting partnerships would be to study parenting during developmental transitions. Such transitions involve substantial change in the child, pose particular challenges to the parenting partnership, and can offset the balance of the parenting system (Cox and Paley, 1997; Minuchin, 1985) thus revealing key foundations and flaws of the system. The transition between infancy and early childhood, marked by autonomy strivings and failed attempts at self-regulation, might be such a transition. It would require parents to renegotiate their conceptualizations of normal child behavior. Consequently, the challenges of the toddler period might pose a more substantial challenge for parenting systems that are less stable and more easily disrupted.

When children are school-aged successful parenting arrangements should relate to child behavioral outcomes, and at the very least predict a relative absence of child behavior problems. The toddler period, however, poses very different challenges. As toddlers face rapid but sometimes uneven development in language, locomotion, autonomy seeking, and emotion regulation there is a normative spike in disruptive behavior associated with the "terrible twos." In a normally developing population, occasional behavior problems in the home context would not be uncommon, and even well adjusted children overall may at times show some elevation in behavior problems.

Parents face difficult decisions, then, in determining the line between normative difficulties with this transition to emotional and behavioral self-regulation, and problematic behavior that warrants a stronger response (Gable et al., 1992). Agreement between parents on the degree of problematic behavior a child is showing is vital at this age, so that parents have a shared perspective on the need for nurturance, socialization, or disciplinary efforts. A truly effective parenting partnership should involve a shared perspective on the nature and frequency of child behavior problems. Consequently, one metric on which parenting partnerships might differ is the degree to which they predict agreement between parents on child behavior problems.

Research on interparental agreement on child behavior problems has been plentiful, so much so that two meta-analyses have been conducted on this topic (Achenbach, McConaughy, and Howell, 1987; Duhig, Renk, Epstein, and Phares, 2000). Achenbach and colleagues (1987) reported that interparental agreement was significant and reached moderate levels. They also reported that agreement was better for reports on younger children, ages 6-11, than for adolescents. Few of the reviewed studies, however, included any children under the age of six, and none focused exclusively on the toddler period. A subsequent meta-analysis by Duhig and colleagues (2000) confirmed the estimates of agreement, although they found that agreement was lower for internalizing behavior than for externalizing behavior. They failed to replicate the child age finding, instead finding that interparental agreement was generally *lower* for younger children than for adolescents, although the youngest child age was again older than the toddler period. Two individual studies, Earls (1980) and Christensen, Margolin, and Sulloway (1992) did include younger children in their samples and also found that mothers and fathers agreed moderately well on behavior problems. Thus agreement between parents about child behavior problems is generally moderate, but little has been done that includes children under the age of three.

THE TODDLERHOOD PROJECT

The Toddlerhood Project was initiated as a study exploring the nature and correlates of the "terrible twos." The main focus of the study was how parents view child temper tantrums and behavior problems during this sometimes difficult transition between infancy and early childhood. The reasons for this exploratory study were twofold. First, anecdotal evidence from a variety of research studies suggested that the toddler period posed new difficulty for some parents who had seemed to be parenting very effectively during infancy, yet research on changes in parent-child relationships did not seem to be capturing the impetus for these changes (Weinfield, Whaley, and Egeland, 2004). Second, parents themselves seemed to differ widely in their thoughts about child behavior during the toddler period, with some parents interpreting the autonomy-seeking and tantrums characteristic of this age as normal and expectable, and others seeing it as intolerable bad behavior.

Research Questions

The two competing hypotheses about coparenting, the similarity hypothesis and the complementarity hypothesis, are tested here using data from the Toddlerhood Project. With regard to the similarity hypothesis, then, parents who adhere to the same parenting style would be expected to show greater agreement about child behavior than those who differ in parenting style. With regard to the complementarity hypothesis, different parenting styles should combine to produce a cohesive whole. Specifically, dyads with at least one parent who engages in the more optimal and flexible authoritative style would be expected to produce a balanced partnership and thus show greater consensus than dyads without an authoritative parent. In keeping with a theoretical perspective that suggests that cohesive parenting partnerships are separable from marital harmony, parenting configurations that relate to greater agreement about child behavior are expected to do so above and beyond variance that could be explained by the tendency to agree on things in general in the marriage.

Participants

Participants in the study were 102 parents from 51 families with 30-month-old children (child gender 49% male, 51% female). Families were contacted through birth records and pediatricians' offices in a small southern city. All but one of the families included a married mother and father; one family consisted of the mother and the child's great grandmother as the two custodial parents; as a secondary caregiver, the great grandmother is included with the "father" group in analyses and this dyad is not included in analyses considering marital relationship qualities. Two families were excluded from all interparental analyses due to incomplete data by one parent. Forty-one percent of the toddlers were firstborn. Toddler race was reported by the primary caregiver as 82% Caucasian, 8% African-American, 6% multiracial, 2% other race, and 2% not disclosing race. Household income ranged from less than $20,000 per year to over $100,000 per year, with a median of $65,000.

Procedures

Both parents in each family completed questionnaires about themselves, their family relationships, and their toddler's behavior. Packets were delivered and measures were explained during a brief home visit, at which time consent was also obtained from each parent independently. Packets were subsequently returned by mail or retrieved by a researcher.

Parents were instructed not to discuss the questionnaires until after both of them had completed and returned the packets. Families were compensated modestly for their time.

Measures

Parenting Behavior

Parenting behavior was assessed through the Parent Behavior Checklist (PBC; Fox, 1994). The PBC is a 100-item checklist of activities the parent engages in with the child and developmental expectations the parent has of the child. For each item parents indicate whether the item is never, sometimes, frequently, or always/almost always true for them. Because the measure asks for the individual parent's behavior and expectations rather than family practices, the resulting data cover only the respondent's parenting. The PBC yields three scale scores: Expectations, Discipline, and Nurturance. Raw scores are converted to normalized T scores based on an age-specific norming sample (Fox, 1994). The PBC has been found to be unrelated to measures of social desirability (Peters and Fox, 1993), and can be discriminated from more general measures of attitudes about parenting (Fox and Bentley, 1992). Thus the PBC taps parenting practices, rather than attitudes, across the following three dimensions of behavior:

Expectations. The Expectations scale is a 50-item scale that captures the parent's expectations of the child regarding developmental abilities and maturity level. Questions inquire about behaviors the parent expects the child to carry out at this age (e.g., "My child should be able to use a spoon without making a mess"). T scores around the mean indicate developmentally appropriate expectations, whereas high scores indicate expectations that exceed the age of the child and low scores indicate expectations that lag behind the age of the child. Internal consistency reliability was alpha = .90 for mothers and alpha = .91 for fathers.

Discipline. The Discipline scale is a 30-item scale that captures the parent's punitive and restrictive discipline strategies in response to perceived child misbehavior. Questions tap parental responses to problematic child behavior (e.g. "I yell at my child for whining"). High T scores indicate a greater use of punitive disciplinary tactics, whereas low T scores indicate few restrictive disciplinary actions. Internal consistency reliability was alpha = .85 for mothers and alpha = .80 for fathers.

Nurturance. The Nurturance scale is a 20-item scale that reflects the parent's engagement in warm or supportive activities that encourage the child's psychological or emotional development. Questions tap parental behavior that encourages child exploration, and behavior that is intended to make the child happy or to comfort the child (e.g., "I read to my child at bedtime"). High T scores indicate multiple, frequent acts of nurturance, whereas low scores indicate a lack of nurturing engagement. Internal consistency reliability was alpha = .81 for mothers and alpha = .86 for fathers.

Parenting Style Clusters. Most studies of parenting examine specific dimensions of parenting such as supportiveness, punitiveness, or expectations for maturity (Maccoby and Martin, 1983). Baumrind (1967), however, argued that looking at features of parenting behavior as separable dimensions, rather than as coherent organizations, would eclipse the essential structure of the parenting style. Consequently, data were cluster analyzed to classify parents into parenting style groups. Because three parenting styles could be expected based on a priori theoretical and empirical grounds – authoritative, permissive, and authoritarian – k-means cluster analysis was conducted. K-means cluster analysis is most useful when confirming and describing a theoretically identified number of groups, and when the data represent the dimensions on which the groups should be based (Aldenderfer and Blashfield, 1984; Everitt, Landau, and Leese, 2001). In this case, the individual parenting scales represented key dimensions identified by Baumrind, and a three cluster solution was expected. Mothers' and fathers' parenting data were clustered separately based on theoretical and empirical work suggesting that mothers and fathers engage in distinctive behaviors within the parenting styles (Baumrind, 1967; Lamb, Frodi, Frodi, and Hwang, 1982), particularly during the toddler years (Grossmann et al., 2002). Clustering identified groups that fit Baumrind's parenting styles (see Table 1 for cluster centers and standard deviations). The first maternal group (n = 21), corresponding to the authoritative style, had high expectations, moderate discipline, and high nurturance. The second maternal group (n = 19), corresponding to the permissive style, had low expectations, low discipline, and moderate nurturance. The third maternal group (n = 9), corresponding to the authoritarian style, had moderate expectations, high discipline, and low nurturance. The paternal groups differed only slightly from the maternal groups, and still confirmed the three expected styles. The paternal authoritative group (n = 15) had moderate expectations, moderate discipline, and high nurturance. The paternal permissive group (n = 13) had low expectations, moderate discipline, and low nurturance, matching Baumrind's (1967) finding that permissive fathers are uninvolved rather than nurturing. The paternal authoritarian group (n = 21) had high expectations, high discipline, and low nurturance.

Table 1. Cluster Centers and Standard Deviations on Parenting Scales for Maternal and Paternal Parenting Clusters

	Parenting Clusters					
Parenting Scale	Authoritative		Permissive		Authoritarian	
	M	(SD)	M	(SD)	M	(SD)
Mothers						
Expectations	49.67	(5.42)	32.16	(4.92)	41.22	(9.34)
Discipline	39.00	(4.67)	36.47	(4.96)	51.78	(5.95)
Nurturance	57.67	(6.39)	54.21	(7.71)	43.89	(5.99)
Fathers						
Expectations	43.93	(10.60)	33.92	(5.69)	50.14	(7.00)
Discipline	39.07	(5.11)	40.84	(6.76)	46.19	(6.84)
Nurturance	57.53	(5.96)	38.15	(5.40)	38.15	(5.40)

Child Behavior Problems

Toddler behavior problems were assessed using the Child Behavior Checklist 2-3 (CBCL; Achenbach, 1992), a widely used 100-item parent-report checklist of child behavior problems. For each item, parents indicated whether the behavior was not true, sometimes true, or often true of their child during the past two months. The CBCL yields three major scales of child behavior problems: Internalizing (comprising anxious/depressed and withdrawn behaviors), Externalizing (comprising aggressive and destructive behaviors), and Total

Problems (comprising internalizing problems, externalizing problems, and sleep and somatic problems). Raw scores are converted to T scores based on a large norming sample. Higher scores indicate more problems, and T scores above 60 may be considered borderline clinical or clinical range problems. The CBCL has been shown to discriminate between clinic-referred and non-clinic-referred children (Achenbach, Edelbrock, and Howell, 1987).

Marital Consensus

General agreement in the parents' marital relationship was assessed using the Dyadic Adjustment Scale (DAS; Spanier, 1989). The DAS is a 32-item scale on which an individual reports agreement, activities, and satisfaction within the marital relationship. For the present study one subscale of the DAS, the Dyadic Consensus subscale, was used. Dyadic consensus consists of 13 items that address agreement on a variety of issues, including finances, activities, religion, priorities, and life goals. Parenting issues are not included in dyadic consensus, thus the scale captures agreement between spouses in general, but does not seek to capture agreement on childrearing specifically. Raw scores are converted to normalized T scores based on a norming sample of married couples. Higher scores indicate greater perceived consensus in the relationship. Internal consistency reliability for the dyadic consensus scale was *alpha* = .77 for fathers, and *alpha* = .82 for mothers. The DAS has been widely used in both research and clinical settings, and has convergent validity established with other paper and pencil measures of marital functioning (Spanier, 1976), and with observed marital communication patterns (Ting-Toomey, 1983).

Analysis Plan

Analyses proceed in several phases. First, the parenting clusters are described and interparental agreement on parenting clusters is explored. Second, descriptive information about maternal and paternal reports of behavior problems are presented, and interparental agreement on behavior problems is investigated. Third, analyses explore the relation between individual parenting styles and interparental agreement on toddler behavior problems to test whether a particular maternal or paternal parenting style are associated with disagreement about child behavior, regardless of the other parent's parenting practices. Fourth, analyses examine the relation between different configurations of parenting and interparental agreement on toddler behavior problems, using the parenting cluster agreement to predict consensus about child behavior. Both the similarity hypothesis and the complementarity hypothesis of parenting are tested to establish which model of parenting is the best predictor of a unified view of toddler behavior. Finally, analyses are conducted controlling for marital consensus more generally to determine if it can account for any relation between parenting patterns and consensus on child behavior problems.

RESULTS AND DISCUSSION

Parenting Styles

The modal parenting style for mothers was authoritative parenting (42.9%). Fewer mothers fell into the permissive (38.8%) and authoritarian (18.3%) styles. The modal parenting style for fathers was the authoritarian parenting style (42.9%), with smaller percentages falling into the authoritative (30.6%) and permissive (26.5%) styles. This pattern suggests that fathers, as compared to mothers, may engage in a stricter, less warm form of parenting with their toddlers.

Similarity of parenting styles within families was assessed through examination of categorical matches (see Table 2). Overall, analyses revealed significant matching of parenting style, with 46.9% of the mothers and fathers in the same families showing similar parenting styles, *kappa* = .228, p = .014. Nonetheless, over half of the parenting dyads did not have similar parenting styles, leaving substantial variability in parenting configurations for exploration.

Table 2. Interparental Matching on Parenting Style Clusters

Maternal Parenting Clusters	Paternal Parenting Clusters: Authoritative	Permissive	Authoritarian	Total
	Observed frequency (expected frequency)			
Authoritative	10	2	9	21
	(6.4)	(5.6)	(9.0)	
Permissive	4	8	7	19
	(5.8)	(5.0)	(8.1)	
Authoritarian	1	3	5	9
	(2.8)	(2.4)	(3.9)	
Total	15	13	21	49

Child Behavior Problems

Internalizing Behavior. Descriptive information on T scores of mothers' and fathers' reports of toddler internalizing behavior appear in Table 3. Only three mothers and four fathers identified their children as having serious levels of behavior problems, falling at or above the subclinical threshold of 60 (Achenbach, 1992), confirming that in this community sample parents are agreeing or disagreeing about primarily normal-range, yet undesirable, child behavior. The correlation between maternal and paternal reports of internalizing was not significant, r (49) = .20, ns, and a paired t-test revealed no significant mean difference between maternal and paternal reports, t (48) = .48, ns. There was no overlap in the cases identified by parents as meeting or exceeding the subclinical threshold. Thus levels of agreement between parents on toddler internalizing behavior were low, although neither mothers nor fathers were seeing the toddlers as having more internalizing behavior on average. To examine the magnitude of the disagreements between parents, a discrepancy score was derived by computing the absolute value of the difference between T scores in each parental dyad. The discrepancy scores range from 0 to 33 (M = 8.04, SD = 7.25).

Externalizing Behavior. Descriptive data on mothers' and fathers' reports of externalizing behavior appear in Table 3. Mothers' reports of toddler externalizing behavior were somewhat higher than reports of internalizing behavior. Nine mothers indicated that their children met or exceeded the subclinical threshold T score of 60. Fathers' reports were similar, and nine fathers reported children's behavior at or above the subclinical threshold. There was a significant correlation between maternal and paternal reports, r (49) = .47, p = .001. A paired t-test revealed no significant mean difference between maternal and paternal reports, t (48) = .73, ns. In five families both the mother and the father identified their toddler as falling in the subclinical or clinical range. Parents showed greater agreement about externalizing behaviors in their toddlers, although neither mothers nor fathers are identifying more behavior problems on average. Again, the small number of children showing substantial behavior problems suggests that parents were agreeing or disagreeing about normal range, but possibly undesirable, behaviors. A discrepancy score was again derived by computing the absolute value of the T score differences in each dyad. Discrepancies on externalizing behavior ranged from 0 to 24 (M = 6.47, SD = 5.45).

Total Behavior Problems. Descriptive data for total behavior problems, which combines internalizing, externalizing, sleep, and somatic problems, appear in Table 3. Means for total behavior problems fell, as expected, between the levels of internalizing and externalizing. Seven children were rated by their mothers and five children were rated by their fathers as falling into the subclinical or clinical range. There was a significant correlation between maternal and paternal reports, r (49) = .30, p = .03. A paired t-test revealed no significant mean differences between maternal and paternal reports, t (48) = .41, ns. In two families both the mother and father identified their toddler as falling in the subclinical or clinical range. A discrepancy score was computed using the same procedures as were used for internalizing and externalizing behavior. Discrepancies ranged from 0 to 33, (M = 7.35, SD = 6.53).

Table 3. Descriptive Statistics on Maternal and Paternal Reports of Child Behavior Problems

Variable *Reporter*	*Minimum*	*Maximum*	*Mean*	*SD*
Internalizing				
Mother	30	71	46.78	8.56
Father	30	70	46.08	8.60
Externalizing				
Mother	36	70	49.98	8.62
Father	34	69	49.10	7.70
Total				
Mother	33	75	49.04	8.75
Father	35	71	48.47	7.93

Thus, mothers and fathers agreed moderately on toddler behavior problems. The pattern of findings mirrors those of Duhig et al. (2000) in that parental reports of internalizing behaviors were less strongly correlated than reports of externalizing behaviors, and there were no significant mean differences on paired t-tests between mothers' and fathers' reports suggesting that neither mothers nor fathers systematically identified more behavior problems. It does seem, then, that there was some subjectivity in within-family perceptions of toddler behavior problems based on the moderate interparental correlations.

Relation between Parenting and Agreement on Child Behavior Problems

Individual Parenting Styles. It is possible that some sub-optimal parenting styles, when present in even one parent, would be sufficient to create disagreements on child behavior regardless of the second parent's predilection. To explore whether agreement on child behavior problems could be accounted for by either maternal or paternal parenting style alone, analyses were conducted on the relation between individual parenting styles and child behavior difference scores. ANOVAs were conducted exploring whether child behavior difference scores differed first across maternal parenting styles, then across paternal parenting styles. Maternal parenting style predicted differences in child externalizing reports with marginal significance, $F\ (2,46) = 2.83$, $p = .07$. Follow up analyses indicated that the difference was between the authoritative and permissive groups, with the permissive group showing marginally greater disagreement on child externalizing behavior (mean difference scores 4.57 and 8.53 respectively). Paternal parenting style analyses yielded no significant group differences on child behavior difference scores.

Individual maternal or paternal parenting styles did not seem to explain much of the variance in interparental agreement on child behavior problems. Families with permissive mothers did show marginally more disagreement than families with authoritative mothers, but not more than families with authoritarian mothers. Other individual parent qualities, including symptoms of psychopathology, have been found to relate to disagreement on child behavior problems in previous studies (Earls, 1980; Phares, Compas, and Howell, 1989). Although more extreme individual parent characteristics like psychopathology might contribute to disagreements about toddler behavior, the normal range parenting style of only one parent might not be sufficient to result in such divergence in interparental perceptions of the child.

It seems that having one parent who engages in suboptimal parenting does not upset the parenting partnership enough to result in disagreements about child behavior. This leaves open the possibility, however, that convergences or clashes between parents in their parenting styles might still result in differing views of their toddler. The next step, then, was to determine whether either similarity or complementarity of parenting styles was associated with greater agreement on child behavior.

Dyadic Similarity of Parenting Styles. To evaluate the relation between similarity of parenting style and agreement on child behavior problems, families were divided into two groups: those where the parents had similar parenting styles (n=23), and those where the parents differed in their parenting styles (n=26). MANOVA was conducted predicting the three child behavior difference scores from the parenting agreement groups. The multivariate test was significant, $F\ (3,45) = 2.96$, $p = .042$. Univariate follow up tests indicated that parenting style similarity predicted agreement on child internalizing, $F\ (1,47) = 8.31$, $p = .006$, and agreement on total behavior problems, $F\ (1,47) = 5.24$, $p = .027$, with those with similar parenting styles showing *less* agreement about child behavior problems than those with different parenting styles (see Table 4 for descriptive data).

Table 4. Descriptive Data on Child Behavior Problem Difference Scores by Parenting Style Groupings

Parenting Style	Child Behavior Problem Difference Scores					
	Internalizing		Externalizing		Total	
Groupings	M	(SD)	M	(SD)	M	(SD)
Similarity						
Similar	11.00	(8.17)	7.48	(7.08)	9.52	(7.80)
Dissimilar	5.42	(5.19)	5.58	(3.35)	5.42	(4.47)
Complementarity						
With Authoritative	6.15	(3.71)	4.77	(3.30)	6.08	(3.81)
Without Authoritative	10.17	(9.50)	8.39	(6.72)	8.78	(8.51)

To further understand this finding, and to explore whether quality of parenting style on which the parents are similar may be relevant for agreement on child behavior problems, follow up planned contrasts were conducted within the parenting similarity groups. To determine if similarity on optimal parenting differs from similarity on less optimal parenting, contrasts compared the authoritative-authoritative group with the combined permissive-permissive and authoritarian-authoritarian groups on child internalizing difference scores and on total behavior problems difference scores. Contrasts revealed a marginally significant difference between the groups predicting child internalizing difference scores, t (14.56) = -1.87, p = .082, with the authoritative-authoritative parents showing more agreement on child internalizing than the permissive-permissive/authoritarian-authoritarian group. No significant difference was found for the contrast predicting total behavior problems. Thus it seems that similar parenting styles may not promote consensus on child behavior problems, although similarity between mothers and fathers on a more optimal parenting style predicted somewhat better agreement on child behavior than similarity between parents on a less optimal parenting style.

Dyadic Complementarity of Parenting Styles. Analyses were conducted examining whether parents with complementary parenting styles, involving at least one authoritative parent, agreed more about child behavior problems than noncomplementary, seemingly mismatched dyads. To test this, MANOVA was conducted comparing the parenting dyads that included at least one authoritative parent to parenting dyads that did not include an authoritative parent on the three behavior problem difference scores. The multivariate test was significant, F (3,45) = 3.50, p = .023. Univariate results indicated that complementary parenting dyads had marginally more agreement than the noncomplementary parenting dyads on child internalizing, F (1,47) = 3.98, p = .052, and significantly more agreement on child externalizing, F (1,47) = 5.94, p = .019. Thus dyads that contained at least one parent with a more optimal parenting style agreed better than parents where neither parent had an optimal parenting style (see Table 4 for descriptive data).

It was somewhat surprising that families where the parents had similar parenting styles showed *less* agreement on child behavior problems than families where the parents differed in their parenting styles. It may be that similarity is not nearly as important as balance in forming an effective parenting partnership. If parents engage in complementary but somewhat non-overlapping parenting behaviors, they may form a functioning system through the combination of parenting efforts; this system may differ somewhat from the individual parenting styles. Consequently rather than both parents engaging in equal amounts of discipline or nurturance, or both parents pushing the child's developmental limits, one parent may discipline more whereas the other engages in more nurturing activities. This would then result in similar parenting styles combining less effectively than complementary parenting styles. This complementarity seemed particularly successful for families that contained at least one parent who is authoritative, perhaps because only the authoritative parents brought flexibility and high nurturance to the partnership along with their other parenting qualities, thus bringing the potential to cover all essential dimensions of parenting within the partnership.

The Role of Marital Consensus

To determine whether the relations between parenting style configurations and agreement on child behavior problems could be accounted for by general agreement in the marital relationship, analyses were conducted covarying out maternal and paternal reports of marital consensus.

Preliminary analyses on the marital consensus variables demonstrated that maternal and paternal marital consensus were significantly intercorrelated r (47) = .54, p = .000. Paired t-test analysis revealed that fathers reported marginally significantly less consensus than mothers, t (46) = 1.87, p = .068. Because of the relatively high correlation between the consensus variables, covariate analyses were conducted separately for maternal and paternal consensus.

Simple correlations between the marital consensus variables and the child behavior problem difference scores were conducted initially. Maternal report of marital consensus was not significantly related to agreement on internalizing, r (48) = -.10, externalizing, r (48) = -.09, or total problems, r (48) = -.03. Paternal report of marital consensus, however, was significantly related to agreement on internalizing, r (48) = -.36, p = .012, externalizing, r (48) = -.33, p = .023, and total problems, r (48) = -.39, p = .006.

Covariate analyses were conducted only for those dependent variables that had emerged as significantly or marginally significantly predicted in the prior MANOVA analyses. Thus in covariate analyses predicting from similarity in parenting style, only child internalizing difference scores and total behavior problems difference scores were used as dependent variables. In covariate analyses predicting from complementarity in parenting style, only child internalizing difference scores and child externalizing difference scores were used as dependent variables.

Covariate analyses were conducted on the previously significant predictions from dyadic similarity in parenting style to child internalizing difference scores and total behavior problems difference scores. Two ANCOVAs were conducted comparing the child internalizing behavior difference scores between the group where parents had similar parenting styles and the group where parents had dissimilar parenting styles. When maternal report of marital consensus was covaried out in the first ANCOVA the covariate itself was not significant, F (1,45) = .35, *ns*, and the main effect of parenting style similarity remained significant, F (1,45) = 7.05, p = .011. When paternal report of marital consensus was covaried out in the second ANCOVA the covariate was significant, F (1,45) = 6.72, p = .013, but the main effect of parenting style similarity still remained significant, F (1,45) = 7.97, p = .007. Next, two ANCOVAs were conducted comparing total behavior difference scores across these two parenting groups. In the first ANCOVA predicting agreement on total behavior problems maternal report of marital consensus was entered as a covariate, and was not significant, F (1,45) = .01, *ns*, and the main effect of parenting style similarity remained significant, F (1,45) = 5.04, p = .03. When paternal report of marital consensus was covaried out in the second ANCOVA the covariate was significant, F (1,45) = 7.91, p = .007, and the main effect of parenting style similarity remained significant, F (1,45) = 4.40, p = .042. Adjusted means confirmed the previous findings that those parents who shared similar parenting styles agreed less about child behavior problems than parents who differed in their parenting styles. Thus agreement in the marital relationship broadly did not account for the findings on parenting agreement.

Covariate analyses were also conducted on significant findings regarding dyadic complementary and noncomplementary parenting style pairings. First, predictions to internalizing difference scores were conducted. When maternal marital consensus was entered as a covariate it was not significant, F (1,45) = .28, *ns*, and the main effect of parenting style group maintained marginal significance, F (1,45) = 3.06, p = .087, with complementary parenting pairs agreeing marginally better than noncomplementary parenting pairs. When paternal marital consensus was entered as a covariate predicting internalizing difference scores it was significant, F (1,45) = 5.39, p = .025, and the main effect of parenting style group maintained marginal significance, F (1,45) = 2.92, p = .094, again indicating that dyads with complementary parenting styles agreed better about child behavior than did dyads with noncomplementary parenting styles. Next, analyses were conducted predicting externalizing behavior difference scores. When maternal marital consensus was entered as a covariate it was not significant, F (1,45) = .17, *ns*, and the main effect of parenting style group remained significant, F (1,45) = 6.27, p = .016, with complementary dyads agreeing significantly better on externalizing behavior than noncomplementary dyads. When paternal marital consensus was entered as a covariate it was significant, F (1,45) = 4.10, p = .049, and the main effect of parenting group remained significant, F (1,45) = 5.15, p = .028, again indicating that complementary dyads agreed better than noncomplementary dyads.

Overall results indicate that marital consensus, when covaried out of the predictions between parenting and agreement on behavior problems, did not change the predictions substantially. Paternal marital consensus was related to child behavior agreement, but although the parenting configurations were reduced in their predictive value they generally remained significant predictors. As suggested by Belsky, Woodworth, and Crnic (1996), parenting consensus and agreement in the marital relationship more broadly may indeed be separable constructs.

This finding should not be taken as a contradiction of other findings that suggest that the marital relationship might be related to the parenting system (Cummings, Goeke-Morey, and Graham, 2002). Marital *conflict* seems clearly related to quality of parenting in the existing literature on slightly older children (Cummings et al., 2002; Cowan et al., 1991). In the present study, however, marital *consensus* and adaptive parenting partnerships are separable, suggesting that even parents who disagree about other areas of their marriage, such as finances or leisure activities, might be able to form effective parenting partnerships, or conversely otherwise harmonious marriages might encounter difficulty in coparenting.

The toddler period is a transition period for parenting, and likely for the marital relationship as well, so during the toddler years these systems may be more separable than at other ages (Belsky, Woodworth, and Crnic, 1996; Gable et al., 1992). Agreement about parenting a toddler, or even the existence of an effective partnership for parenting a toddler, may not have the same correlates in the marital relationship as it does in older children. It is possible, though, that diverging views of child behavior and incompatible parenting strategies might prompt more disagreement within the marital relationship over time. The toddler period may be an important transition not only for the toddler, but also for the parents as the parenting system adjusts to new demands from the child and new areas of potential conflict within the marital relationship.

CONCLUSION

Too often when studying parenting researchers isolate the activities of one parent, transforming what is often practiced within a parenting partnership into an individual activity. Parenting systems should have a cohesiveness that allows the partnership to achieve a completeness or balance that one person's behavior could not capture (Minuchin, 1985); individual contributions may be less meaningful unless combined with complementary efforts of a partner. Thus considering one parent's behavior outside the context of the other parent may inaccurately assume that an individual's parenting occurs independently rather than interdependently (Cox and Paley, 1997; Minuchin, 1985). Much like focusing on one person's efforts during a tango, an individual focus with regard to parenting has variability and some logic, yet gives incomplete information.

The data presented from the Toddlerhood Project explored whether particular configurations of parenting styles are associated with differing degrees of consensus about child behavior. Consensus about the nature of child behavior and the degree to which the behavior is problematic is particularly salient during the toddler period, as it is the foundation for decisions about emergent socialization issues. Maternal or paternal parenting alone did not predict agreement on toddler behavior in this sample, suggesting that information on only one parent is insufficient as an indicator of the parenting system.

The similarity hypothesis, which suggests that parents who have the most similar parenting styles will have the most cohesive parenting partnerships, was not supported. Not only did similarity on parenting fail to predict better agreement on child behavior problems, but parents with similar parenting styles showed less consensus on child behavior than parents with dissimilar parenting styles. Follow up analyses revealed that parents who share a more optimal parenting style show marginally better consensus on child problems than parents who share a sub-optimal parenting style.

The complementarity hypothesis, which suggests that some combinations of different parenting styles may be effective expressions of a shared vision for parenting that has been split into differentiated duties across two people, was supported. As hypothesized, parenting systems that contained at least one authoritative parent did show significantly more consensus on child behavior problems than systems that did not contain an authoritative parent.

Several avenues for future research are indicated based on the work presented in this chapter. The Toddlerhood Project data are drawn from a relatively small, primarily middle class sample of mostly intact families. It will be important to explore the issues raised about complementary parenting systems and their relation to indices of effective parenting partnerships in larger samples, and in samples that cover a broader range of family configurations and socioeconomic status. Parents who are divorced, for example, may have very different configurations of parenting systems because they engage in less day-to-day coparenting and more individual parenting activities that must nonetheless be coordinated (Emery and Tuer, 1993). Low-income parents, whose children live in more stressful and dangerous environments, also tend to engage in stricter, authoritarian parenting (McLoyd, 1990), thus what styles are modal or constitute effective partnerships may differ from those of middle-income families. Longitudinal work to ascertain the predictive meaning of cohesive parenting partnerships and interparental consensus on toddler behavior problems is also necessary. Disagreement about the presence or severity of child problems may have long-term consequences not only for the marital relationships, but for parental decisions about child socialization, for decisions to seek treatment, and for the persistence of child behavior problems.

References

Achenbach, T. (1992). *Manual for the Child Behavior Checklist/2-3 and 1992 Profile.* Burlington, VT: University of Vermont Department of Psychiatry.

Achenbach, T., Edelbrock, C., and Howell, C. (1987). Empirically based assessment of the behavioral/emotional problems of 2- and 3-year-old children. *Journal of Abnormal Child Psychology, 15,* 629-650.

Achenbach, T., McConaughy, S., and Howell, C. (1987). Child/adolescent behavioral and emotional problems: Implications of cross-informant correlations for situational specificity. *Psychological Bulletin, 101,* 213-232.

Aldenderfer, M., and Blashfield, R. (1984). *Cluster Analysis.* Newbury Park, CA: Sage.

Bateson, G. (1972). *Steps to an ecology of mind.* New York: Ballantine.

Baumrind, D. (1967). Child care practices anteceding three patterns of preschool behavior. *Genetic Psychology Monographs, 75,* 43-88.

Baumrind, D. (1966). Effects of authoritative parental control on child behavior. *Child Development, 37,* 887-907.

Belsky, J., Putnam, S., and Crnic, K. (1996). Coparenting, parenting, and early emotional development. In J. McHale and P. A. Cowan (Eds.), *New Directions for Child Development (Winter 74): Understanding how family-level dynamics affect children's development: Studies of two-parent families* (pp.45-55). San Francisco: Jossey-Bass.

Belsky, J., Woodworth, S., and Crnic, K. (1996). Trouble in the second year: Three questions about family interactions. *Child Development, 67,* 556-578.

Block, J.H., Block, J., and Morrison, A. (1981). Parental agreement-disagreement on child-rearing orientations and gender-related personality correlates in children. *Child Development, 52,* 965-974.

Bosormenyi-Nagy, I., and Spark, G. (1984). *Invisible loyalties: Reciprocity in intergenerational family therapy.* New York: Brunner/Mazel.

Christensen, A., Margolin, G., and Sulloway, M. (1992). Interparental agreement on child behavior problems. *Psychological Assessment, 4,* 419-425.

Cowan, C., Cowan, P., Heming, G., and Miller, N. (1991). Becoming a family: Marriage, parenting, and child development. In P. Cowan and E.M. Hetherington (Eds.), *Family Transitions* (pp.79-109). Hillsdale, NJ: Erlbaum.

Cox, M., and Paley, B., (1997). Families as Systems. *Annual Review of Psychology, 48,* 243-267.

Cummings, M., Goeke-Morey, M., and Graham, M. (2002). Interparental relations as dimensions of parenting. In J. Borkowski, S.L. Ramey, and M. Bristol-Power (Eds.), *Parenting and the Child's World: Influences on Adademic, Intellectual, and Social-Emotional Development* (pp.251-263). Mahwah, NJ: Erlbaum.

Deal, J., Halverson, C., and Wampler, K.S. (1989). Parental agreement on child-rearing orientations: Relations to parental, marital, and child characteristics. *Child Development, 60,* 1025-1034.

Dienhart, A. (2001). Make room for daddy: The pragmatic potentials of a tag-team structure for sharing parenting. *Journal of Family Process, 22,* 973-999.

Duhig, A., Renk, K., Epstein, M., and Phares, V. (2000). Interparental agreement on internalizing, externalizing, and total behavior problems: A meta-analysis. *Clinical Psychology: Science and Practice, 7,* 435-453.

Earls, F. (1980). The prevalence of behavior problems in 3-year-old children. *Journal of the American Academy of Child Psychiatry, 19,* 439-452.

Emery, R., and Tuer, M. (1993). Parenting and the marital relationship. In T. Luster and L. Okagaki (Eds.), *Parenting: An ecological perspective* (pp.121-148). Hillsdale, NJ: Erlbaum.

Everitt, B., Landau, S., and Leese, M. (2001). *Cluster Analysis, 4th Edition.* New York: Oxford University Press.

Fagot, B. (1995). Classification of problem behaviors in young children: A comparison of four systems. *Journal of Applied Developmental Psychology, 16,* 95-106.

Fivaz-Depeursinge, E., Frascarolo, F., and Corboz-Warnery, A. (1996). Assessing the triadic alliance between fathers, mothers, and infants at play. In J. McHale and P. A. Cowan (Eds.), *New Directions for Child Development (Winter 74): Understanding how family-level dynamics affect children's development: Studies of two-parent families* (pp.27-44). San Francisco: Jossey-Bass.

Fox, R., and Bentley, K. (1992). Validity of the parenting inventory: Young children. *Psychology in the Schools, 29,* 101-107.

Fox, R. (1994). *Parent Behavior Checklist.* Brandon, VT: Clinical Psychology Publishing Company.

Gable, S., Belsky, J., and Crnic, K. (1992). Marriage, parenting, and child development: Progress and prospects. *Journal of Family Psychology, 5,* 276-294.

Gable, S., Crnic, K., and Belsky, J. (1994). Coparenting within the family system: Influences on children's development. *Family Relations, 43,* 380-386.

Gjerde, P. (1988). Parental concordance on child rearing and the interactive emphases of parents: Sex-differentiated relationships during the preschool years. *Developmental Psychology, 24,*700-706.

Grossmann, K., Grossmann, K.E., Fremmer-Bombik, E., Kindler, H., Scheuerer-Englisch, H., and Zimmermann, P. (2002). The uniqueness of the child-father attachment relationship:

Fathers' sensitive and challenging play as a pivotal variable in a 16-year longitudinal study. *Social Development, 11,* 307-331.

Jouriles, E., Murphy, C., Farris, A., Smith, D., Richters, J., and Waters, E. (1991). Marital adjustment, parental disagreements about child rearing, and behavior problems in boys: Increasing the specificity of the marital assessment. *Child Development, 62,* 1424-1433.

Lamb, M., Frodi, A., Frodi, M., and Hwang, C. (1982). Characteristics of maternal and paternal behavior in traditional and nontraditional Swedish families. *International Journal of Behavioral Development, 5,* 131-141.

McLoyd, V. (1990). The impact of economic hardship on black families and children: Psychological stress, parenting, and socioemotional development. *Child Development, 61,* 311-346.

Maccoby, E., and Martin, J. (1983). Socialization in the context of the family: parent-child interaction. In E.M. Hetherington (Ed.) *Handbook of Child Psychology: Vol.4. Socialization, Personality, and Social Development, 4th edition* (pp. 1-101). New York: Wiley.

Minuchin, P. (1985). Families and individual development: Provocations from the field of family therapy. *Child Development, 56,* 289-302.

Minuchin, P. (1988). Relationships within the family: A systems perspective on development. In R. Hinde and J. Stevenson-Hinde (Eds.), *Relationships within families: Mutual influences* (pp.7-26). New York: Oxford University Press.

Peters, C., and Fox, R. (1993). Parenting inventory: validity and social desirability. *Psychological Reports, 72,* 683-689.

Phares, B., Compas, B.E., and Howell, D.C. (1989). Perspectives on child behavior problems: Comparisons of children's self-reports with parent and teacher reports. *Psychological Assessment, 1,* 68-71.

Spanier, G. (1976). Measuring dyadic adjustment: New scales for assessing the quality of marriage and similar dyads. *Journal of Marriage and the Family, 38*, 15-28.

Spanier, G. (1989). *Manual for the dyadic adjustment scale.* North Tonawanda, NY: Multi-Health Systems, Inc.

Ting-Toomey, S. (1983). An analysis of verbal communication patterns high and low marital adjustment groups. *Human Communication Research, 9*, 306-319.

Weinfield, N.S., Whaley, G.J.L., and Egeland, B. (2004). Continuity, discontinuity, and coherence in attachment from infancy to late adolescence: Sequelae of organization and disorganization. *Attachment and Human Development, 6,* 73-97.

In: Parent-Child Relations: New Research
Editor: Dorothy M. Devore, pp. 121-141
ISBN 1-60021-167-4

Chapter 7

FAMILY UNPREDICTABILITY

Lisa Thomson Ross
College of Charleston

ABSTRACT

Research on parent-child relations has often focused on the quality of interactions (e.g., parental nurturance) or magnitude of a characteristic present in the interaction (e.g., parental warmth). The present work focuses on the *predictability* (i.e., consistency) of parenting characteristics and family life rather than the *degree* (i.e., amount) of that characteristic. Thus, family unpredictability is defined as a lack of consistency in the behaviors and regulatory systems of a family (Ross and Hill, 2000). How family unpredictability relates to family functioning is reviewed and summarized. Theoretical foundations are described, including attachment theory and learned helplessness. Several possible correlates pertaining to origins of family unpredictability are highlighted, namely parental transitions, residential instability, parental divorce, and parental alcoholism. It is possible that the negative outcomes of these family patterns may be due in greater part to the unpredictability associated with them, rather than the condition per se. Particular attention is given to the research conducted by the author over the past decade, including the development of the Family Unpredictability Scale (FUS) and the Retrospective Family Unpredictability Scale (Retro-FUS). Finally, future research ideas are suggested and prevention, treatment, and policy implications are discussed.

Much of the research on parent-child relations has focused on the quality of interactions (e.g., degree of parental nurturance) or amount of a characteristic present in the interaction (e.g., level of perceived family support). Researchers have paid less attention to the consistency or predictability of parenting and family life, and more attention to the degree of a particular characteristic, despite the presumed importance of consistency and predictability in our lives. Social psychologist David Myers writes "One of the most human of tendencies is our urge to explain behavior, to attribute it to some cause, and therefore make it seem orderly, predictable, and controllable" (1990, p. 138d).

The present article summarizes research on family unpredictability, including the correlates and behavioral consequences of this construct. Family unpredictability is defined as inconsistent family behavior patterns and regulatory systems (Ross and Hill, 2000). Family unpredictability results when parental figures are unable or unwilling to consistently fulfill their familial responsibilities, such as providing affection and sustenance. Family unpredictability also occurs when mechanisms for regulating behavior or maintaining expectations break down (e.g., when consequences for rule violations no longer occur). Parents and primary caretakers are in key positions to contribute to family unpredictability, especially in families with younger children. Unpredictability can refer to more objective and easily quantifiable forms such as number of residential moves or parental separations (including death or divorce), or they can come in more subjective forms such as perceptions of inconsistent discipline or inconsistent affection.

THEORETICAL FOUNDATIONS

The construct of family unpredictability derives from both attachment theory and learned helplessness theory. According to attachment theory (Bowlby, 1978), infants are influenced by both the warmth/coldness and the consistency/inconsistency of their caregivers' responsiveness. Attachment theory predicts that infants whose mothers inconsistently respond to their needs (e.g., sometimes warmly and sometimes coldly or harshly) will develop an insecure-anxious attachment style; indeed, research confirms that these infants are less likely to explore their surroundings and are harder to comfort during stressful situations (Ainsworth, Blehar, Waters, and Wall, 1978). In contrast, consistent and warm caregiving fosters secure attachment, allowing children to believe their behavior affects their environment (Lewis and Goldberg, 1969). Thus, the belief system pertaining to the unpredictability or predictability of one's caregiver meeting one's needs appears to be established in infancy.

Another prediction of attachment theory is that our early relationships with primary caregivers influence the expectations and experiences we have with subsequent relationships. Davies and Cummings (1994) would interpret this in terms of the child's emotional security within the family, suggesting that "over time these response processes and internalized representations of parental relations that develop have implications for children's long-term adjustment" (p. 387). Elicker, Englund, and Stroufe (1992) demonstrated support for this prediction with their longitudinal study when they found that early attachment had an ongoing impact on relationships and social skills. Elicker and colleagues classified toddlers when they were 12 and 18 months old, then followed them over time and measured their functioning during a month-long summer camp when the children were 10 and 11 years old. The insecurely attached children developed fewer friendships and were rated by counselors and peers as less popular, prosocial, self-assured, emotionally healthy, and socially competent, compared to the securely attached children. Also, compared to children classified as securely attached, insecure-anxious children spent less time with peers and more time alone or with adults only, and were ranked as having less self-esteem and self-confidence, and being more dependent upon adults. Furthermore, the insecure-anxious children were rated as demonstrating less "interpersonal sensitivity" (degree of understanding others' feelings and thoughts) compared to their securely attached peers (Elicker et al., 1992).

Learned helplessness theory also contributes to an understanding of family unpredictability. Learned helplessness develops when chronic and unavoidable punishment decreases one's motive to maintain control over one's life (Seligman, 1975), so people come to believe that external forces and persons determine their destiny (Overmier and LoLordo, 1998). This occurs when events, especially negative events, are both unpredictable and uncontrollable (as opposed to uncontrollable yet predictable, see Tiggeman and Winefield, 1987). This belief system contributes to several negative consequences, including poorer emotional and physical health (Cohen, 1980).

In a very clever study demonstrating the importance of predictability relative to a sense of control, Schultz (1976) randomly assigned nursing home patients to two conditions; some patients were informed when a visitor was scheduled to come (i.e., the predictability group), whereas others were able to determine the times for the visits themselves (i.e., the controllability group). Shultz found it was the *predictability* but not necessarily the *controllability* of the visits per se that was associated with nursing home residents' well being. Mineka and Henderson (1985) point out that "it is this added predictability inherent in control that produces all of the beneficial consequences of having control, and conversely that it is the unpredictability inherent in not having control that produces ... negative consequences" (p. 509).

Ross and Hill (2002) suggest that children who grow up in a chaotic environment, especially in an unpredictable family, develop an unpredictability schema or belief system. This schema, whether due to having needs inconsistently met (i.e., an insecure attachment) or due to experiences that chronically suggest the locus of control in their life is external (i.e., learned helplessness), has the power to "cloud" interpretations of future relationships and events. We defined this schema as "a pervasive belief that people are undependable and the world is chaotic" (Ross and Hill, 2002, p. 458). We propose that this schema increases the probability that an individual will engage in a variety of risk-taking behaviors, including aggression, unprotected sexual intercourse, risky hobbies, and not wearing seat belts. Thus, the model helps explain how risk factors are associated with such behaviors. We outline our model and provide preliminary support for various paths in this model (Ross and Hill, 2002). Currently, there are many constructs related to an unpredictability schema (e.g., self-efficacy, locus of control, causal uncertainty, interpersonal trust, and future orientation), however it is not being measured directly. Jennifer McDuff and I are in the process of developing an Unpredictability Schema Scale to assess its correlates and consequences.

Measuring Parental Inconsistency/Family Unpredictability

Observations

Family unpredictability is conceptualized and measured in a variety of ways. Sometimes researchers observe directly the behaviors of parents and rate them on the basis of their consistency. Using home observations, Gardner (1989) defined maternal inconsistency as occurring when, during an episode of conflict, a mother either refused (at first) to comply with her child's command and then complied, or when a mother insisted (at first) on a prohibition or command, and then did not follow through. Mothers of children who had been rated by their teachers as having behavior problems were more inconsistent in their conflict management, as compared to mothers of children not labeled as having behavior problems. Dishion and Loeber (1985) also used home observations to rate inept discipline (defined as not following up on commands and being inconsistent in discipline) and found it was related to more frequent alcohol (but not marijuana) use among 7th and 9th grade boys. Conger and colleagues (1993) used observer ratings of discipline during in-home tasks assigned to parents and children; inconsistent discipline from either parent was associated with more self-reported hostility/aggression and with less self-confidence among adolescent girls.

Parental Reports

Observing parents behaviors may provide rich information, however, it is often not cost-effective and so researchers and clinicians may depend on surveys asking parents to report their behavior. Stoneman, Brody and Burke (1989) asked parents to describe how consistent they were in enforcing discipline and limits, based on the Block Q-sort procedure for child rearing practices. Mothers' inconsistency scores correlated with their negative behaviors toward their younger daughters (but not with sons), based on ratings of videotaped play interactions. Arnold, O'Leary, Wolfe, and Acker (1993) found that self-reported laxness in discipline (e.g., "when my child won't do what I ask, I often let it go or end up doing it myself," p. 140) was associated with more marital discord and more externalizing, acting-out behavior among children. Family researchers in Sweden have included chaos-related adjectives (i.e., confusion, nervousness, and instability) in their measure of family climate (Hansson, Ryder, and Johnsson, 1994); they discovered that families describing more chaos also report that their children's diabetes is more poorly managed than families with less chaos, whose children's diabetes is more optimally managed. Deliberate family process, or the ability to plan and carry out rituals and routines, is measured via a focused, one-hour interview (Bennett, Wolin and Reiss, 1988). Fiese and Kline (1993) build upon the work of Bennett and colleagues to create the Family Ritual Questionnaire, which assesses family settings (e.g., dinnertime, religious holidays, vacations) and dimensions or behaviors associated with rituals (e.g., roles, deliberateness, routines). Family Ritual Questionnaire scores correlated with cohesion and system maintenance aspects of family dynamics. Although the impact of family rituals on child behavior and adjustment has not yet been examined using this scale, it appears that parents who report more meaningful family rituals with their preschool children also report more marital satisfaction (Fiese, Hooker, Kotary, and Schwagler, 1993).

Matheny, Wachs, Ludwig, and Phillips (1995) developed a Confusion, Hubbub and Order Scale (CHAOS) to assess variables such as commotion, loudness and tension within the family; CHAOS scores were associated with observations of having the television on, more noise, more crowding and having a higher traffic pattern. In addition, CHAOS scores were associated with a variety of behaviors among the parents of toddlers, including ignoring their child's attempts to get their attention, interfering with their child's attempts to explore the environment, not naming objects for the child, and not giving objects to the child (Matheny et al., 1995). Dumas and colleagues (2005) gave European American mothers of preschoolers the CHAOS inventory. They found more family chaos correlated with more dysfunctional (i.e., harsh and/or inconsistent) discipline as well as with two child outcomes: anger-aggression symptoms and attentional focusing problems. Dumas and colleagues also gave the CHAOS to African American mothers and found more family chaos was associated with more internalizing and externalizing problems among their third graders (2005).

Stoneman and colleagues (1989) included a second measure of inconsistency *between* parents (i.e., mothers' scores subtracted from fathers' scores on four other Block subscales - belief in nonpunishment, authoritarian control, control through anxiety induction, and rational guidance strategies) in their research. They found that the more mothers and fathers disagreed on these parenting dimensions, the more negative behaviors observed between mothers and daughters (but not with sons) (Stoneman et al., 1989). Others have defined parental inconsistency as the difference between parents' intensity of punishment and found this discrepancy correlated with teachers' ratings of maladjustment (e.g., moodiness and aggression) among elementary school children (Gordon, Jones, and Nowicki, 1979).

Parental Reports: The Family Unpredictability Scale

For the past 13 years, I have been investigating family unpredictability – how to measure it, what its correlates are, and what the potential long-term outcomes are. Early work in this area yielded the Family Unpredictability Scale (FUS; Ross and Hill, 2000), which was developed to help us understand this aspect of family dysfunction. The FUS data began as 123 items in the original survey, and an iterative series of reliability analyses and factor analyses suggested 4 meaningful factors related to unpredictability: meals, money, nurturance, and discipline. This 22-item scale was free from social desirability. Here are sample items from the FUS: "It's hard to predict what time meals will be." (meals); "Some months we have plenty of money to spend, other months we're quite poor." (money); "I show my children the same amount of affection from day to day." (nurturance); and "Whether or not I discipline the children when they act up depends on my mood at the time." (discipline).

To begin establishing validity for the FUS, we assessed how it related to other aspects of personal and family functioning. Elizabeth Hill and I discovered that parents who reported more family unpredictability, overall, were also more likely to report having a child with an emotional or behavioral problem, compared to parents not reporting such a problem among their children. The pattern of results held for the overall (i.e., total) FUS scores, as well as for all subscales except meals. Also, parents who reported more family unpredictability also had higher self-reported scores on the Brief Symptom Inventory (Derogatis and Melisartos, 1983), which assesses depression and anxiety (Ross and Hill, 2000).

As expected, more unpredictable families reported fewer routines (as measured by the Family Routines Inventory; Jensen,. James, Boyce, and Harnett, 1983); all subscale correlations were significant, with the strongest relationship between lack of family routines and more unpredictable discipline.

Higher family unpredictability was associated with more inconsistent affection (as measured by the Love Inconsistency Scale; Schwartz and Zuroff, 1982) and with more inconsistent discipline and more parental disagreement (as measured by self-report versions of Scheck's (1979) Inconsistent Parental Discipline Scale and Parental Disagreement on Expectations for their Children Scale). Also, family unpredictability correlated with general family dysfunction (as measured by the McMaster Family Assessment Device; Epstein, Baldwin, and Bishop 1983), including less affective involvement, more role confusion, poorer problem solving and communication.

Children's Reports

Other research designs have asked children to describe parental inconsistency. Concurrent perceptions of parental inconsistency are associated with a variety of negative outcomes. Kohlmann, Schumacher, and Streit (1988) found seventh graders' reports of mothers' and fathers' inconsistency, as measured by questions such as "my mother promises me a reward and then later forgets about it," were associated with more self-reported anxiety. Perry and Millimet (1977) found similar results; in summarizing their findings they report that high anxiety children come from families "characterized by parental inconsistency, disagreement, criticism, and lack of definition of family rules" (p. 201). Krohne (1980) reported perceived inconsistent maternal behavior was associated with daughters' decreased intelligence and academic achievement, and with sons' greater anxiety and sensitization, which is an unhealthy, defensive coping style that is overly concerned with potential danger cues. Hall, Herzberger, and Skowronski (1998) found that children aged 10-15 who reported weak expectations for punishment if they misbehave reported more aggressive behavior. Older children's perceptions of inconsistent parental discipline are associated with their alcohol and marijuana use (Vicary and Lerner, 1986; Dielman, Campanelli, Shope, and Butchart, 1987). Finally, family chaos has been linked to self reports of family stress in a sample of young adults in Australia (Craddock, 2001).

In a remarkable longitudinal study, Hightower (1990) followed participants from age 13 to age 50 and found that teen-agers who perceived that their parents were reasonable and consistent in their attitudes and rules toward them had better psychological health at age 50. It is interesting to note that other parental domains assessed at age 13, such as feeling nurtured and secure at home, perceiving ones parents as admirable individuals, and perceiving them as respected community members, did not relate to subsequent psychological health (Hightower, 1990). Perhaps the consistency and predictability (as well as fairness) that was assessed when the participants were teenagers were markers of a schema for how people are treated, and this ongoing perception of consistency helped explain subsequent mental health.

Occasionally the perceived inconsistency that children describe is based on retrospective reports. Scalf-McIver and Thompson (1989) found that retrospective accounts of inconsistent maternal and paternal affection positively correlated with depression and bulimic eating behavior among undergraduate women. Reports of inconsistent parental affection were also linked to increased self-criticism among nursing students (McCranie and Bass, 1984). Male psychiatric inpatients' retrospective reports of family instability were a better predictor of recent self-destructive behavior than various forms of family losses in one's childhood (Yesavage and Widrow, 1985).

Children's Reports: The Retrospective Family Unpredictability Scale

Much of my research in the past decade has revolved around the Retrospective Family Unpredictability Scale (Retro-FUS; Ross and McDuff, under review). I developed this version to compliment the original FUS by assessing young adults' recollections of family functioning while growing up. As with the original FUS, the Retro-FUS has four dimensions dealing with family unpredictability: meals, money, nurturance, and discipline. By administering the Retro-FUS with college students, we gain insight as to what might contribute to family unpredictability and what the consequences of family unpredictability might be. According to the self-reports of college students, childhood correlates of unpredictability include corporal punishment (which correlated with higher FUS total, money, discipline, and nurturance scores), residential instability (which correlated with FUS total and money scores), fathers' problem drinking (which correlated with unpredictable nurturance); and not living with both biological parents (which was associated with more discipline, money and nurturance unpredictability) (Ross, 1999). Military college students with higher Retro-FUS scores also reported lower family support while growing up (Ross, 2003). Among outpatient mental health clients, Retro-FUS scores were associated with parentification, which occurs when children take on parental roles within the family (Burnett, Jones, Bliwise and Ross, 2006).

In addition, my research using the Retro-FUS has found that college students' recollections of earlier family unpredictability are associated with a variety of more recent problems they are facing. Research projects in my lab have revealed, for example, that aspects of family unpredictability relate to: lower levels of relationship satisfaction quality (Shurling et al., 1998), lower levels of interpersonal trust (McDowell et al., 1998), and more risky sexual behaviors (Wells et al., 1998). Also, when college students assessed their attachment style in romantic relationships (using Hazan and Shaver's [1987] classification question), we found that those with insecure-anxious or insecure-avoidant attachment styles reported more family unpredictability (overall, and regarding nurturance and discipline) than did their securely attached peers (Todd and Ross, 1999). Ross and Gill (2002) discovered that family unpredictability, as measured by the Retro-FUS, was associated with both anxiety and eating disorder symptoms. Statistical analyses tested two possible relationships, and we found that anxiety mediated the relationship between having unpredictable discipline while growing up and reporting eating disordered behavior among college women. In other words, the relationship between unpredictable discipline and eating disorders was no longer significant when the effects of anxiety were controlled statistically (Ross and Gill, 2002). More recent research suggests that eating disordered symptoms are most consistently associated with unpredictable maternal discipline and unpredictable paternal nurturance, and that the relationship between family unpredictability while growing up and recent eating disorders may be due in part to feelings of ineffectiveness (Furr and Ross, 2006). Finally, Retro-FUS scores positively correlated with binge drinking and alcohol misuse (i.e., negative consequences from drinking) but not recent frequency or quantity of drinking among students at a military college (Ross, 2003).

CORRELATES

Parental Transitions (Divorce, Separation, Death, New Partners)

Probably the most researched topic pertaining to parental changes is parental divorce. On average, it appears that children whose parents divorce experience a variety of problems, including those pertaining to social relations, internalizing behaviors such as depression and anxiety disorders, and externalizing behaviors such as aggression, resistance to authority, non-compliance, delinquency, and substance use (see Amato and Keith, 1991, and Amato,

2001, for reviews). Heatherington, Stanley-Hagan, and Anderson (1989) report that during and after a divorce, custodial mothers become more inconsistent in their punishment. They monitor their children less and tend to give "many instructions with little follow-through" (Heatherington, 1989, p.5). However, divorce is part of a series of events, pre and post-divorce, which typically reflect stress or disruption in children's and parents' lives, and should not be interpreted as a single event (Hetherington, 1993). Researchers often find pre-divorce conflict in families that later divorce, including less intimate relationships with parents, as reported by adolescents (Sun, 2001) and relationship difficulties, as reported by parents (Amato and Booth, 1996).

Perhaps it is not the divorce per se that has such detrimental outcomes, but rather the unpredictability associated with the divorce. In her study on attachment and suicide risk among college students, de Jong (1992) suggests that family instability is a stronger risk factor than parental divorce for suicidality. In addition, experiencing parental divorce was not a risk factor for criminality among Danish males if the divorce was followed by a stable family constellation, however divorce was a risk factor if it was followed by changes in one's family structure (Mednick, Baker, and Carothers, 1990). Unpublished analyses from my lab suggests that among college students, parental divorce is unrelated to anxiety and depression, however, young adult children from divorced families reported more family unpredictability, and family unpredictability does correlate with more anxiety and depression. Interestingly, the most common mediating link among these variables had to do with finances: unpredictable money scores were higher among children of divorce, and unpredictable money scores correlated with both depression and anxiety.

Ross and McDuff (2006) found that students with divorced parents reported more family unpredictability on the Retro-FUS compared to their peers whose biological parents remained married; follow-up analyses determined that these groups differed on unpredictable meals, money, nurturance and discipline, as well as on total scores of family unpredictability. Financial unpredictability and unpredictable paternal nurturance were especially heightened for children of divorce. Miller and Ross (2006) also found more unpredictable money and meals among children of divorce; the lack of findings for the other dimensions of family unpredictability could be related to the fact that comparison group in this study was more broadly defined as *all* students who did not experience a parental divorce. In turn, Retro-FUS scores have been associated with numerous unhealthy or undesirable correlates, as described earlier.

Other disruptive variables pertaining to parental transitions also appear to impact children's functioning, including an increased number of mother's romantic partners, separations from parents, and the creation of stepfamilies. Research suggests that the more times a child's mother has a new partner (boyfriend or husband), the worse the child's adjustment (Capaldi and Patterson, 1991). Adam and Chase-Lansdale (2002) found that African American adolescent girls with more separations from a mother or father figure also reported more sexual activity and more externalizing symptoms (including both minor delinquent acts such as drinking and more serious delinquent acts such as damaging property). Adam, Bouckoms, and Streiner (1982) found that adults who attempted suicide were more likely to report forms of parental loss, especially parental divorce or separation or death of one's father, than were nonsuicidal matched control participants (see Yang and Clum, 1996, for a review of family factors, including instability, linked to suicide).

Capaldi and Patterson (1981) found that parental transitions impacted boys' adjustment due to increased maternal antisocial behavior and less parental involvement. Family instability has been associated with parents using less effective forms of behavior management, including less monitoring and more inconsistent discipline (Roberts, 1989) . Kurdek, Fine, and Sinclair (1994) found that increased parental involvement and supervision helped offset the negative impact of parental transitions on their children's adjustment. Parental separations from either mother or father figures have been associated with poorer adjustment among low-income adolescent girls (Adam and Chase-Lansdale, 2002).

Forman and Davies (2003) extended the findings of Adam and Chase-Lansdale among middle-class boys and girls and used a broader definition of family instability. They found aspects of family instability (i.e., residence changes, changes in caregivers or their romantic relationships, jobs, or health status) related to adolescents' internalizing symptoms (e.g., anxiety, depression, and low self-esteem) and externalizing symptoms (e.g., aggression and substance use) directly and indirectly, via adolescents' reports of feeling insecure in their family. Thus, "even relatively modest levels of family instability in our middle-class sample were associated with adolescent internalizing and externalizing symptoms" (Forman and Davies, p. 102).

Ross and Hill (2000) found more family unpredictability among stepfamilies than biologically "intact" families. We did not control for how long ago the stepfamilies were formed in our analyses, however, stepfamilies had to have been living together for at least two years in order to participate in the study. Hetherington (1989) points out that "it is important to distinguish between those stepfamilies in the early stages of remarriage, when they are still adapting to their new situation, and those in later stages, when family roles and relationships should have been worked through and established" (p. 6).

Poverty

Hill, Ross, and Low (1997) found that parents who are less likely to keep promises or carry out family activities in their present families also reported more economic adversity in their childhoods, defined by questions related to perceived poverty, lower prestige of parents' occupation, not being the firstborn child, and having more than one sibling . Ross and McDuff (under review) asked students four questions about going without food, light, heat, telephone services, or new clothing while growing up and compared those who replied no to all situations with students reporting yes to one questions and finally students reporting yes to two or more questions. Overall these three groups differed and follow-up analyses determined group differences, not surprisingly, for all three groups on unpredictable money. Both the medium and high adversity groups reported more family unpredictability than did students in the low adversity group on meals, maternal and paternal nurturance, maternal discipline, and overall family unpredictability (Ross and McDuff, 2006).

In her review of economic hardship among Black families, McLoyd (1990) points out that mothers who live in poverty are more likely to use inconsistent discipline, even if they know it is less effective. Others point out that poorer parents are more likely to utilize harsh, overactive parenting techniques (Felner et al., 1995). According to Conger and his colleagues (1993), economic pressures among rural families increased parental depression, which related to poorer adolescent adjustment directly as well as indirectly via increased marital conflict and less nurturant/involved parenting.

In addition, poverty has been associated with divorce. Economic adversity is likely more common among families when parents divorce (Simons, Lin, Gordon, et al., 1999), and couples with fewer economic resources may be at greater risk for subsequent divorce (Sun, 2001). Divorce likely contributes to unreliable income as well as a reduction of available resources due in part to the division of wages and separation of the household.

Residential Instability

It appears that "residential moves affect adolescents' lives both inside and outside the home and affect multiple spheres of functioning" (Adam and Chase-Lansdale, p. 802). For example, in their study, Adam and Chase-Lansdale found residential instability was associated with a variety of adjustment problems among adolescent African American girls, including sexual activity, educational problems and delinquency, even after controlling for potential confounding factors, such as parental separations and other family and environmental characteristics (2002). Wood, Halfon, Scarlata, Newacheck, and Nessim (1993) linked more frequent moves to both behavioral problems and likelihood of repeating a grade in a national sample of children and their families. In my research, the number of times college students reported moving while growing up was positively associated with money and total family unpredictability scores (Ross, 1999). It is important to note that researchers typically tally the number of moves without delving into the reasons for the move. Perhaps some moves are more disruptive than others, and perhaps some individuals are more resilient than others when families move. Related to these individual differences in reacting to a move, Humke reviewed this literature and concluded that "one of the most influential factors was parental attitude toward the move, since children were found to mirror their parents' attitude" (1995, p. 16).

Parental Alcoholism

Another contribution to family unpredictability comes from parental alcoholism. Clinicians and researchers have described families with an alcoholic parent as chaotic or unpredictable (Beletsis and Brown, 1989; Black, 1981; Elkin, 1984; Hill, Steinhauer, and Zubin, 1992; Velleman and Orford, 1990). In his book *Families Under the Influence*, Elkin writes "Given the fact that the most consistent factor in drunken behavior is its unpredictability, it is safe to assume that drunkenness will be very disabling to a parent trying to enforce discipline" (1984, p. 51). This unpredictability among alcoholic parents takes many forms, including more parental separation and divorce (Black, Bucky, and Wilder-Padilla, 1986; Menees and Segrin, 2000), parental unemployment and economic difficulties (Fitzgerald and Zucker, 1995), parental psychiatric illnesses (Helzer and Pryzbeck, 1988; Reiger et al., 1990), premature parental and sibling death (Black et al., 1986), family conflict and arguments (Black et al., 1986; Reich, Earls, and Powell, 1988; Tubman, 1993) and emotional (Tweed and Ryff, 1991), physical, and sexual abuse by parents (Jones and Houts, 1992). Bennett, Wolin and Reiss (1988) characterize families with an alcoholic parent as being less likely to exhibit deliberate family process, in other words they are unable to plan and/or carry out family rituals. In addition, daughters of alcoholics report perceptions of less consistent parental expressions of love and affection (Benson and Heller, 1987).

It is important to note that unpredictability in these families may be more intense or detrimental when the alcoholic parent is an episodic or binge drinker (Jacob, Krahn, and Leonard, 1991) or has relapsed (Moos and Billings, 1982), as the nature of binge drinking and relapsing each have connotations of instability. Furthermore, alcoholic parents who are classified as "antisocial," "Type II," or "Type B" alcoholics are likely to contribute to more family unpredictability than alcoholic parents designated "Type I" or "Type A" because they also tend to be more impulsive (Ichiyama, Zucker, and Fitzgerald, 1994) and have more unstable employment and relationships (Zucker, Fitzgerald, and Moses, 1995; Cloninger, Bohman, and Sigvaardson, 1981; Babor et al., 1992). These unpredictable events, which are more common among families with an alcoholic parent, likely contribute to an internalized perception about whether or not the world and people are fundamentally unpredictable.

Ross and Hill (2002) examined the alcohol use and retrospective ratings of perceived parental inconsistency (perceiving parents as unpredictable, inconsistent regarding rules and discipline, not acting on threats, and delaying punishment) among young adult children of alcoholics and non-alcoholics. Parental inconsistency mediated the relationship between having a parent diagnosed with alcoholism and frequent high school drinking and heavier lifetime drinking. Thus, problematic drinking was not simply associated with having an alcoholic parent per se, but rather with the greater parental unpredictability reported by the adult children of alcoholics, because the impact of their parental alcoholism was diminished and nonsignificant when parental undependability was controlled statistically. Menees and Segrin (2000) found a moderating effect: college students reporting parental alcoholism did not have disturbed family relationships any more than peer controls with no family stressors. However, those with parental alcoholism and another stressor (e.g., parental divorce, death, separation, etc.) did have disturbed family relationships compared to their peers without any of these stressors.

Ross and Hill (2004) expanded upon the retrospective research described above and compared alcoholics who had recently entered treatment with a control sample of community parents on FUS scores. Alcoholic parents reported more unpredictable nurturance, finances, discipline, as well as more total family unpredictability, and they tended to report more meal unpredictability. This appears to be a unique study on unpredictability among families with an alcoholic parent in that it measured multiple dimensions of unpredictability and the unpredictability was assessed by the alcoholic parents themselves. The group differences for discipline and overall unpredictability held even after controlling for sex and education level, as the alcoholic group was overrepresented by men and those with less education. The relationship between parental alcoholism and unpredictable nurturance was partly explained by the fact men reported more unpredictable nurturance than women, and there were more male than female alcoholic parents. Similarly, the relationship between parental alcoholism and unpredictable finances was explained in part by the association between unpredictable finances and education, as alcoholics reported less education.

The Clustering of Correlates

Family sources of unpredictability, unfortunately, appear to cluster together, in that families who experience some forms tend to experience other forms of unpredictability. For example, Mundy, Robertson, Greenblatt, and Robertson (1989) report associations among residential instability (many domicile moves), parental separation, physical abuse, and caregiver neglect for adolescent psychiatric inpatients. Smith, Twemlow, and Hoover (1999) noted that 100% of the elementary-school children described as bullies or victims came from "divorced, single parent homes, many of which were chaotic" (p. 35), compared to 11% of the children from a control sample. Scores on the CHAOS scale are associated with less maternal education, more parenting stress, lover family income, and more negative neighborhood characteristics such as crime and vandalism (Dumas et al., 2005).

In Werner's (1993) longitudinal study of resilient Hawaiian children, a majority of those with four or more risk factors early in life (e.g., perinatal stress, parental discord, divorce, or psychopathology) had a variety of negative outcomes by age 18, including pregnancy, delinquency, or mental health problems. Mundy and colleagues (1989) found that the cumulation of risk factors has a multiplicative rather than an additive influence on subsequent functioning. Similarly, Rutter (1979) examined children's families in terms of severe marital discord, low SES, overcrowding or large family size, paternal criminality, maternal psychiatric disorder, and being under the care of a local authority. Not only did childhood psychopathology increase as the number of family risk factors increased, but that children with only one of these risk factors were no more likely to have psychiatric problems than children without any risk factors (Rutter, 1979). Other researchers have found similar effects of multiple family risk factors on fourth grade boys' social emotional and academic adjustment (Capaldi and Patterson, 1991), and on adults' insecure attachment (Hill, Young, and Nord, 1994). In all these examples, I argue that the common underlying process that is contributing to negative outcomes is family unpredictability; the lack of consistency in family behaviors and regulatory systems for one reason or another (residential instability, less consistent access to resources due to poverty or large family size, parental disruptions, abuse, conflict, alcoholism or other mental illness) has a negative impact on the offspring.

CONCLUSION

This chapter summarizes a variety of research findings pertaining to family unpredictability. Adam (2004) points out that research on instability and unpredictability among families is relatively rare for a variety of reasons, including the difficulty of assessing change with cross-sectional designs and the difficulty of recruiting and tracking highly chaotic families over time. Nonetheless, I have attempted to synthesize the work of many authors from many fields of inquiry (including myself, a social psychologist) and we all seem to reach a very similar conclusion: family unpredictability, in its various forms, appears detrimental to the overall well-being of the family system as well as the individual members of the family.

One could argue that family unpredictability is not inherently pathological: perhaps families may be unpredictable in a fun and healthy way. Constantine's (1986) family paradigms model would describe this as a *creative* random family rather than a *chaotic* random family. Conversely, families with very low scores on measures such as the Family Unpredictability Scale might be maladaptively rigid. This does not seem to be the case, however, as very rarely has something positive or healthy been associated with family unpredictability, at least as it is conceptualized and measured in this chapter. In the past decade, I have mentored several student projects and investigated the relationship between the Retro-FUS and dozens of variables. In my work I have discovered only one finding to contradict the conclusion that family unpredictability is bad for us: in one study, students who reported more unpredictable maternal nurturance also reported more social/dating assertiveness (Miller and Ross, under review). One other exception I was able to find in the literature was reported by Taylor, Roberts, and Jacobson (1997), who found that family disruption (including death or moving) was associated with mothers using more firm control of their child's behavior. They speculated that following family disruption, there were increased attempts "to control and regulate adolescents' behavior to enhance family stability and to enhance and preserve their resources (i.e., to enhance their sense of self-esteem and competence)" (p.444).

The present overview leads to many questions, and many caveats are necessary. First, we must be cautious not to jump to causal conclusions. The research studies presented here are correlational in nature. Therefore, it is unknown whether family unpredictability is a cause or a consequence of other conditions like parental transitions, poverty, or parental alcoholism; more longitudinal and prospective research is needed to determine the directionality (if not the causality) of this relationship. For example, it is easy to imagine how the stress of an unpredictable family life may contribute to drinking and perhaps problematic drinking. On the other hand, when people who struggle with alcoholism become parents, they likely have difficulty fulfilling parental duties and responsibilities in a consistent manner. Similarly, the mental health and adjustment correlates of all these various forms of family unpredictability and disruptions may or may not be causal outcomes. Dumas and colleagues conclude that "although the processes linking chaos to its many parent and child correlates are largely unknown, we speculate that some of them may be causal and, therefore, that confusion and disorganization in the home may have detrimental effects on parents and children (2005, p. 102).

Is family unpredictability similarly detrimental across socioeconomic status levels and ethnic groups, and are tools like the FUS and R-FUS appropriate to use with less educated and more ethnically diverse samples? The over-reliance of middle-class families for most of this research restricts the generalizability of the findings, and may be dampening researchers' ability to detect results, as presumably middle and upper-class families are more stable in some ways. Indeed, Ross and Hill (2000) examined how the three hallmark characteristics of socioeconomic status (income, education level and occupational status) related to the Family Unpredictability Scale. We found that not only did participants with higher income have lower FUS-money scores, they had lower discipline unpredictability scores as well (although there was no relationship with nurturance, meal and overall unpredictability scores). Also, more educated participants reported lower discipline, money and total family unpredictability. FUS scores did not correlate with occupational prestige, however.

Future attention is needed to look at details regarding family functioning and family unpredictability. What are the mechanisms that link family unpredictability to negative outcomes? Ross and Hill (2002) argue that early environmental chaos, including family unpredictability, contributes to an unpredictability schema, which in turn impacts risk taking and mental health. Dumas and colleagues (2003) suggest two possible outcomes of increased family chaos: that it either impacts many aspects of parenting behavior or that it is especially impactful on parents' organizational and planning skills, which then has pervasive effects on family functioning. Repetti, Taylor, and Seeman (2002) provide a very different explanation, one rooted in biology. They provide support for the hypothesis that a risky family environment leads to social and emotional deficiencies via "disturbances in physiologic and neuroendocrine system regulation that can have cumulative, long-term adverse effects" (p. 330) and children cope with these dysregulations by engaging in health-threatening behaviors, including substance use and promiscuous sexual behavior. Some of the biologically-based difficulties more common among children in risky families include problems with emotion regulation and heightened hormonal and cardiovascular reactivity to stress. Although they characterize families as risky for mental and physical health if they are high in conflict (i.e., aggressive and angry) and low in nurturing (i.e., neglectful, unsupportive, and cold) and they do not address unpredictability directly as a source of family risk, their model could be applied to the area of family unpredictability.

One developmental question that needs research attention is how might family unpredictability and its impact differ depending on the age of the children? Ross and Hill (2000) found that older parents (who also had older children) reported more meals, nurturance, and overall family unpredictability. This may reflect developmental processes, as families with older children are more likely to have irregular afternoon and evening routines due to activities and clubs, etc. and adolescents begin spending less time with parents and more time with peers (Larson and Richards, 1991). In addition, as Adam (2004) points out, there may be critical developmental periods in which there is a heightened sensitivity to family unpredictability, and Hetherington (1989) notes that "early adolescence may be a particularly difficult age in which to gain acceptance of stepparents by stepchildren (p. 7). Compared to younger children and older adolescents, young adolescents may be more vulnerable to problems in the family (Hetherington et al., 1989). Perhaps "normative changes that take place during individual development, such as those associated with puberty, also are important aspects of instability and may increase the impact of external events" (Adam, 2004, p. 212).

A related issue is whether very young childhood, including infancy, is a time of heightened sensitivity during which family unpredictability may have a long lasting effect, as predicted by attachment theory. Also, must family unpredictability be ongoing to have detrimental effects? Mednick, Baker, and Carothers (1990) found that Danish males with chronic family instability during their adolescent years were at greatest risk for criminality. Similarly, Ackerman, Kogos, Youngsrom, Schoff and Izard (1999) found that children with greater family instability at both ages 5 and 7 demonstrated more internalizing behaviors at age 7 than did children with persistently low instability or with changes in their instability status over this period of time. On the other hand, after thoroughly reviewing the literature on childhood poverty, Evans (2004) concludes that "persistent, early childhood poverty has more adverse impact relative to intermittent poverty exposure" (p. 88). Thus it is not clear whether ongoing instability is more detrimental than shorter-lived instability, however it seems children can overcome the negative effects of family instability if their family life becomes more stable (e.g., in this study, few changes in residence or primary caregiver's partners).

Also, research is needed to examine each parent's contribution to family unpredictability versus predictability. In the case of alcoholism, for example, the non-alcoholic parent (providing there is one) may be critical for establishing more family predictability, which should be beneficial for the well-being of all family members. Having a very consistent nonalcoholic parent in the home may help break the transgenerational cycle of alcoholism (Ross and Hill, 2001).

Family unpredictability research has a variety of applications. One set of implications pertains to family-related social policies. For example, Smith (1997, in Smith, Twemlow, and Hoover, 1999) noted that when aggressive children were removed from chaotic and inconsistent family systems and placed in structured foster care settings, the rules and enforcement of discipline dramatically changed children's behavior, One 16-year old boy remarked "it's nice to know that when they say it, they mean it" (Smith et al., 1999, p. 31).

Other applications pertain to prevention and treatment programming. The importance of consistency, routines, rituals and predictability is implied in many prevention and treatment programs aimed at parents (Dumas et al., 2005). In terms of primary prevention, parents need to be educated regarding predictable behaviors and their importance. Parents intuitively know about the importance of being warm and loving with their children. Is the importance of consistency and predictability as intuitive for parents? With regard to secondary prevention, scales such as the FUS and the Retro-FUS may be used to detect at-risk families, and educational programs could be offered to interested parents. Finally, as far as treatment, family therapists can target family unpredictability, however measured, as an area for change. Research is needed to confirm that as unpredictable families become less so, then the family dynamics become healthier and the parents and the children within the system become better adjusted.

ACKNOWLEDGEMENTS

Thanks to Thomas P. Ross and Tom Hutchinson for editorial assistance.

REFERENCES

Ackerman, B.P., Kogos, J., Youngstrom, E., Schoff, K., and Izard, C. (1999). Family instability and the problem behaviors of children from economically disadvantaged families. *Developmental Psychology, 35*, 258-268.

Adam, E.K. (2004). Beyond quality: Parental and residential stability and children's adjustment. *Current Directions in Psychological Science, 13*, 210-213.

Adam, E.K., and Chase-Lansdale, L. (2002). Home sweet home(s): Parental separations, residential moves, and adjustment problems in low-income adolescent girls. *Developmental Psychology, 38,* 792-805.

Adam, K. S., Bouckoms, A. and Streiner, D. (1982). Parental loss and family stability in attempted suicide. *Archives of General Psychiatry, 39*, 1081-1085.

Ainsworth, M. D. S. (1979). Infant-mother attachment. *American Psychologist, 34,* 932-937.

Ainsworth, M.D.S., Blehar, M.C., Waters, E., and Wall, S. (1978). Patterns of attachment: A psychological study of the strange situation. Hillsdale, NJ: Lawrence Earlbaum.

Amato, P. R. (2001). Children of divorce in the 1990's: An update of the Amato and Keith (1991) meta-analysis. *Journal of Family Psychology, 15,* 355-370.

Amato, P. R. and Booth, A. (1996). A prospective study of divorce and parent-child relationships. *Journal of Marriage and the Family, 58,* 356-365.

Amato, P. R., and Keith, B. (1991). Parental divorce and the well-being of children: A meta-analysis. *Psychological Bulletin, 110,* 26-46.

Arnold, D.S., O'Leary, S.G., Wolfe, L.S., and Acker, M.W. (1993). The Parenting Scale: A measure of dysfunctional parenting in discipline situations. *Psychological Assessment, 5,* 137-144.

Babor, T.F., Hoffman, M., DelBoca, F.K., Hesselbrock, V., Meyer, R.E., Dolinsky, Z.S., and Rounsaville, B. (1992). Types of alcoholics, I: Evidence for an empirically derived typology based on indicators of vulnerability and severity. *Archives of General Psychiatry, 49,* 599-608.

Beletsis, S., and Brown, S. (1989). A developmental framework for understanding the adult children of alcoholics. In S. Brown, S. Beletsis, and T. Cermak (Eds.), *Adult children of alcoholics in treatment.* Deerfield Beach, FL: Health Communications.

Benson, C.S., and Heller, K. (1987). Factors in the current adjustment of young adult daughters of alcoholic and problem drinking fathers. *Journal of Abnormal Psychology, 96,* 305-312.

Bennett, L.A., Wolin, S.J., and Reiss, D. (1988). Deliberate family process: A strategy for protecting COAs. *British Journal of Addiction, 83,* 821-829.

Black, C. (1981). *It will never happen to me.* New York: Ballantine.

Black, C., Bucky, S.F., and Wilder-Padilla, S. (1986). The interpersonal and emotional consequences of being an adult child of an alcoholic. *International Journal of the Addictions, 21,* 213-231.

Bowlby, J. (1969). *Attachment and loss: Volume 1. Attachment.* New York: Basic Books.

Burnett, G., Jones, R. Bliwise, N., and Ross, L.T. (2006). Family unpredictability, parental alcoholism and the development of parentification. *Submitted for publication.*

Capaldi, D.M., and Patterson, G.R. (1991). Relation of parental transition to boys' adjustment problems: I. A linear Hypothesis. II. Mothers at risk for transitions and unskilled parenting. *Developmental Psychology, 27,* 489-504.

Cloninger, C.R., Bohman, M., and Sigvaardson, S. (1981). Inheritance of substance abuse: Cross-fostering analysis of adopted men. *Archives of General Psychiatry, 38,* 861-867.

Cohen, S. (1980). Cognitive processes as determinants of environmental stress. In I.G. Sarason and C.D. Spielberger (Eds.), *Stress and anxiety, Vol. 7* (pp. 171-183). Washington: Hemisphere Publishing Corp.

Conger, R.D., Conger, K.J., Elder, G.H., Jr., Lorenz, F.O., Simons, R.L., and Whitbeck, L.B. (1993). Family economic stress and adjustment of early adolescent girls. *Developmental Psychology, 29,* 206-219.

Constantine, L. (1986). Family paradigms. New York: Guilford.

Craddock, A. E. Family system and family functioning: Circumplex model and FACES IV. *Journal of Family Studies, 7,* 29-39.

Davies, P.T. and Cummings, M. (1994). Marital conflict and child adjustment: An emotional security hypothesis. *Psychological Bulletin, 116,* 387-411.

de Jong, M.L. (1992). Attachment, individuation, and risk of suicide in late adolescence. *Journal of Youth and Adolescence, 21*, 357-373.

Derogatis, L., and Melisartos, N. (1983). The Brief Symptom Inventory: An introductory report. *Psychological Medicine, 13*, 595-605.

Dielman, T.E., Campanelli, P.C., Shope, J.T., and Butchart, A.T. (1987). Susceptibility to peer pressure, self-esteem, and health locus of control as correlates of adolescent substance abuse. *Health Education Quarterly, 14*, 207-221.

Dishion, T.J., and Loeber, R. (1985). Adolescent marijuana and alcohol use: The role of parents and peers revisited. *American Journal of Drug and Alcohol Abuse, 11,* 11-25.

Dumas, J.E., Nissley, J., Nordstrom, A., Smith, E.P., Prinz, R.J., and Levine, D.W. (2005). Home chaos: Sociodemographic, parenting, interactional, and child correlates. *Journal of Clinical Child and Adolescent Psychiatry, 34*, 93-104.

Elicker, J., Englund, M.,and Stroufe, L.A., (1992). Predicting peer competence and peer relationships in childhood from early parent-child relationships.. In R. Parke and G. Ladd (Eds.*), Family-peer relations: Modes of linkage* (pp. 77-106). Hillsdale, N.J.: Earlbaum.

Elkin, M. (1984). *Families under the influence: Changing alcoholic patterns.* New York: W.W. Norton.

Epstein, N.B., Baldwin, L.M., and Bishop, D.S. (1983). The McMaster Family Assessment Device. *Journal of Marital and Family Therapy, 9,* 171-180.

Evans, G.W. (2004). The environment of childhood poverty. *American Psychologist, 59*, 77-92.

Felner, R.D., Brand, S., DuBois, D.L., Adan, A.M., Mulhall, P.F., and Evans, E.G. (1995). Socioeconomic disadvantage, proximal environmental experiences, and socioemotional and academic adjustment in early adolescence: Investigation of a mediated effects model. *Child Development, 66,* 774-792.

Fiese, B.H., Hooker, K.A., Kotary, L., and Schwagler, J. (1993). Family rituals in the early stages of parenthood. *Journal of Marriage and the Family, 55,* 633-642.

Fiese, B.H., and Kline, C.A. (1993). Development of the Family Ritual Questionnaire: Initial reliability and validity studies. *Journal of Family Psychology, 6*, 290-299.

Fitzgerald, H.E., and Zucker, R.A. Socioeconomic status and alcoholism: The contextual structure of devepmental pathways to addition. In H.E. Fitzgerald, B.M. Lester, and B.S. Zuckerman (Eds.) Children of poverty: Research, health, and policy issues. New York, NY, US: Garland Publishing, Inc, 1995. pp. 125-148.

Forman, E.M., and Davies, P.T. (2003). Family instability and young adolescent maladjustment: The mediating effects of parenting quality and adolescent appraisals of family security. *Journal of Clinical Child and Adolescent Psychology, 32,* 94-105.

Furr, A. and Ross, L.T. (2006). *Ineffectiveness as a mediator of family unpredictability in the development of eating disorders in college women.* Manuscript in preparation.

Gardner, F.E.M. (1989). Inconsistent parenting: Is there evidence for a link with children's conduct problems? *Journal of Abnormal Child Psychology, 17*, 223-233.

Gordon, D.A., Jones, R.H., and Nowicki, S. (1979). A measure of intensity of parental punishment. *Journal of Personality Assessment, 43,* 485-496.

Hall, J.A., Herzberger, S.D., and Skowronski, K.J. (1998). Outcome expectancies and outcome values as predicators of children's aggression. *Aggressive Behavior, 24,* 439-454.

Hansson, K., Ryden, O. and Johnsson, P. (1994). Parent-related family climate: A concomitant to metabolic control in juvenile IDDM? *Family Systems Medicine, 12,* 405-413.

Hazan, C., and Shaver, P. (1987). Romantic love conceptualized as an attachment process. *Journal of Personality and Social Psychology, 52,* 511-524.

Helzer, J.E., and Pryzbeck, T.R. (1988). The co-occurrence of alcoholism with other psychiatric disorders in the general population and its impact on treatment. *Journal of Studies on Alcohol, 49,* 219-224.

Hetherington, E.M. (1989). Coping with family transitions: Winners, losers, and survivors. *Child Development, 60,* 1-14.

Heatherington, E.M., Stanley-Hagan, M., and Anderson, E. (1989). Marital transitions: A child's perspective. *American Psychologist, 44,* 303-312.

Hightower, E. (1990). Adolescent interpersonal and familial precursors of positive mental health at midlife. *Journal of Youth and Adolescence, 19,* 257-275.

Hill, E.M., Ross, L.T., and Low, B. (1997). The role of future unpredictability in human risk-taking. *Human Nature, 8,* 287-325.

Hill, E.M., Young, J.P. and Nord, J.L. (1994). Childhood adversity, attachment security, and adult relationships: A preliminary study. *Ethology and Sociobiology, 15,* 323-338.

Hill, S.Y., Steinhauer, S.R., and Zubin, J. (1992). Cardiac responsitivity in individuals at high risk for alcoholism. *Journal of Studies on Alcoholism, 53,* 378-388.

Humke, C. (1995). Relocation: A review of the effects of residential mobility on children and adolescents. *Psychology: A Journal of Human Behavior, 32,* 16-24.

Ichiyama, M.A., Zucker, R.A., and Fitzgerald, H.E. (1994, June). *The structure of self-concept and social behavior among antisocial and non-antisocial alcoholic men.* Paper presented at the Research Society on Alcoholism, Maui.

Jacob, T., Krahn, G.L., and Leonard, K. (1991). Parent-child interactions in families with alcoholic fathers. *Journal of Consulting and Clinical Psychology, 59,* 176-181.

Jensen, E.W., James, S.A., Boyce, W.T., and Harnett, S.A. (1983). The Family Routines Inventory: Development and validation . *Social Sciences and Medicine, 17,* 201-211.

Jones, D.C., and Houts, R. (1992). Parental drinking, parent-child communication, and social skills in young adults. *Journal of Studies on Alcohol, 53,* 48-56.

Kohlmann, C.-W., Schumacher, A., and Streit, R. (1988). Trait anxiety and parental child-rearing behavior: Support as a moderator variable? *Anxiety Research, 1,* 53-64.

Krohne, H.W. (1980). Parental child-rearing behavior and the development of anxiety and coping strategies in children. In C.D. Spielberger and I.G. Sarason and (Eds.), *Stress and anxiety,* Vol. 7 (pp. 233-245). Washington: Hemisphere Publishing Corp.

Kurdek, L.A., Fine, M.A., and Sinclair, R.J. (1994). The relation between parenting transitions and adjustment in young adolescents: A multisample investigation. *Journal of Early Adolescence, 14,* 412-431.

Larson, R., and Richards, M.H. (1991). Daily companionship in late childhood and early adolescence: Changing developmental contexts. *Child Development, 62,* 284-300.

Lewis, M., and Goldberg, S. (1969). Perceptual-cognitive development in infancy: A generalized expectancy model as a function of the mother-infant interaction. *Merrill-Palmer Quarterly, 15,* 81-100.

Matheny, A.P., Wachs, T.D., Ludwig, J.L., and Phillips, K. (1995). Bringing order out of chaos: Psychometric characteristics of the Confusion, Hubbub, And Order Scale. *Journal of Applied Developmental Psychology, 16,* 429-444.

McCranie, E.W., and Bass, J.D. (1984). Childhood family antecedents of dependency and self-criticism: Implications for depression. *Journal of Abnormal Psychology, 93,* 3-8.

McDowell, S., Ross, L.T., Gill, J., Shurling, D., and Wells, J. (1998, April). *Childhood unpredictability and interpersonal trust in adulthood.* Paper presented at the Carolinas Psychology Conference, Raleigh.

McLoyd, V. (1990). The impact of economic hardship in black families and children: Psychological distress, parenting and socioemotional development, *Child Development, 61,* 311-346.

Mednick, B.R., Baker, R.L., and Carothers, L.E. (1990). Patterns of family instability and crime: The association of timing of the family's disruption with subsequent adolescent and young adult criminality. *Journal of Youth and Adolescence, 19,* 201-220.

Menees, M.M. and Segrin, C. (2000). The specificity of disrupted processes in families of adult children of alcoholics. *Alcohol and Alcoholism, 35*, 361-367.

Miller, J. R. and Ross, L.T. (2006). *Parental divorce and college students: The impact of family Unpredictability and perceptions of divorce*. Manuscript submitted for publication.

Mineka, S., and Henderson, R.W. (1985). Controllability and predictability in acquired motivation. *Annual Review of Psychology, 36,* 495-529.

Moos, R.H., and Billings, A.G. (1982). Children of alcoholics during the recovery process: Alcoholic and matched control families. *Addictive Behaviors, 7,* 155-163.

Mundy, P., Robertson, J., Greenblatt, M. and Robertson (1989). Residential instability in adolescent inpatients. *Journal of the American Academy of Child and Adolescent Psychiatry, 28*, 176-181.

Myers, D.G. (1990). *Social psychology* (2nd Ed.). New York: Worth.

Overmier, J.B. and LoLordo, V. M. (1998). Learned helplessness. In W.T. O'Donohue (Ed.) *Learning and behavior therapy.* (pp. 352-373). Boston: Allyn and Bacon.

Paolino (1978).

Perry, N.W., and Millimet, C.R. (1977). Child-rearing antecedents of low and high anxiety eighth-grade children. In C.D. Spielberger and I.G. Sarason and (Eds.), *Stress and anxiety,* Vol. 4 (pp. 189-204). Washington: Hemisphere Publishing Corp.

Reich, W., Earls, F., and Powell, J. (1988). A comparison of the home and social environments of children of alcoholic and on-alcoholic parents. *British Journal of Addiction, 83*, 831-839.

Reiger, D.A., Farmer, M.E., Rae, D.S., Locke, B.Z., Keith, S.J., Judd, L.L. and Goodwin, F.K. (1990). Comorbidity of mental disorders with alcohol and other drug abuse: Results form the Epidemiologic Catchment Area (ECA) study. *Journal of the American Medical Association, 264,* 2511-2518.

Repetti, R.L., Taylor, S.E., and Seeman, T.E. (2002). Risky families: Family social environments and the mental and physical health of offspring. *Psychological Bulletin, 128*, 330-366.

Roberts, W.L. (1989). Parents' stressful life events and social networks: Relations with parenting and children's competence. *Canadian Journal of Behavioural Science, 21*, 132-146.

Ross, L.T. (1999). *Measuring Family of Origin Unpredictability.* Paper presented at the Southeastern Psychological Association conference, Savannah, GA.
Ross, L.T. (2003, April). *Alcohol consumption: The role of family support and family unpredictability.* Paper presented at the Southeastern Psychological Association conference, New Orleans, LA.
Ross, L.T. and Gill, J.L. (2002). Family unpredictability, anxiety and eating disorders among college women. *Psychological Reports, 91*, 289-298.
Ross, L.T., and Hill, E.M. (2000). The Family Unpredictability Scale: Reliability and validity. *Journal of Marriage and the Family, 62*, 549-562.
Ross, L.T., and Hill, E.M. (2001). Drinking and parental unpredictability among adult children of alcoholics: A pilot study. *Substance Use and Misuse, 36,* 609-638.
Ross, L.T., and Hill, E.M. (2002). Childhood environmental unpredictability, schemas for unpredictability, and risk taking. *Social Behavior and Personality: An International Journal, 30*, 453-474.
Ross, L.T. and Hill, E.M. (2004). Comparing alcoholic and non-alcoholic parents on the Family Unpredictability Scale. *Psychological Reports, 94,* 1358-1391.
Ross, L.T. and McDuff, J.A. (2006). *The Retrospective Family Unpredictability Scale: Reliability and validity.* Manuscript submitted for publication.
Rutter, M. (1979). Protective factors in children's responses to stress and disadvantage. In G.W. Albee and J.M. Joffee (Eds.) *Primary prevention of psychopathology Vol. 3: Social competence in children.* Hanover, N.H.: University Press of New England.
Seligman, M.E.P. (1975). *Helplessness: On depression, development and death.* San Francisco: Freeman.
Scalf-McIver, L., and Thompson, J.K. (1989). Family correlates of bulimic characteristics in college females. *Journal of Clinical Psychology, 45,* 467-472.
Scheck, D.C. (1979). Two measures of parental consistency. *Psychology, 16,* 37-39.
Schultz, R. (1976). Some life and death consequences of perceived control. In J. Carrol and J. Payne (Eds.), *Cognition and social behavior.* Hillsdale, N.J..: Lawrence Earlbaum.
Schwartz, J. and Zuroff, D.C. (1982). Family structure and depression in female college students: Effects of parental conflict, decision-making power, and inconsistency of love. *Journal of Abnormal Psychology, 88*, 398-406.
Shurling, D., Ross, L.T., Gill, J., McDowell, S., and Wells, J. (1998, April). *Childhood unpredictability and dependence in romantic relationships.* Paper presented at the Carolinas Psychology Conference, Raleigh.
Simons, R.L., Lin, K.-H., Gordon, L.C., Conger, R.D., and Lorenz, F.O. (1999). Explaining the higher incidence of adjustment problems among children of divorce compared with those in two-parent families. *Journal of Marriage and the Family, 61*, 1020-1033.
Smith, J., Twemlow, S.W., and Hoover, D.W. (1999). Bullies, victims, and bystanders: A method of in-school intervention and possible parental contributions. *Child Psychiatry and Human Development, 30*, 29-37.
Stoneman, Z., Brody, G.H., and Burke, M. (1989). Marital quality, depression and inconsistent parenting: Relationship with observed mother-child conflict. *American Journal of Orthopsychiatry, 59,* 105-117.
Sun, Y. (2001). Family environment and adolescents' well-being before and after parents' marital disruption: A longitudinal analysis. *Journal of Marriage and the Family, 63,* 697-713.

Taylor, R.D., Roberts, D., and Jacobson , L. (1997). Stressful life events, psychological well-being and parenting in African American mothers. *Journal of Family Psychology, 11*, 436-446.

Todd, J. and Ross, L.T. (1999, April). *Family unpredictability and attachment in relation to social risks.* Poster presented at the South Carolina Psychological Association conference, Myrtle Beach.

Tubman, J.G. (1993). Family risk factors, parental alcohol use, and problem behaviors among school-age children. *Family Relations, 42,* 81-86.

Tweed, S.H., and Ryff, C.D. (1991). Adult children of alcoholics: Profiles of wellness amidst distress. *Journal of Studies on Alcohol, 52,* 133-141.

Velleman, R., and Orford, J. (1990). Young adult offspring of parents with drinking problems: Recollections of parents' drinking and its immediate effects. *British Journal of Clinical Psychology, 29*, 297-317.

Vicary, J.R., and Lerner, J.V. (1986). Parental attributes and adolescent substance abuse. *Journal of Adolescence, 9,* 115-122.

Wells, J., Ross, L.T., Gill, J., McDowell, S., and Shurling, D. (1998, April). *Sexual behavior among college students: The role of childhood unpredictability.* Paper presented at the Carolinas Psychology Conference, Raleigh.

Werner, E. (1993). Resilience in development. *Current Directions in Psychological Science, 4,* 81-85.

Wood, D., Halfon, N., Scarlata, D., Newacheck, P. and Nessim, S. (1993) Impact of family relocation on children's growth, development, school function, and behavior. *JAMA: The Journal of the American Medical Association, 270,* 1334-1338.

Yang, B.U. and Clum, G.A. (1996). Effects of early negative life experiences on cognitive functioning and risk for suicide: A review. *Clinical Psychology Review, 16,* 177-195.

Yesavage, J.A., and Widrow, L.A. (1985). Early parental discipline and adult self-destructive acts. *Journal of Nervous and Mental Disease, 173*, 74-77.

Zucker, R.A., Fitzgerald, H.E., and Moses, H.D. (1995). Emergence of alcohol problems and the several alcoholisms: A developmental perspective on etiologic theory and life course trajectory. In D. Ciccetti and D.J. Cohen (Eds.), *Developmental psychopathology, Vol. 2: Risk, disorder, and adaptation* (pp. 677-711). New York: Wiley.

In: Parent-Child Relations: New Research
Editor: Dorothy M. Devore, pp. 143-156
ISBN 1-60021-167-4

Chapter 8

CAREGIVING CONFLICT AND RELATIONSHIP STRATEGIES OF AGING PARENTS AND ADULT CHILDREN

Paula M. Usita,[1*] Jonathan C. Davis [2] and Scott S. Hall[3]

[1] Associate Professor, Graduate School of Public Health,
San Diego State University, 5500 Campanile Drive, San Diego, CA
[2] Assistant Professor, Department of Family Studies, Samford University: 800
Lakeshore Dr. Birmingham, AL 35229-2239
[3] Assistant Professor, Department of Family and Consumer Sciences,
Ball State University, Muncie, IN 47306

ABSTRACT

Contentious family conflicts may frequently arise when families provide care to dependent elders. However, few studies have examined caregiving conflict according to specific theoretical models; sparse research has been conducted on caregiving conflict among aging parent and adult child caregivers. The purpose of this study was to investigate caregiving conflict and relationship strategies of aging parent and adult child caregivers using Rusbult's relationship investment model as the conceptual framework. A total of 16 aging parent caregivers and adult child caregivers participated in individual or joint interviews about caregiving conflict. Content analysis of the interview data showed that 56% of parent and child caregivers reported the presence of conflict. Parent and child caregivers favored constructive approaches in dealing with caregiving conflict. Fear, protection, and relationship history guided caregivers in their reactions to caregiving conflict. Implications of these findings for theoretically driven research on intergenerational ties are discussed.

---

* Address correspondence to Paula M. Usita, PhD, Associate Professor, Graduate School of Public Health, San Diego State University, 5500 Campanile Drive, San Diego, CA 92182-4162; E-mail: usita@mail.sdsu.edu

INTRODUCTION

Spouses and adult children are usually the first responders of the informal support system to assist dependent elders with their personal care needs. Contentious family conflicts are not uncommon when families provide personal care to dependent elders. Little systematic research is available however, on how family caregivers react when faced with problems and why they react to family caregiving tension in the way they do. Moreover, the majority of studies of family conflict in elder care scenarios focus upon the views of only the primary caregiver—the person who provides the majority of care. As has been suggested by others, the viewpoints of those who supplement the care given by the primary caretaker must also be examined (Ingersoll-Dayton, Neal, Ha, and Hammer, 2003). In the present study, we examined conflict within caregiving families where duties were shared between aging parent primary caregivers and adult child secondary caregivers. We sought to understand how older adults and adult children involved in elder care might be expected to behave when they are upset with each other. The questions that guided our research were: How do aging parent and adult child caregivers react when faced with caregiving conflict? What types of relationship strategies do they employ? What explanations do caregivers provide for their reactions to caregiving conflict? We employed Rusbult's (1980) model of relationship investment as a framework to explore caregiver relationship strategies in the face of conflict; extant literature on intergenerational relationships in adulthood were used to explore reasons for caregiver relationship strategies.

PREVALENCE OF FAMILY CONFLICT IN CAREGIVING

According to several published studies, conflict among family caregivers is a frequent occurrence. Researchers have found that among adult child dementia caregivers, 56% of those studied reported experiencing conflict (Rabins, Mace, and Lucas, 1982). Studies with minority caregivers who were in middle adulthood and caring for family members with dementia, indicated that among those studied, 78% of Chinese American and African American caregivers reported the presence of conflict (Weitzman, Chee, and Levkoff, 1999). In a study of middle aged adult child caregivers to elder family members who had a variety of illness conditions (e.g., dementia, stroke, frailty, cardiovascular disease, arthritis, mental illness, cancer, and other), 40% of caregivers reported experiencing a relatively serious conflict with another family member over caregiving (Strawbridge and Wallhagen, 1991). Note that studies involving dementia caregivers have a higher percentage of caregivers with reported conflict--this may be a result of the increased difficulties associated with caring for a demented elder who has significant behavioral and personality disturbances.

Dimensions of Conflict in Eldercare

In previous research on family conflict, researchers identified three distinct dimensions of conflict in elder care based on interviews with 20 primary caregivers to noninstitutionalized patients with Alzheimer's disease: (1) conflict about definitions of the illness and strategies for care, (2) conflict regarding family member attitude toward the care recipient, and (3) conflict about family member action and attitudes toward the caregiver (Semple, 1992). When the three dimensional scale was assessed among 555 caregivers who were closely related to the care recipient, it was found that more adult children (82%) than spouses (55%) reported conflict on at least one dimension of family conflict. Other studies report family conflicts that fall into the aforementioned dimensions (Smerglia, Deimling, and Schaefer, 2001; Strawbridge and Wallhagen, 1991; Weitzman et al., 1999).

Conflict Type, Its Effects, and Caregiving Processes

Concern over family conflict and its effects have led researchers to examine a number of questions, including how responses to family conflict affects the health of caregivers and the help that families provide to their ill elder members. Conflict involving family member attitude and behaviors toward the caregiver has been found to be most closely associated with depression, and conflict revolving around family member attitude toward the care recipient has been found to be most closely associated with anger (Semple, 1992). Other studies indicate that degree of upset with members of the social network is associated with caregiver depression and burden (Barusch and Spaid, 1989; Pagel, Erdly, and Becker, 1987; Strawbridge and Wallhagen, 1991), however, positive interactions with members of the social network reportedly are not associated with depression among caregivers (Pagel et al., 1987).

Use of avoidant family conflict strategies and guilt as a means to control other family members has been shown to negatively affect the health and well-being of adult offspring over a period of two years (Fisher and Lieberman, 1996). With regard to helping an ill elder family member, families caring for an elder with Alzheimer's disease who displayed positive conflict resolution methods and focused decision making skills provided more help to elders (Lieberman and Fisher, 1999). In a study of over 1,500 caregivers, researchers found that dementia caregivers reported greater impacts of family conflict than nondementia caregivers (Ory, Hoffman, Yee, Tennstedt, and Schulz, 1999). When the impact of family conflict on the institutionalization of care recipients was assessed among dementia caregivers, researchers reported that family conflict pre nursing home placement was among the predictors of difficulty with the family search process for institutionalization (Gaugler, Pearlin, Leitsch, and Davey, 2001) and pre nursing home family conflict predicted depression among wife caregivers after nursing home placement (Gaugler, Zarit, and Pearlin, 1999).

One study of responses to family conflicts that used a specific theoretical model as a guiding framework illustrated that interpersonal resolution frameworks were beneficial for understanding caregiver reactions to family conflict. In a study comparing 10 African American and 10 Chinese American caregivers to patients with dementia, researchers employed an interpersonal negotiation strategies model (Weitzman et al., 1999). An underlying feature of this model is the adoption of social cognitive competency skills, or the degree to which an individual can understand another's point of view in conflict and integrate it with one's own (Weitzman et al., 1999). Similar interpersonal negotiation strategies and social cognitive competencies were found among the two groups of minority caregivers. Interestingly, a higher level of social cognitive competency was found among caregivers who were more satisfied with the division of caregiving responsibilities (Weitzman et al., 1999).

In summary, family conflict surrounding caregiving can be harmful to the well-being of caregivers. Families caring for elders who suffer from conditions such as dementia may be worse off than families caring for elders with other illness. Although researchers have suggested that secondary caregivers' viewpoints should also be examined in caregiving studies, few studies have included both primary and secondary caregivers. Moreover, most studies of family conflict in caregiving have not used theoretical models to understand conflict management styles of caregivers.

Model of Relationship Investment

This investigation of family conflict strategies during intergenerational caregiving employed Rusbult's (1980) relationship investment model as the conceptual framework. The relationship investment model was developed to differentiate between those romantic relationships that would dissolve over time from those that would not (Rusbult, 1980), but it has been applied to non romantic relationships, including the ties of healthy aging mothers and their adult daughters (Fingerman, 1998; Usita and Du Bois, 2005). Though caveats have been provided elsewhere about aspects of the model that have limited applicability to intergenerational relationships in adulthood (Fingerman, 1998; Usita and Du Bois, 2005), the model should be tested on non romantic relationships among different segments of the population, including intergenerational dyads under different life situations such as caregiving, so that insights might be offered into conflict of all sorts.

According to the relationship investment model, individuals respond to interpersonal tension based on their level of regard for or satisfaction with the relationship. Persons with a high level of relationship regard or those who are satisfied with the relationship are more likely to use constructive approaches rather than destructive ones. Moreover, in conjunction with constructive or destructive approaches, individuals respond to their relationship problems in active or passive ways. Thus, the four possible responses to interpersonal conflict as described in the relationship investment model are: (1) *voice* or verbalize behavior in a way that is believed to improve the relationship (constructive, active); (2) *loyalty* or keep information to self with the hope that the relationship will improve over time (constructive, passive); (3) *exit* or leave the relationship (destructive, active), and (4) *neglect* or ignore the other or engage in behaviors that are damaging but not disbanding to the relationship (destructive, passive) (Rusbult, 1980). Exit approaches are said to be less relevant to the ties of aging parents and adult children (Fingerman, 1998) because adult intergenerational relationships are rarely severed (Roberts, Richards, and Bengtson, 1991).

Studies of interpersonal conflict among mothers and their adult daughters that have been framed by the relationship investment model indicate that constructive approaches are favored, and that both voice and loyalty strategies are employed (Fingerman, 1998; Usita and Du Bois, 2005). However, the Rusbult model does not account completely for the use of constructive approaches. For example, a common finding across both of the studies was that responses to conflict in mother-daughter relationships appeared to be driven by more than just the level of regard for the relationship. Mothers and daughters who did not have a high level of regard for their relationship also used loyalty and voice approaches, for example. Alternate explanations for the use of constructive approaches have been posited: understanding that the other's behavior will likely not change, need to control one's own emotions, and keen awareness of the other's life history and understanding how that history has affected the other's point of view and ways of living (Fingerman, 1998; Usita and Du Bois, 2005). In all, the available research to date suggests that constructive approaches predominate over destructive tendencies, exit approaches appear to be less relevant to adult parent-child relationships, and level of relationship investment may not be the sole factor responsible for reactions to relationship problems in adult parent-child relationships. We now turn to other bodies of literature to gain further insight into factors which may account for intergenerational reactions to caregiving problems.

Adult Intergenerational Relationships and Expectations of Care Literature

A perspective on family caregiving that highlights historical patterns of family interactions is vital to understanding current beliefs and behaviors of caregivers (Merrill, 1996). Caregiving interactions are anchored, in part, by family history. The quality of past ties may play a role in current patterns of affection and support, including support that a parent caregiver receives from an adult child. Perceptions that parents were unfair in the past may influence how adult children feel and behave toward their dependent parents (Bedford, 1992; Hoyert, 1991; Whitbeck, Hoyt, and Huck, 1994), although one study indicated that earlier reports (3 years) of conflict did not interfere with contemporary exchanges of help and support (Parrot and Bengtson, 1999).

Caregiving research which acknowledges the interdependence among family members' life histories is vital to achieving a clearer understanding of relationship patterns and reactions. Increasingly, research is revealing the role that interdependency appears to play in adult family ties. Mutual exchange of different personal commodities appears to more accurately describe the interactions within families (Becker, Beyene, Newsom, and Mayene, 2003; Usita, 2001; Usita and Blieszner, 2002). Family caregiving research shows that caregivers have the mental and emotional capacity to take into account others' perspectives and needs, and adjust their personal expectations of giving and receiving support from other family members. That is, family members appear to be willing both to give in and to provide help where necessary. For example, older adults have been shown to adjust their expectations for care based upon the demands in the adult child's life (Peek, Coward, Peek, and Lee, 1998) and secondary caregivers have been shown to adjust the level of care to be in balance with the needs of the entire family (Piercy, 1998). These findings suggest that in the face of interpersonal problems such as conflict over the level of care provided, caregivers may alter their expectations for care and choose to remain quiet about their feelings of disappointment or frustration.

The Present Study

The present study uses the model of relationship investment to explore aging parent and adult child caregivers' responses to caregiving conflict. We expect that aging parent and adult child caregivers will favor constructive approaches. We anticipate that a complex set of factors, involving more than just relationship investment, will be involved in caregivers' reactions to caregiving tension. The research questions which we address are the following:

How do aging parent and adult child caregivers react when faced with caregiving conflict? What types of relationship strategies do they employ? What explanations do caregivers provide for their reactions to caregiving conflict?

METHODS

Participants

The 16 caregivers (8 caregiver dyads) who participated in this study were recruited from respite care agencies whose services they used, caregiver support groups, home care agencies, radio announcements, newspapers, and community announcement boards. The primary caregivers were parents of the secondary caregivers. By definition, the primary caregivers provided the majority of care, whereas the secondary caregivers provided supplemental care. The extent of support provided by the secondary caregivers varied across the families.

Primary caregivers where white females (n = 7) and a male (n = 1) between the ages of 50 and 76, most were married (88%), and retired. All of the primary caregivers were high school graduates. Secondary caregivers were white females (n = 8) between the ages of 20 and 53, most were married (63%), and employed part-time or full-time. All of the secondary caregivers were high school graduates; two of the secondary caregivers were college graduates.

The study participants cared for persons with a variety of illness conditions: heart attack, traumatic brain injury, stroke, chronic mental health problems, Parkinson's disease, cardiovascular problems, and Alzheimer's disease. Caregivers had been providing care from between 6 months to 6 years. Care recipients and primary caregivers shared a residence; secondary caregivers had a separate residence. In seven of the eight dyads (88%), the care recipient was the spouse of the primary caregiver. In one dyad, the care recipient was the parent of the primary caregiver.

Procedures

In-depth interviews were conducted with each caregiver using the same interview guide and protocol. Interviews were conducted individually or jointly, depending upon the wishes of the family. All interviews were audiotaped. Five major topics were covered in the interview guide: caregiving involvement, effects of caregiving on the caregiver's life, family relationships with the care-recipient and the other caregiver, meaning and motivation with regard to caregiving, and preparation for future caregiving. Interviews took between two to three hours to complete. Caregivers were interviewed more than once, if their schedules permitted. Some caregivers also participated in informal telephone conversations and in-personal discussions. Two of the authors completed all of the interviews.

Data Analysis

Data from the interviews, informal telephone conversations, and in-person discussions concerning family conflict and relationship strategies were analyzed.

Audiotaped Interviews Were Transcribed

Two of the authors served as analysts. They were assigned to read the transcripts and to perform content analysis (Clark and Anderson, 1967). Analysts used open coding procedures to identify core categories in the data pertaining to conflict and relationship strategies. Analysts wrote code notes or memos that tracked the development of their identification of core categories. Thereafter, the analysts read the same selected transcripts that appeared to reflect the core categories and discussed the core categories. Labels reflective of subjects' own words were assigned to the core categories. Properties and ranges of categories were identified and documented. After all coding had been completed, the transcripts and codes were entered into QSR Nud*ist (1997). QSR Nud*ist is able to screen written text to ensure thorough searching of the data set for exemplars of identified coding categories. Themes and causal relationships among the core categories were identified. One of the analysts examined the conflict passages and categorized the responses according to the model of relationship investment, and compared the responses to other literature that had used the model to understand aging parent-adult child relationships.

RESULTS

Caregiver Reports of Family Conflict

A total of 56% (n = 9) of the primary and secondary caregivers reported interpersonal conflict with the other caregiver. Primary caregivers reported conflicts over level of responsibility, caretaking philosophy, competing for sympathy, not initiating caregiving, and how much help is offered. Secondary caregiver reports of conflicts centered upon: financial costs, value of taking medication, caretaking philosophy, piddly stuff, and asking others for help. Caretaking philosophy was the only conflict topic that was reported by both parent and adult child caregivers. The majority of the caregiver reports of conflict in this study are consistent with caregiver reported conflict in other research (Strawbridge and Wallhagen, 1991; Weitzman et al., 1999). Importantly, however, some of this sample's reported conflict topics, such as the financial cost of caregiving, do not easily fit into the dimensions of conflict identified in previous research.

Approaches to Caregiving Conflict

Across the primary and secondary caregiver groups, caregivers relied heavily upon the constructive approaches of voice and loyalty. No examples of destructive approaches were provided by any of the caregivers. A total of 63% of parent caregivers who reported conflict described the use of voice approaches and 100% of the parent caregivers who reported about the presence of conflict described strategies that were consistent with loyalty approaches. The results were the same for the adult child caregivers. A total of 63% of adult child caregivers who reported conflict described the use of voice approaches and 100% of these participants described using loyalty approaches. Most parent and adult child caregivers used a combination of voice and loyalty approaches. Importantly, of parents and adult children who reported caregiving conflict and who used constructive approaches were caregivers who were satisfied with and caregivers who were dissatisfied with their relationship with the other caregiver. The finding that aging parents and their offspring who were not satisfied with their relationship also chose constructive responses to caregiving conflict suggests that positive regard for the relationship does not provide a complete explanation of caregiver reactions to conflict. It is necessary to search caregiver narratives for additional explanations for their selection of voice and loyalty approaches.

Relationship Strategies and Explanations

Caregivers' narratives contained reports of three major reasons why they chose to respond to conflict through voice or loyalty means: fear, protection, and relationship history. The following text annotations were used: __ words were spoken with greater volume and ( ) explanations or replacements provided by the author.

Fear. Fear of hurting the relationship and jeopardizing caregiving led caregivers to choose constructive approaches. In discussing a past conflict, a secondary caregiver reported that she was afraid to bring up the conflict issue with her mother because she thought it would be the end of the world if she and her mother were to acknowledge the conflict that they had. For the secondary caregiver, the conflict issue between her mother and herself involved not knowing if her mother wanted her to help or if her mother did not want her to help. Regarding the past conflict, the secondary caregiver reported:

> When she tells me not to come out, that's when she's having a bad day, that's when she needs me the *most.* So, you know it's a win-lose situation, or *lose*-lose situation, because I can't read her sometimes. I can't tell if she's telling me, if she's having a bad day, (trying to) please me, or not.

Not knowing of her mother's true wishes for and need for help, the secondary reported, "I was walking on *eggshells* because I didn't want her to blow up." The secondary caregiver was very concerned about her relationship with her mother. She reported, "I think the worst part was thinking that, if she does blow up, what will happen? You know? Will I not come out here anymore? You know, what will happen?" One day, the blow up happened. In reflecting upon that day, the daughter reported, "It did happen, we're close, its okay." After the blow up, the daughter reported that she and her mother were closer than they have ever been before. At first, waiting things out seemed like a strategy to get along in the relationship. But, as the secondary caregiver reported, voicing concerns enabled her mother and herself to put the issue behind them, and to move forward in their relationship.

Protection. For a primary caregiver who experiences conflict with levels of support and involvement of the secondary caregiver, keeping her feelings of disappointment to herself is important so that she may protect the relationship between herself and the secondary caregiver. In the past, the secondary caregiver had an incident in which she felt overwhelmed and broke down to her mother, and since then, the mother has been hesitant to ask her to fill in. Subsequently, a strategy for dealing with the knowledge that the secondary caregiver is overwhelmed is to take on more caregiving tasks or to seek volunteer or professional assistance. For the primary caregiver, it is important that her daughter does not look back on times of caregiving and feel exploited. As reported by the primary caregiver:

> Yeah, I don't want to take advantage of my daughter. I don't want her to think in terms of, 'Mom took advantage of me when Dad was ill. I have to be there, and do this, and this, and this.' I don't want that. I want my loving daughter that I've always had. And don't want hard feelings in years to come.

The mother wants to maintain the close relationship that they have had for a long time. In essence, she wants to protect the relationship from hard feelings that could arise in the future because of the potential burden that could be placed upon her daughter. She takes the burden of caregiving upon herself and will call paid professionals or volunteers before she will expect more from her daughter. This type of reaction, to adjust expectations for care based upon the demands in the adult child's life, is consistent with prior research (Peek et al., 1998).

Relationship history. Adult children who used constructive approaches described the importance of the relationship history as a factor in their decision to remain silent and behave in a nondestructive manner. As pointed out by one adult child in this study, standing up to her caregiving parent has never been easy, and it has not become any easier. When she was a child, she never questioned her parents, and if she ever did, her father yelled at her.

> *My* biggest challenge, because he was always—whatever Dad says goes, no questions, no ifs, ands, or buts….*I never ever* back talked to my parents, Mom or Dad. If I did I usually would keep it to myself and I would leave the room and leave angry.

Now, as a grown child who is also a caregiver, she is careful to offer suggestions to her father about the types of actions he can take to improve the overall care of her mother and enhance the quality of her mother's and his daily lives. But, while her father will listen, he will not act upon the suggestions which she has offered.

For this adult child caregiver, a constant struggle with her father has been his inability or unwillingness to make regular trips to the grocery store and ensure that meals were prepared for himself and his wife. Her mother and father had clearly delineated role responsibilities when both were physically and mentally healthy. "Mom was in control of everything, and so now, she's not in control of anything." Since the onset of her mother's illness, her mother has been unable to manage the household duties, including shopping for groceries. Her father has not assumed responsibility for the tasks his wife is no longer able to complete. When asked what usually happens when she initiates a suggestion to her father, the daughter responded:

> He will typically, well, it's like, 'That's a good idea.' But, he won't act on it. Or, 'That's nice and I appreciate the gesture.' 'I think we're doing okay.' But, there's still nothing in the refrigerator (laugh). He's listening but he's not acting on any of the suggestions that we make (referring to husband and self). That's the way I feel about it.

In addition to taking on grocery shopping responsibilities, her father has not been able to oversee her mother's medication regime. When asked if those kinds of things are settled in her mind or if they are unresolved, the adult child responded, "It's unresolved." Eventually, the adult child foresees herself purchasing the groceries for her father and mother. And, because she is the only adult child who lives close to her parents, she reported that eventually "I'll have to resolve it somehow." This adult daughter is aware of her parents' role histories, and she is also aware her that her father's health has deteriorated over the past few years. The daughter reported that two years prior to the interview, her father received open heart surgery. So, for this adult child, voice has become one of her adopted approaches, but voice is carried out gently and without too much pressure placed upon her father. Loyalty is also involved in this adult daughter's strategy repertoire--loyalty usually comes soon after she has voiced her concerns and her father has not taken action.

For another adult child caregiver, the relationship history also played itself out in response to interpersonal tension in caregiving. The adult child caregiver is the only offspring from a large family who is providing help to her parents. She does not have a happy past with her parents and keeps a superficial relationship with them as a caregiver. She helps her mom with her dad's Alzheimer's and bad knees, but her mom had a stroke and is aged and needs to be checked on for her own sake as well. The secondary caregiver has come to terms with her painful childhood and sees her parents as elderly people who need help more than she sees them as her own parents with whom she can have a meaningful bond. However, the mother reports a very positive relationship, especially throughout adulthood with her daughter. The daughter lives next door to her parents and has daily contact. She drives them most places, and she works full time.

This adult child described the importance of separating the past from the present regarding her relationship to her parents. An area of caregiving conflict for this family is inconsistent beliefs about the care recipient's autonomy. Inconsistent beliefs about caregiving have been shown to exist in caregiving families (Semple, 1992; Strawbridge and Wallhagen, 1991; Weitzman, 1999). Previous research provides detailed information about the role of developmental factors in shaping inconsistent intergenerational beliefs about the care recipient's autonomy (Usita, Hall, and Davis, 2004). The adult child caregiver wants her father to do as much for himself as he can, whereas the mother intervenes more and does more for him. When they are in the presence of each other and care differently for the care recipient, they have different reactions. The mother becomes upset, whereas the daughter lets things go. For the daughter, letting things to not only helps her deal with her past hurt so that she can allow herself to care for her parents, but this is also a relationship strategy of sorts because her past could lead to current conflict with her mother, but she lets it go.

In summary, the results revealed that loyalty and voice approaches were popular among the study group. Our qualitative approach enabled us to examine the reasons behind caregiver reactions to conflict. Our research confirmed that intergenerational caregiving dyads take into account the dynamics of the relationship and the other caregiver's stress when responding to caregiving conflict.

CONCLUSION

Content analysis of conflict reports of family caregivers showed that participants in this study were more likely to use constructive than destructive approaches. Across the 16 caregiver narratives, 56% reported the presence of conflict. This proportion fits within the range of conflict frequency reported in other studies (Rabins et al., 1982; Strawbridge and Wallhagen, 1991; Weitzman et al., 1999). The model of relationship investment was used as a framework to examine caregiving conflict and the relationship strategies of parents and adult children. Constructive approaches of loyalty and voice were the conflict responses used by the study sample. Caregivers provided varied reasons for their loyalty and voice reactions to caregiving conflict: fear, protecting the relationship, and separating the past from the present were among the reasons provided.

A limitation of past research on caregiving conflict was the absence of models in guiding the research (Weitzman et al., 1999). Rusbult's model of relationship investment was primarily useful in this study for categorizing caregivers' reactions to tension. Based on extant literature, we predicted that constructive approaches would be the overwhelming favored choice of our study sample. Indeed, that was the case. Interestingly, we also found evidence for what other intergenerational scholars had written--that regard for the relationship does not provide a complete representation of conflicted caregiver motives. More and more, researchers are finding evidence of interdependency in the relationships of aging parents and adult children (Becker et al., Usita, 2001; Usita and Blieszner, 2002). Research and theory development that focuses upon the role of interdependency in intergenerational ties as a motive to explain reactions to conflict could lead to greater insights into conflict reactions across the generations.

Two key findings emerged from this study. First, primary and secondary caregivers often took the perspective of the other caregiver into consideration when caregiving conflict arose. None of the caregivers described situations where they completely overlooked the position and life demands of the other. As reported in other studies (Weitzman et al., 1999), caregivers who are satisfied with the division of caregiving labor tend to integrate others' concerns with their own. In this study, a slightly different finding surfaced—caregivers who were not satisfied with the division of caregiving labor and caregivers who did not have a high level of regard for their relationship were also able to consider the other's position. What enabled these caregivers to understand the position of the other even when relationship satisfaction was low and levels of support were perceived as inadequate? What was the process by which these caregivers were able to integrate the other's position and move to a more collaborative caregiving arrangement? It will be important to tease out these kinds of matters in future research so that strategies can be identified which may assist caregivers in handling relationship problems, and possibly reducing the level of caregiving stress in their lives.

The second key finding of this study is that when confronted with caregiving conflict, secondary caregivers considered the current and anticipated changes in the primary caregiver's health. Adult child caregivers displayed an awareness of the overall health of the family caregiving unit. Many primary and secondary caregivers in this study displayed a sense of concern about the wear and tear that caregiving, or caregiving and the aging process itself were exerting upon the health of the other caregiver. This finding is significant because it portrays the complexity of aging parent and adult child caregivers' reactions to caregiving conflict. It appears that not only is the relationship history of the caregivers important to understanding how caregiving conflict is addressed in families (Merrill, 1996), but that acknowledging the current health status of the other caregiver and anticipating the future of the individual parties in the relationship also figures prominently in intergenerational reactions to caregiving conflict.

Though our study is limited in its generalizability because of its use of a convenience sample, our findings nonetheless suggest the need for additional research on caregiving conflict among aging parent and adult child caregivers in the following areas. First, greater attention to the financial stress in caregiving families should be examined. Among our sample, study participants cited the financial cost of caregiving as a source of caregiving conflict. The economic value of caregiving has been written about, with data from the late 20th century showing the economic value of informal caregiving was $196 billion in 1997 (Arno, Levine, and Memmott, 1999). Knowing the market value of informal caregiving is important, but it is also important to understand how the economics of caregiving are played out within families. We must ask questions such as: What are the sources of financial distress among caregiving families? How significant are financial costs to the problems which family caregivers report? To what degree do financial issues affect how caregivers get along with each other? How have caregiving families dealt with financial problems in the past, and what are caregiving families currently doing do address financial distress? Second, assessment of the nature of family histories and futures is vital for understanding current attitudes and behaviors towards other caregivers and the care recipient. Our research clearly demonstrated that in order to understand caregivers' reactions to conflict, it is necessary to be familiar with the histories of the caregivers and their families, as well as the current and anticipated health of family members. Third, approaching future studies of conflict in caregiving families with an understanding that interdependent bonds may underlie the use of constructive approaches may help to advance current understanding about conflict management styles of caregiving families.

Our research suggests some possible topics for interventions with caregivers. Educational sessions about the importance of relationship history and its potential impact on caregivers would be beneficial for caregivers as it may help them to anticipate their own personal reactions to distress associated with caregiving. Also, as we had suggested in our previous research (Usita et al., 2004) addressing the importance of communication between caregivers as a way to circumvent caregiving problems is also ideal. Caregiver conflict surrounding differences in attitudes and behaviors towards care recipients, for example, could be addressed in educational sessions.

Conflict within caregiving families is a topic worthy of attention in future research because of the stress associated with caregiving and the outcomes of family conflict on the parties involved in giving and receiving care. In this study we addressed researchers' call for future studies to investigate more than just the primary caregiver experience in family conflict (Ingersoll-Dayton et al., 2003), and we subsequently observed the complexity of intergenerational reactions to caregiving problems, about which others (Merrill, 1996) had written.

Authors' Note

The authors thank the individuals who participated in this study. The research project was supported by a grant from the Purdue Research Foundation. A version of this paper was presented at the meeting of the Gerontological Society of America, November 2002, Boston, MA.

References

Arno, P. S., Levine, C., and Memmott, M. M. (1999). The economic value of informal caregiving. *Health Affairs, 18*(2), 182-188.

Barusch, A. S., and Spaid, W. M. (1989). Gender differences in caregiving: Who do wives report greater burden? *The Gerontologist, 29*, 667-676.

Becker, G., Beyene, Y., Newsom, E., and Mayen, N. (2003) Creating continuity through mutual assistance: Intergenerational reciprocity in four ethnic groups. *Journal of Gerontology: Social Sciences, 55B*(3), S151–S159.

Bedford, V. H. (1992). Memories of parental favoritism and the quality of parent-child ties in adulthood. *Journal of Gerontology: Social Sciences, 47*, S149-S155.

Clark, M. M., and Anderson, B. (1967). *Culture and aging*. Springfield, IL: Charles C. Thomas.

Fingerman, K. L. (1998). Tight lips? Aging mothers' and adult daughters' responses to interpersonal tensions in their relationships. *Personal Relationships, 5*, 121-138.

Fisher, L., and Lieberman, M. A. (1996). The effects of family context on adult offspring of patients with Alzheimer's disease: A longitudinal study. *Journal of Family Psychology, 10*, 180-191.

Gaugler, J. E., Pearlin, L. I., Leitsch, S. A., and Davey, A. (2001). Relinquishing in-home dementia care: Difficulties and perceived helpfulness during the nursing home transition. *American Journal of Alzheimer's Disease, 16*(1), 32-42.

Gaugler, J. E., Zarit, S. H., and Pearlin, L. I. (1999). Caregiving and institutionalization: Perceptions of family conflict and socioemotional support. *International Journal of Aging and Human Development, 49*(1), 1-25.

Hoyert, D. L. (1991). Financial and household exchange between generations. *Research on Aging, 113*, 205-225.

Ingersoll-Dayton, B., Neal, M. B., Ha, J., and Hammer, L. B. (2003). Redressing inequity in parent care among siblings. *Journal of Marriage and the Family, 65*(1), 201-212.

Lieberman, M. A., and Fisher, L. (1999). The effects of family conflict resolution and decision making on the provision of help for an elder with Alzheimer's disease. *The Gerontologist, 39*(2), 159-166.

Merrill, D. M. (1996). Conflict and cooperation among adult siblings during the transition to the role of filial caregiver. *Journal of Social and Personal Relationships, 13*(3), 399-413.

Ory, M. G., Hoffmann III, R. R., Yee, J. L., Tennstedt, S., and Schulz, R. (1999). Prevalence and impact of caregiving: A detailed comparison between dementia and nondementia caregivers. *The Gerontologist, 39*(2), 177-185.

Pagel, M. D., Erdly, W. W., and Becker, J. J. (1987). Social networks: We get by with (and in spite of) a little help with our friends. *Journal of Personality and Social Psychology, 53*, 793-804.

Parrott, T. M., and Bengtson, V. L. (1999). The effects of earlier intergenerational affection, normative expectations and family conflict on contemporary exchanges of help and support. *Research on Aging, 21*, 73-105.

Peek, M. K., Coward, R. T., Peek, C. W., and Lee, G. R. (1998). Are expectations of care related to the receipt of care? Analysis of parent care among disabled elders. *Journal of Gerontology: Social Sciences, 53B*, S127-S136.

Piercy, K. W. (1998). Theorizing about family caregiving: The role of responsibility. *Journal of Marriage and the Family, 60*, 109-118.

QSR Nud*ist. (1997). QSR Nud*ist (Version 4.0). [Computer software]. Thousand Oaks, CA: Sage.

Rabins, P. V., Mace, N. L., and Lucas, M. J. (1982). The impact of dementia on the family. *Journal of the American Medical Association, 248*, 333-335.

Roberts, R. E. L., Richards, L. N., and Bengtson, V. L. (1991). Intergenerational solidarity in families: Untangling the ties that bind. *Marriage and Family Review, 16*, 11-46.

Rossi, A. S., and Rossi, P. H. (1990). *Of human bonding: Parent–child relations across the life course.* New York: Aldine de Gruyter.

Rusbult, C. E. (1980). Commitment and satisfaction in romantic associations: A test of the investment model. *Journal of Experimental and Social Psychology, 16,* 172-186.

Semple, S. J. (1992). Conflict in Alzheimer's caregiving families: Its dimensions and consequences. *The Gerontologist, 32*(5), 648-655.

Smerglia, V. L., Deimling, G. T., and Schaefer, M. L. (2001). The impact of race on decision-making satisfaction and caregiver depression: A path analytic model. *Journal of Mental Health and Aging, 7*(3), 301-316.

Strawbridge, W. J., and Wallhagen, M. I. (1991). Impact of family conflict on adult child caregivers. *The Gerontologist, 31*(6), 770-777.

Usita, P.M. (2001). Interdependency in immigrant mother-daughter relationships. *Journal of Aging Studies, 15*, 183-199.

Usita, P.M., and Blieszner, R. (2002). Communication challenges and intimacy strategies of immigrant mothers and adult daughters. *Journal of Family Issues, 23*(2), 266–286.

Usita, P. M., and Du Bois, B. C. (2005). Conflict sources and responses in mother-daughter relationships: Perspectives of adult daughters of aging immigrant women. *Journal of Women and Aging, 17*(1/2), 151-165.

Usita, P. M., Hall, S. S., and Davis, J. C. (2004). Role ambiguity in family caregiving. *Journal of Applied Gerontology, 23*(1), 20-39.

Weitzman, P. F., Chee, Y. K., and Levkoff, S. E. (1999). A social and cognitive examination of responses to family conflict by African-American and Chinese-American caregivers. *American Journal of Alzheimer's Disease, 14*, 343-350.

Whitbeck, L. B., Hoyt, D. R., and Huck, S. M. (1994). Elderly family relationships, intergenerational solidarity, and support provided to parents by their adult children. *Journal of Gerontology: Social Sciences, 49*, S89-S94.

In: Parent-Child Relations: New Research
Editor: Dorothy M. Devore, pp. 157-174
ISBN 1-60021-167-4

Chapter 9

STROKE, CONSEQUENCES FOR THE FAMILY AND RECOMMENDATIONS FOR REHABILITATION

Anne Visser-Meily ***and Anne Marie Meijer*****

*Rehabilitation specialist, Department of Rudolf Magnus Institute of Neuroscience, University Medical Centre and Rehabilitation Centre De Hoogstraat, Utrecht, The Netherlands

**Psychologist, University of Amsterdam, Faculty of Social and Behavioral Sciences, Department of Education, Amsterdam, The Netherlands

ABSTRACT

This study is concerned with the psychological and/or behavioral problems that children of stroke patients suffer. The study is designed to assess the clinical course of children's functioning during the first year after parental stroke, and to discover factors which predict children's suffering at 1 year post-stroke.

Results show that depression of the healthy parent was the most significant predictor of all outcome scores, and that support was most frequently given to children with a more severely disabled parent. These findings confirm the need of a family-centered rehabilitative process in which all family members take part.

REVIEW OF LITERATURE

Stroke

Stroke is the third major cause of death and disability in industrialised societies after ischaemic heart disease and cancer [1]. The incidence of stroke in the Netherlands is at least 30,000 persons per year [2] and the prevalence is estimated to be over 120,000 persons [3]. Despite the huge burden that cerebrovascular disease places on communities, there is less reliable data on the incidence throughout the world. In many cases stroke has severe

* Email: a.visser@dehoogstraat.nl

consequences for the patient's physical and mental health as well as their behavioural functioning. Motor symptoms, such as 'weakness', 'heaviness' and 'clumsiness', are the most common symptoms described by stroke patients; 80% in acute phase to 50% six months after stroke. Patients may complain of speech difficulty due to an articulatory and /or a language disturbance; understanding or expressing spoken or written language, such as reading and writing can be difficult. Cognitive changes are seen among 40 - 75% of the patients. These impairments are less visible than the other impairments but have more influence on social activities. Besides, these problems are the ones most disruptive to the lives of all those involved. Cognitive impairments can influence negatively rehabilitation efforts. There is poor agreement between patient and relatives about these changes [3]. Stroke patients may have a reduced insight into their problems. Each patient has a unique blend of impairments and disabilities. Rehabilitation is a complex process because of the multiplicity of problems. Daily life and participation in society can be seriously hindered after a stroke. Yet a stroke not only affects the patients, but also their families. Up until now researchers have paid relatively little attention to the family members of stroke patients.

Caregivers-Spouses

Most stroke survivors return home after discharge. In the home setting, care is mostly provided by informal caregivers such as the spouse, close family members or neighbours. Informal care varies from physical help with activities of daily living to psychosocial support for coping with the sometimes dramatic changes to daily life. Ongoing efforts to reduce the length of institutionalisation (early discharge) and to promote community care have increased the health care system's reliance on informal caregivers. In many cases the success of returning home is more dependent on the characteristics of the primary caregiver than on the characteristics of the stroke patient [4-5] However, informal caregiving is burdensome and may cause health problems [6] and emotional distress [7] Moreover, caregiver burden and depression might have a negative effect on the outcome of the stroke patient's rehabilitation [8]. In cross-sectional studies, caregiver burden, depression or low quality of life are associated with the patient's disability and the caregiver's psychological functioning [9-10]. A cross-sectional design limits the possibilities for early identification of risk factors for poor caregivers' quality of life at a later stage. In a prospective study, 'passive coping strategy' of the caregiver was the most important predictor for burden one year after stroke [11]. It is still unknown how each of the characteristics of the patient and the caregiver may contribute to the caregiver's quality of life.

Young Caregivers

In families with a young stroke patient not only the spouse but also the children may experience many changes. During the past decade, health care research has increasingly paid attention to children whose parents suffer from physical illness, resulting in three reviews. Armistead et al [12] noted that the way parents' physical illnesses may affect children's functioning can vary with a number of different dimensions of illness: onset (acute or gradual), course (progressive, constant, episodic), impairments (physical or cognitive) and outcome (morbidity or mortality). Kelly et al [13] speculated that children of parents with disabilities are at risk for numerous maladies, though few empirical studies have assessed this problem. The review by Korneluk et al [14] included 17 studies that evaluated the impact of parents' physical illness on children under the age of 18. The authors examined available evidence for the influence of three sets of variables: illness variables, individual variables (patient and child characteristics) and family variables. With respect to illness variables, they found that the mere presence of parental illness per se did not inevitably lead to child adjustment difficulties. Although there is sufficient evidence showing that children are distressed by their parents' illness, the majority of children of ill parents do not have psychological problems in the clinical range. With respect to the individual variables, adolescents in particular appear at risk for emotional problems when parents fall ill, and this risk is most pronounced for adolescent girls. Only six articles have examined family variables, and these studies offer preliminary evidence that variables relating to the family's functioning and coping strategies (marital adjustment, parental depression and parent-child relationships) play a role in the adjustment to parental illness [14].

Profile of Young Carers

Dearden and Becker [15] presented data of a research on 2303 young carers conducted in 1997 in UK. These data included the profile of young carers, types of tasks and effects of caregiving.

Profile. The age of these young carers, supported by projects for young carers, ranged from three to 18 years. The average age of young cares was 12; 86% are of compulsory school age. Fifty seven per cent of the young carers in this survey were girls. Over half of the young carers lived in lone-parents families. This was significantly above the national figure for lone-parent families (23 % of all children were living in lone-parent families in 1995 in UK). The majority of care recipients were mothers. This could be anticipated, given the large number of young carers living in lone-parent households, which most are headed by women. If the fathers did have an illness of disability, their female partners were more likely to take on the role of carer. The majority of young carers (63%) were caring for people with physical health problems, the most commonly occurring single condition being Multiple Sclerosis.

Understanding caring. There are different types of tasks young people can undertake; domestic (for example washing dishes), general (giving medicine), intimate (helping to use the toilet), emotional (listening, talking) and child care tasks (caring for younger siblings). A number of key factors [15] have been shown to influence and determine the type and extent of caring roles.

- *age:* the likelihood of performing domestic tasks, general and intimate care increases with age.
- *gender*: girls are more likely to be involved in all aspects of care than boys, but especially domestic tasks and intimate care.
- *ethnicity*: more carers from minority communities are caring for members of the extended family; and among black and Asian young carers girls are in the majority.Effects of caring. Caring may have effects on the children but also on the

parents and the parent-child contact. In short we summarize some effects in this paragraph.

- *educational effects:* One out of four children has educational difficulties. These can consist of difficulties in getting to school in time, absence from school and difficulties in completing homework.
- *friendships and social activities*: some young carers find it difficult to find the time to socialise with friends because of their responsibilities in the home and a lack of external support. Others feel their friends do not understand their situation, which can lead to embarrassment or discomfort.
- *emotional effects*: Not surprisingly, the illness or disability of a family member can cause emotional upset for all members of that family, including and possibly especially, for children. Often the emotional upset is related to their feelings of being in charge at a young age, fears about the future or regret that their family has been affected by illness and disability. They can worry about the deterioration of parental health, the possible death of a close relative or hospitalisation, but also about their own future if anything should happen to their parent, e.g. who will care for them of where they will live if their parents become incapacitated before they, the children, are old enough to be fully independent.
- *health:* caring can cause physical health problems as a result of lifting and carrying, fatigue and sleeping problems.

Young Carers and Stroke

The majority of studies among the children of parents with a physical illness or disability has been conducted outside of the field of medical rehabilitation, though a few studies have been published about spinal cord injury [16] and multiple sclerosis [17]. In 2000, Teasell et al [18] paid attention to parental stroke and stated that the impact of stroke on the young children of stroke patients had yet to be studied. Although stroke mostly affects the elderly, young patients are over-represented in the group selected for rehabilitation and they often have young children living at home.

A Case: a mother describes one family's experience in coping with stroke.

> "From the moment of the fateful telephone call informing us of Richard's stroke, our daughter (11-year-old) was involved. She went to the hospital with me where she saw her daddy lying nonresponsive on a gurney in the emergency room. Our daughter needed stability, but I needed to be with my husband as much as possible. I had arranged for her to stay with two different family friends because I was worried about imposing on just one family. No doubt she felt frightened and abandoned, given that throughout this 2-week period. After Richard was released from acute care, I spent more time at home, but it was still difficult to give Elizabeth the attention she needed. A telephone answering machine full of messages, mail that could not be ignored, and ordinary household tasks consumed much of my time and energy at home. Six weeks after stroke Richard returned home and Elizabeth had different changes to face. At this point, Richard still relied on a wheelchair for trips out of the house, even though he could walk short distances with a cane. The physical issues, however, were not as difficult for Elizabeth as her father's vacant stares, his lability while watching television, his slow responses, and his inability to communicate. It became apparent that Elisabeth was beginning

to retreat. There were occasional blow-ups where her anger, frustration, and sense of loss were obvious. She was embarrassed by her father and avoided having her friends see him."

From: Addressing the needs of adolescent children when a parent becomes aphasic: one family's experiences. Ann Harlow, Laura Murray [19].

Parental Stroke: Our Own Research Findings

Introduction

Between 2000 and 2002, 338 stroke patients were included in the so-called FuPro stroke study [20]. This study had the aim to determine which outcome measures are most appropriate (responsive) for the assessment of Functional outcome and to determine Prognostic determinants of functional outcome. This project gave us a unique opportunity to link measurement data from stroke patients and family caregivers; spouses and young children ≤ 18 years old. The main research questions to be answered were:

- What is the clinical course of children's functioning (depression, behaviour problems and health status) during the first year after parental stroke?
- Which factors can predict children's functioning at 1 year post-stroke?
- Which children receive support form a rehabilitation team during inpatient rehabilitation?
- What are the daily hassles of children of chronically ill parents three years after stroke?

After the description of the results of our study below, we present a family-centred approach for stroke rehabilitation and clinical practice guidelines to support young caregivers.

Method

Stroke patients consecutively admitted to nine Dutch rehabilitation centers between April 2000 and July 2002 were included in the FuPro-Stroke cohort. Inclusion criteria for patients were: first-ever stroke, supratentorial and one-sided lesion, and age over 18. Exclusion criteria for patients were: prestroke Barthel Index (BI) below 18 (assessment independency of daily living) and inability to speak Dutch. If the patient had a spouse, he or she was also asked to participate in the study. Exclusion criteria for spouses were: BI of the spouse below 16 and/or having a very serious chronic illness. If the couple had young children (4–18 years) who were living at home, these children were also invited to participate in the study. Exclusion criteria for children were: having a serious chronic illness and having behavioral problems for which professional help had been obtained before the parental stroke.

A total of 338 patients were included in the FuPro study, of whom 68% had a spouse. Of these spouses, 211 (92%) participated in the present study. Fifty-nine couples had young children. Three families refused to participate with their children, and one family received professional help for their child's behavioral problems before the stroke. A total of 82 children of 55 families participated in the first assessment (T1), of whom 77 also participated in the second (T2) and 71 in the third assessment (T3). Seven children were excluded because their parents were excluded from the FuPro study due to recurrent stroke (4x) or divorce (3x) and four children refused further participation. To answer the question of the daily hassles of children of chronically ill parents we interviewed 29 children in the chronic phase (T4).

Procedure: At the start of inpatient rehabilitation, patients, spouses and children were invited by their rehabilitation specialists to participate in the study. The first assessment was conducted as soon as possible after informed consent had been given. Spouses and children individually completed a series of pencil-and-paper questionnaires in a face-to-face interview. For children aged 4–7 years, we used parent-report measures only. The same researcher interviewed all spouses and children at home about two months after the patients had been discharged from the rehabilitation center (second assessment), 1-year post-stroke (third assessment) and three years after stroke (fourth assessment). The medical ethics committees of the University Medical Centre Utrecht and the participating rehabilitation centers approved the study, and informed consent was obtained from all participating patients, spouses and children.

Child measures. Behavior problems of the child were assessed using the Child Behavior Check List (CBCL) [21], a parent-report measure for children aged 4–18 years. Items were summed to obtain scores for internalizing symptoms (i.e., withdrawn somatic complaints, and anxiety/depression) and externalizing symptoms (i.e., delinquent and aggressive behavior). Raw scores were transformed into T-scores that are standardized for gender and age. Cut-off scores of T-values were used to mark behavior as 'clinical'; indicating a need for professional help' (≥64), 'subclinical'; indicating considerable problems just outside the clinical range (60–63), and 'normal' (≤59).

Depression was measured using the Child Depression Inventory (CDI) [22]. The CDI is a 27-item child self-report measure for children aged 8–18 years. A total score of 20 or higher indicates clinical depression and scores between 13 and 19 subclinical depression.

We used the 14-item parent-report version of the Functional Status (FS-II) [23] to assess the child's health status. The FS-II was developed for children aged 0–16 years, and consists of 14 items like fatigue, sleep disturbance, energy and intractable behavior. The FS-II score has a range of 0–100; a higher score indicates better health status.

In the second assessment, we asked the children about the support they had received from the rehabilitation team during the period of inpatient rehabilitation. Three types of support were distinguished: one or more consultations with the rehabilitation specialist (1) and/or the social worker (2), and/or attending one or more full-day therapies (3). By adding the 'yes' answers, we constructed a score for the support received from the rehabilitation professionals, ranging from 0 (no support) to 3 (much support), a score of 3 meaning that the child had had all possible contact moments with members of the rehabilitation team.

In the fourth assessment we used the Daily Hassles Questionnaire [24] to quantify the emotions of children on parental chronic disease. The questionnaire consists of 22 items. Children can mark if they recognize the daily hassles, how many times a week they experience these moments and the kind of feelings which come into after these moments.

Disease and parental measures. Patient's data on age, gender, type of stroke, hemisphere involved and length of stay at the rehabilitation center were obtained from medical records. Demographic variables of the spouse and the child were documented at the first assessment.

Stroke patients. Disability (ADL dependency) was assessed using the BI [25]. The ability to communicate was rated on a scale from 1 (no communication possible) to 5 (normal communication), based on the Utrecht Communication Observation (UCO) [26]. The BI and the UCO score were assessed at admission and at the 1-year post-stroke.

Spouses. Depression was measured using the Goldberg Depression Scale (GDS) [27]. This consists of nine questions with yes or no answers. A total score of 2 or higher indicates a clinically important disturbance. The perception of marital relationship between the spouse and patient was assessed using the 17-item Interactional Problem Solving Inventory (IPSI) [28]. The IPSI has a total score range of 17–85, a higher score indicating more harmony. The GDS and IPSI were assessed at all three measurements.

Statistical analysis. The research questions were answered using multilevel analysis, also named hierarchical linear modelling [29]. This is a type of regression analysis that is suitable for longitudinal data with a hierarchical nature (measurements within children, children within families, families within rehabilitation centers) because it corrects for the violation of independence assumption of normal (non-hierarchical) regression analysis. The numbers of observations per individual may vary. Similar to ordinary linear regression, a regression equation is obtained. For each predictor a regression coefficient B is estimated and tested for significance and the amount of explained variance by all predictors together is computed. To identify differences between T1 and T2 and T2 and T3 (the first research question) the outcome variables were related to time which was entered into the analyses as a categorical predictor variable; i.e. converted into dummy variables with the second measurement as a reference (dummy T1-T2; T1=1, T2=0, T3=0; dummy T2-T3; T1=0, T2=0, T3=1). To answer the second question of the prediction of children's functioning at 1-year post-stroke all children who performed T3 measurements were included. The number of families (n=55) and children (n=82) included in this study allowed for a maximum of 6 independent variables in the analyses. Variables were chosen that were most relevant in earlier cross-sectional analyses. Independent variables were: age and gender (child), BI and UCO (patient) and GDS and IPSI (spouse). All four outcome variables at T3 were analyzed twice: with the outcome variable measured at T1 as predictor (to correct outcome differences for baseline differences) and without. Since it is not common practice to assess or screen children of stroke patients, analyses without the assessment of children's functioning are more useful in practice. A backward elimination technique was used to filter significant main relationships ($P \leq 0.05$). To answer the third research question, i.e., which children obtained support, univariate analysis was applied to examine the relation between 'support from the rehabilitation team' and the independent children's and parents' characteristics at baseline. The fourth research question regarded a description of the frequency and perception of the hassles or difficult moments. The analyses were performed using SPSS and MlwiN [30].

RESULTS

Description of the group. Half of the children were girls, and the mean age was 13 years (Table 1). Four children were under 8 years of age. The patients were relatively young (mean age 46) and moderately disabled (mean BI 13) at the start of inpatient rehabilitation. On average, admission to the rehabilitation center was about 1-month post-stroke, and patients remained at the center for about three months. Sixty-six percent of the spouses had a paid job for more than 20 hours a week.

Table 1. Baseline characteristics of children and their parents

Children n=82	
Gender (girls)	51%
Mean age (years) (SD)	13.3 (3.2)
First child in family	39%
School type	
Primary education	25%
Junior general secondary education	20%
Senior general secondary education	20%
Pre-university education	12%
Intermediate vocational education	21%
Patients n=55	
Gender (women)	51%
Mean age (years) (SD)	45.5 (6.0)
Stroke infarction	71%
hemisphere (left)	57%
Mean LOS* in days (SD)	99 (57)
Spouses n=55	
Gender (women)	49%
Mean age (years) (SD)	44.6 (5.5)
Employed for more than 20 h/week	66%
Educational level (high**)	27%

* LOS: length of stay in rehabilitation centre

** Senior general secondary education, pre-university education, higher professional education or university

The Clinical Course of Children's Functioning (Depression, Behaviour Problems and Health Status) During the First Year after Parental Stroke

Results. At the first assessment, 54% of all children showed one or more behavior problems or depression and for 21% these scores were within the clinical range. 30% Showed internalizing symptoms, 18% externalizing symptoms and 13% depressive symptoms (Table 2). At the second and third assessment the proportion of children with one or more of these problems was 23% (12% clinical range) and 29% (20% clinical range) respectively. Between T1 and T2 the internalizing behavioral problems, depression and health status scores improved ($P < 0.001$). Between T2 and T3 we did not find significant differences but the percentage of children with subclinical or clinical scores on depression and internalizing behavior problems increased and there was a decreasing trend in health status ($P=0.06$). Externalizing problem behavior did not change significantly between T1 and T2 or between T2 and T3.

Stroke patients improved significantly on the BI and UCO score between T1 and T3. The spouse's depressive symptoms decreased significantly between T1 and T2, but not between

T2 and T3 (Table 2). Spouse perception of marital relationship did not change between T1 and T2, but decreased significantly between T2 and T3.

Table 2. Scores of the child adjustment measures, variables stroke patient (BI, UCO) and variables of the healthy parent (GDS, IPSI) at T1, T2 and T3

	T1	T2	P value T1–T2	T3	P value T2–T3
Dependent variables					
CBCL int median (IQR)	54 (17)	48 (22)	‡	48 (17)	ns
% ≥60	30%	10%		16%	
CBCL ext median (IQR)	51 (17)	49 (19)	ns	48 (14)	ns
% ≥60	18%	15%		15%	
CDI median (IQR)	5 (6)	3 (5)	‡	3 (6)	ns
% ≥13	13%	7%		12%	
FS-II median (IQR)	86 (16)	93 (12)	‡	89 (18)	ns
Independent variables					
BI median (IQR)	13 (8)			19 (2)	‡[a]
UCO median (IQR)	5 (1)			5 (0)	†[a]
GDS median (IQR)	3 (4)	0 (4)	*	2 (5)	ns
IPSI median (IQR)	71 (14)	68 (17)	ns	63 (21)	*

CDI : Child Depression Inventory; CBCL int: Child Behavior Check List internalizing; CBCL ext: Child Behavior Check List externalizing; FS-II: Functional Status; BI : Barthel Index; UCO: Utrecht Communication Observation; GDS: Goldberg Depression Scale; IPSI: Interactional Problem Solving Inventory

[a] P value change between T1 and T3

multilevel analysis. ns indicates nonsignificant * $P < 0.05$, †$P < 0.01$, ‡$P < 0.001$

Discussion. Children's functioning improved between admission of the stroke patient in the rehabilitation center and 2 months after discharge of inpatient rehabilitation, except for externalizing problem behavior. In the period between 2 months after discharge from inpatient rehabilitation and 1-year post-stroke we found no significant differences in problem behavior, depression and health status, but there was a trend of decreased functioning. The same course was observed for depression of the spouse: in the first period a significant improvement occurred but in the second period there was a trend of more depressive symptoms. The quality of the marital relation as perceived by the healthy spouse also decreased in the second period. According to Rolland [31], diseases with an acute onset, such as a stroke, require the family to accomplish several adaptations in a short period of time. The high percentage of children with clinical and subclinical problems directly after parental stroke might reflect psycho-trauma as a consequence of parental stroke and family crisis. The family tries to find a new balance and after a period of absence (inpatient rehabilitation) the stroke patient comes home. An increase of child problems in the T2–T3 period can be expected, because the family will realize that at least some of the changes will be permanent and that they have to reorganize family routines. Although our results showed a trend in this direction the differences were not significant. This might be because our data set was too small or the follow-up period too short.

Factors Predicting Children's Functioning at 1 year Post-Stroke

Results. Internalizing problem behavior and spouse depression at T1 were significant predictors of internalizing problem behavior at T3 (47% explained variance) (Table 3a).

Externalizing problem behavior and age at T1 predicted externalizing problem behavior at T3 (40% explained variance). Children's depression at T3 was predicted by children's depression, gender, and Barthel Index of the parent with stroke at T1 (58% explained variance). Health status at T3 was predicted by health status, spouse depression and spouse perception of marital relationship at T1 (28% explained variance). The same analyses without the T1 child-functioning scores revealed that depression of the healthy parent at T1 was a significant predictor of all outcome scores (Table 3b).

The spouse's perception of the marital relationship was a significant predictor for children's health status and internalizing problem behavior. The explained variance was between 19% and 22%.

Discussion. Children's functioning at T1 showed to be the most important predictor of functioning at T3. This result may suggest an enduring impact of parental stroke on a child's functioning. The predictive power (amount of explained variance) of the models including children's functioning at T1 was considerable, and much larger than that of the models without this information. Identification of children at risk for long-term problems is therefore best done by screening children for these problems in the early phase of stroke. Ensuring that these children obtain information about the consequences of stroke and its impact on the family, and advice about how to deal with their feelings might support the adjustment process. At a later stage children with persisting adjustment problems can be given professional help if needed.

To the exclusion of children's functioning scores at T1, depression of the healthy parent was clearly the most important early predictor of children's adjustment. Other authors also found a negative relation between parental depression and CBCL scores [32-33]. Vandervalk et al. [34], found a similar negative relation between quality of marital relationship and children's emotional adjustment. Like others [12, 14], we found some indications that individual child characteristics (age and gender) moderate the impact of parental illness. The seriousness of the stroke appears to be of minor importance.

Table 3a. Results of the multilevel analysis to predict CBCL score, CDI score and FS-II at T3 using dependent and independent variables measured at T1 as predictors

	CBCL int T3	CBCL ext T3	CDI T3	FS-II T3
T1	B (95%-CI)	B (95%-CI)	B (95%-CI)	B (95%-CI)
CBCL int T1	0.64 (0.45, 0.83)‡	Not entered	Not entered	Not entered
CBCL ext T1	Not entered	0.50 (0.27, 0.72)‡	Not entered	Not entered
CDI T1	Not entered	Not entered	0.62 (0.46, 0.77)‡	Not entered
FS-II T1	Not entered	Not entered	Not entered	0.25 (0.03, 2.75)*
Age child	-	−0.72 (0.00, −1.44)*	-	-
Gender child	-	-	3.02(1.33, 4.71)‡	-
UCO	-	-	-	-
BI	-	-	−0.21(−0.03, −0.39)*	-
GDS	1.01 (0.04, 1.98)*	-	-	−1.81(−0.05, −3.12)†
IPSI	-	-	-	0.26(0.00, 0.52)*
Expl variance	47%	40%	58%	28%

CBCL int: Child Behavior Check List internalizing; CBCL ext: Child Behavior Check List externalizing; CDI: Child Depression Inventory; FS-II: Functional Status; BI:Barthel Index; UCO: Utrecht Communication Observation; GDS: Goldberg Depression Scale; IPSI: Interactional Problem Solving Inventory

* $P < 0.05$, † $P < 0.01$, ‡ $P < 0.001$

B: regression coefficient. Expl variance: % of the variance of the dependent variable that is jointly explained by the predictor variables in the analysis.

Table 3b. Results of the multilevel analyses to predict CBCL score, CDI score and FS-II at T3, using independent variables measured at T1 (without the CBCL, CDI and FS-II scores at T1)

	CBCL int T3	CBCL ext T3	CDI T3	FS-II T3
T1	B (95%-CI)	B (95%-CI)	B (95%-CI)	B (95%-CI)
Age child	-	−1.28 (−0.57, −2.00)‡	-	-
Gender child	-	-	3.16 (0.86, 5.46)†	-
UCO	-	-	-	-
BI	-	-	−0.31 (−0.07, −0.55)*	-
GDS	2.22 (0.93, 3.51)‡	1.28 (0.16, 2.41)*	0.59(0.07, 1.11)*	−2.31 (−0.98, −3.64)‡
IPSI	−0.27 (−0.01, −0.55)*	-	-	0.32 (0.05, 0.59)*
Expl variance	19%	20%	19%	22%

CBCL int: Child Behavior Check List internalizing; CBCL ext: Child Behavior Check List externalizing; CDI: Child Depression Inventory; FS-II: Functional Status; BI : Barthel Index; UCO: Utrecht Communication Observation; GDS: Goldberg Depression Scale; IPSI: Interactional Problem Solving Inventory

* P <0.05, † P <0.01, ‡ P <0.001.

B: regression coefficient. Expl variance: % of the variance of the dependent variable that is jointly explained by the predictor variables in the analysis.

Support of Children from a Rehabilitation Team during Inpatient Rehabilitation

Results. About half of the children (54%) obtained at least one type of support from the rehabilitation team: 23%, 15% and 16% of the children had one, two or all three types of contact with the team, respectively. Of the children with deviant scores on the CBCL scales for internalising and externalising behaviour or CDI, 65%, 75% and 62% had had at least one type of support from the rehabilitation team, compared with 46%, 46% and 52% of the children without deviant scores on the scales. These differences in percentages are not statistically significant. The support score only correlated significantly with the patients' Barthel Index (r = -0.263, p = 0.04) (Table 4). More support was given to children with a more disabled parent. We found no correlations between support and any of the children's or spouses' characteristics.

Table 4. Univariate correlation coefficients between baseline characteristics of children and their parents and support measured two months after discharge of the parent with stroke from clinical rehabilitation; multilevel analysis

Characteristics		Support	p-value
Child:	gender	0.150	0.10
	age	-0.056	0.58
	CDI	0.00	1.0
	CBCL int.	0.108	0.32
	CBCL ext.	0.123	0.24
	FS II	-0.082	0.49
Patient :	Barthel Index	-0.263	0.04*
	UCO	-0.225	0.10
	Cognitive imp. (yes)	0.143	0.25
Spouse:	Gender	-0.138	0.31

CDI : Child Depression Inventory; CBCL int. : Child Behaviour Check List internalising; CBCL ext.: Child Behaviour Check List externalising; FS II: Functional Status; UCO: Utrecht Communication Observation

* $p < 0.05$

Discussion. We found that only half of the children had received one or more types of supportive contact from a rehabilitation team. Support received during inpatient rehabilitation did not correlate with the children's or spouses' characteristics, but there was a significant negative correlation with the stroke patients' Barthel Index scores. Apparently, the rehabilitation teams did not pay more attention to children who had adjustment problems, as has been suggested in the literature [14, 35]. The significant relationship between child support and the patients' Barthel Index might indicate that team members do pay extra attention to children who have a seriously disabled parent, perhaps because they expect these children to have more adjustment problems than children of less seriously disabled parents. But from research question two we know that the seriousness of the stroke appears to be of minor importance. An other explanation of the relationship between BI and support score may be that seriously impaired patients stay in inpatient rehabilitation for longer, which simply increases the opportunities for contacts between the teams and the children.

The Daily Hassles of Children of Chronically Ill Parents (Three Years after Stroke)

Results. To get insight into the daily difficult moments of children of chronically ill parents, 29 children from the FuPro-stroke study and 77 children from parents with Parkinson disease were interviewed. The majority of the children (70 – 80%) noticed distress and dependence with their ill parents and stress, fatigue and irritation with their healthy parents at a minimum of once a month. Half of the children also noticed distress with their healthy parent and relational problems between the parents. Nearly half of the children worried about the future and nearly one out of 5 reported receiving little parental recognition for their help. We conclude that the children in this study frequently experienced difficult moments associated with their ill parent, their healthy parent, their parents in relation to each other, and their personal life.

Recommendations

Family Centred Approach in Stroke Rehabilitation and Guidelines

Family centred approach. On the basis of our findings, we recommend supporting not only children from severely disabled parents, but also children from depressed and stressed non-ill parents. In addition, one should support both parents, to improve their competence to participate in family life, to inform them about children's behaviour and self-expression and to assist them in supporting their own children. We would like to emphasise the importance of focusing on the entire family system in case of parental illness. In a family-centred approach the strengths and needs of all family members, the patient with stroke included, are considered throughout all phases of the rehabilitation process and the family dynamics are taken into account. Family-centeredness in stroke rehabilitation means also a central role for the family in terms of assessments, interventions and outcome.

In the diagnostic phase the family system will be assessed. What are the strengths and weaknesses of the system? What about the coping style of the family, the health status, social support and relationships? Interventions should be focused on the family's problems and needs, learning to set goals, problem solving and using active coping strategies. Outcomes should include, but need to go beyond, the stroke patient's physical, emotional, cognitive and social functioning. The children's and spouse's burden, quality of life and satisfaction with the care provided as well as the family functioning should be kept in mind.

The Department of Health Practice Guide (London. UK, 1996) gave tips for assessing a young carer and the family system:

- listen to the child and respect his/her view
- give time and privacy to children who may need this in order to talk about their situation
- acknowledge that this is the way the family copes with the stroke
- acknowledge parents' strengths
- beware of undermining parenting capacity
- consider what is needed to assist the parent in his/her parenting role
- what needs does the child have arising from caring responsibilities
- consider whether the caring responsibilities are restricting the child's ability to benefit from his/her education
- consider whether the child's emotional and social development are being impaired
- remember children must be allowed to be children
- provide information on the full range of relevant support services

Guidelines. We developed practical clinical guidelines [36] to transfer scientific knowledge about care by young caregivers of patients with a stroke into evidence-based interventions. These guidelines were formulated on the basis of systematic literature searches and expert opinion in case evidence was lacking. The research results were ordered according to the following levels of evidence. Level 1 (strong evidence) supported by at least two independent studies such as meta-analyses or high quality randomized controlled trials (RCTs). Level 2 (moderate evidence) supported by at least two independent studies such as RCT's or other studies comparing groups of patients. Level 3 (limited evidence) supported by research other than level 1 or 2 (i.e. cohort studies, descriptive studies, control groups unknown, no blinded outcome assessment). And level 4 (consensus), supported by expert opinion. A Delphi procedure was conducted consisting of two meetings and a final round by mail.

RCT's are not yet executed and therefore level 1 and 2 evidence (supporting young caregivers) is lacking.

Young Children of Stroke Patients

1. The development of young children can be influenced negatively by the possible changes in the family situation after stroke. Children should therefore be supported actively in order to live with the lasting consequences of the stroke of the parent (level 3).
2. Supporting children of patients with stroke should be elaborated in a protocol and should be offered with consent of the parents. In the protocol should be written who, when and how support to the children will be offered (level 4).
3. Both the patient and the healthy parent should be supported in the changes within the family and the role as parent. This should be a regular theme in the support of the individual caregiver and can be a topic of the caregiver support group (level 3).

In the Netherlands these new guidelines were adopted by the National Heart Foundation (2004) and have been integrated in the already existing national guidelines on the rehabilitation after stroke. After publication, the guidelines were offered to many relevant health care organisations and were made available freely on the internet (www.hartstichting.nl). In addition, national journals for health care professionals announced the edition (i.e. general practitioners, nursing home physicians, rehabilitation physicians, social workers, and nurses). And finally, national workshops were organized to facilitate implementation into daily clinical practice.

Conclusion

Children of stroke patients may also suffer from psychological or behavioural problems [37, 38]. At the start of rehabilitation, more than half of all children in our study showed depressive feelings or behavioural problems in the subclinical or clinical range. At follow-up one year post-stroke, about one in four children still had these problems. Depressive symptoms of the healthy parent, a relatively poor perception of marital relationship by the spouse, female gender and young age of the child, and severe disability of the patient at the start of rehabilitation were significant predictors of child adjustment 1 year post-stroke. The amount of explained variance of children functioning 1 year post-stroke was substantial (28–58%). Depression of the healthy parent was the most significant predictor of all outcome scores. Only half of the children obtained at least one type of support from the rehabilitation team: individual consultation with the rehabilitation specialist and/or social worker, or attending therapies. Support was most frequently given to children with a more severely disabled parent. Team members abusively might think that children with a severely disabled parent will have more adjustment problems than children with a mildly disabled parent, what often is not the case. In the chronic phase children frequently appeared to experience difficult moments associated with their ill parent, their healthy parent, their parents in relation to each other, and their personal life. These findings confirm the need to work with a family-centred approach, in which all family members take part. Only in such a setting can be taken into account how family members deal with the ill patient and how they affect each other. It is important to use guidelines and protocols in clinical practice. Although stroke health professionals pay more attention to family members than in the past, supporting the family (including young caregivers) should get a much higher priority.

References

[1] Murray CJ, Lopez AD. Global mortality, disability, and the contribution of risk factors: Global Burden of Disease Study. *Lancet* 1997 17; 349: 1436-42.

[2] Hollander M, Koudstaal PJ, Bots ML, Grobbee DE, Hofman A, Breteler MM. Incidence, risk and case fatality of first ever stroke in the elderly population. The Rotterdam Study. *J Neurol Neurosurg Psychiatry* 2003; 74: 317-321.

[3] Horstenbach J, Prigatano G, Mulder T. Paitents' and relatives' reports of disturbances 9 months after stroke: subjective changes in physical functioning, cognition, emotion, and behaviour. *Arch Phys Med Rehabil august* 2005; 1587-1593.

[4] Meijer R, van Limbeek J, Kriek B, Ihnenfeldt D, Vermeulen M, de Haan R. Prognostic social factors in the subacute phase after a stroke for the discharge destination from the hospital stroke-unit. A systematic review of the literature. *Disabil Rehabil* 2004; 26: 191-7.

[5] Jong de TH, Eijck R. Informal caregivers are the heart of our care system.(Het hart van de zorg, in Dutch). *Medisch Contact* 2002; 57:896-98.

[6] Exel van NJA, Koopmanschap MA, Berg van den B, Brouwer WBF, Bos van den GAM. Burden of informal caregiving for stroke patients. Identification of caregivers at risk of adverse health effects. *Cerebrovasc Dis* 2005; 19: 11-7.

[7] Berg A, Palomäki H, Loönnqvist J, Lehtihalmes M, Kast M. Depression among caregivers of stroke survivors. *Stroke* 2005; 36: 639-43.

[8] Carnwath TCM, Johnson DAW. Psychiatric morbidity among spouses of patients with stroke. *BMJ* 1987; 294: 409-411.

[9] Jönsson AC, Lindgren I, Hallström B, Norrving B, Lindgren A. Determinants of quality of life in stroke survivors and their informal caregivers. *Stroke* 2005; 36: 803-808.

[10] Scholte op Reimer WJM, Haan de RJ, Rijnders PT, Limburg M, Bos van den GAM. The burden of caregiving in partners of long-term stroke survivors. *Stroke*. 1998; 29:1605-1611.

[11] Visser-Meily J, Post MW, Schepers VP, Lindeman E. Spouses' quality of life 1 year after stroke: prediction at the start of clinical rehabilitation. *Cerebrovasc Dis*. 2005;20:443-8.

[12] Armistead L, Klein L, Forehand R. Parental physical Illness and child functioning. *Clin Psychol Review* 1995;15:409-22.

[13] Kelley SDM, Sikka A, Venkatesan S. A review of research on parental disability: Implications for research and counseling practice. *Rehab Couns Bulletin* 1997;41:105-21.

[14] Korneluk YG, Lee CM. Children's Adjustment to Parental Physical illness. *Clin Child Family Psychol Review* 1998;1:179-93.

[15] Dearden D, Becker S. *Young carers in the United Kingdom.* A Profile. Young Carers Research Group. Loughborough University. 1998. ISBN 1 873747 06 3.

[16] Alexander CJ, Hwang K, Sipski ML. Mothers with spinal cord injuries: impact on marital, family, and children's adjustment. *Arch Phys Med Rehabil* 2002; 83:24-30.

[17] Coster GM, Sturge JC, Williams KA, Frank AO. Pilot investigation into the needs of children when one parent has multiple sclerosis (abstract). *Clin Rehabil* 1989; 3: 80.

[18] Teasell RW, McRae MP, Finestone HM. Social issues in the rehabilitation of younger stroke patients. *Arch Phys Med Rehabil* 2000; 81:205-209.

[19] Harlow A, Murray L. Addressing the needs of adolescent children when a parent becomes aphasic: one family's experiences. *Top Stroke Rehabil* 2001;7(4):46-51.

[20] Schepers VM, Visser-Meily JMA, Ketelaar M, Lindeman E. Prediction of social activity 1 year post stroke. *Arch Phys Med Rehabil*. 2005; 86: 1472-6.

[21] Achenbach TM, Edelbrock C. Manual for the Child Behavior Checklist and Revised Behavior Profile. Stowe, VT: University of Vermont, Department of Psychiatry, 1983.

[22] Kovacs M. Rating scales to assess depression in school-aged children. *Acta Paedopsychiatrica* 1980; 46: 305-315.

[23] Stein RE, Jessop DJ. Functional Status II(R). A measure of child health status. *Med Care* 1990;11:1041-1055.

[24] Klauw vd I, Parental stroke. Undergraduate thesis, department of education, University of Amsterdam, The Netherlands 2003.

[25] Wade DT. Measurement in Neurological Rehabilitation. Oxford University Press, 1992.

[26] Pijfers EM, Vries LAd, Messing-Petersen H. Het Utrechts Communicatie Onderzoek (The Utrecht Communication Observation). Westervoort; 1985.

[27] Goldberg D, Bridges K, Duncan-Jones P, Grayson D. Detecting anxiety and depression in general medical settings. *BMJ* 1988; 297: 897-899.

[28] Lange A, Hageman W, Markus E, Vriend M, Hanewald G. Statusverschillen, traditionaliteit en harmonie binnen het huwelijk (Dutch).Differences in status, tradition and harmony within marriage. *Dutch J Psychology*. 1990; 45: 214-220.

[29] Singer JD, Willett JB. Applied longitudinal data analysis: modeling change and event occurrence. New York: Oxford University Press, Inc., 2003.

[30] Rasbahs J, Browne W, Goldstein H, Yang M et al. A user's guide to MLwiN. Multilevel Models Project, University of London. 2000.

[31] Rolland J. Chronic illness and the life cycle: a conceptual framework. *Family Process* 1987; 26: 203-221.

[32] Nelson DR, Hammen C, Brennan PA, Ullman JB. The impact of maternal depression on adolescent adjustment: the role of expressed emotion. *J Consult Clin Psychology* 2003; 71: 935-944.

[33] Langrock AM, Compas BE, Keller G, Merchant MJ, Copeland ME. Coping with the stress of parental depression: parents' reports of children's coping, emotional, and behavioural problems. *J Clin Child Adolescent Psychology* 2002; 31: 312-324.

[34] Vandervalk I, Spruijt E, Goede de M, Meeus W, Maas C. Marital status, marital process, and parental resources in predicting adolescents' emotional adjustment. *J family Issues* 2004; 25: 291-317.

[35] Lewis FM, Woods NF, Hough EE, Bensley LS. The family's functioning with chronic illness in the mother: The spouse's perspective. *Soc Sci Med* 1989;29:1261-9.

[36] Heugten Van C, Visser-Meily J, Post M, Lindeman E. Care for caregivers of patients with stroke: evidence-based clinical practice guidelines. *J Rehabil Med* 2006, in press.

[37] Visser-Meily J, Post MW. Meijer AM, Port van I, Maas C. Lindeman E. When a parent has a stroke: clinical course and prediction of mood, behavior problems and health status of their young children. *Stroke*. 2005; 36: 2436-40.

[38] Visser-Meily JMA, Post MWM, Meijer AM, Maas C, Ketelaar M, Lindeman E. Children's adjustment to a parent's stroke: determinants of health status and psychological problems and the role of support by the rehabilitation team. *J Rehabil Med* 2005; 37: 236-41.

In: Parent-Child Relations: New Research
Editor: Dorothy M. Devore, pp. 175-195
ISBN 1-60021-167-4

Chapter 10

IMPROVING COMMUNICATION INTERACTIONS BETWEEN PARENTS AND CHILDREN WITH DEVELOPMENTAL AND PHYSICAL DISABILITIES

Kathleen Tait[1], Jeff Sigafoos[2*], Mark O'Reilly[3] and Giulio E. Lancioni[4]
[1]University of Sydney
[2]University of Tasmania
[3]The University of Texas at Austin
[4]University of Bari

ABSTRACT

This chapter describes an empirically supported approach for collaborating with parents in the design and implementation of communication intervention for children with developmental and physical disabilities. The approach includes four phases: (a) identifying and verifying prelinguistic behaviors, (b) non-directive collaborative consultation with parents, (c) parent use of functional communication training procedures, and (d) feedback on implementation of intervention strategies. Each phase of the approach is described. This description may enable clinicians to collaborate more effectively with parents. Emerging evidence suggests that this approach may enhance the communicative interactions and social relations between parents and their child with developmental and physical disabilities.

INTRODUCTION

In this chapter we review literature related to the social-communicative relations between parents and children with developmental and physical disabilities. We also describe an

* Correspondence: Jeff Sigafoos, School of Education, University of Tasmania, Private Bag 66, Hobart, Tasmania 7001, Australia. Jeff.Sigafoos@utas.edu.au

empirically supported approach for enhancing the communicative interactions and social relations between parents and their children with developmental and physical disabilities. Parents often need assistance in engaging the child in positive social-communicative interactions. In terms of meeting this intervention need, professionals need empirically validated approaches for guiding their collaborations with parents in the design and implementation of communication intervention programs. This collaborative approach focuses on enhancing parent-child relations in the area of social-communication interactions. The focus on parent-child relationships in the area of communication interaction is viewed as one way of promoting more meaningful and successful communicative interactions and social relations between parents and their child with a disability.

There are several phases or activities associated with this approach, including (a) identifying and verifying the child's prelinguistic behaviors, (b) a non-directive, collaborative consultation approach with parents, (c) parent use of functional communication training procedures, and (d) provision of feedback to the parents on their implementation of the intervention strategies. Each phase of the approach is described. This description may enable clinicians to collaborate more effectively with parents in the design and implementation of communication interventions for children with developmental and physical disabilities. By doing so, clinicians may assist in prompting better social-communicative interactions between parents and their child with a developmental and physical disability.

Developmental and Physical Disabilities

Many children with developmental and physical disabilities experience difficulties initiating and maintaining social-communicative interactions (Hogg, 1996; van der Pijl, 2000). This is due in part to the fact that these children typically lack effective communication skills. While the child may have acquired some informal prelinguistic acts (e.g., reaching, leading. vocalizing), such acts are often subtle and difficult for parents to recognize and interpret. In addition, for some children with developmental and physical disabilities, restrictive patterns of general motor impairment might not only affect the children's abilities to produce clear communication signals, but also complicate the parents' attempt to engage the child in social-communicative interactions.

For example, Dunst (1985) reported that parents adapt their style of communication interaction to gain some feelings of efficacy about their interaction with their children. That is, they may offer their children only certain types of communication opportunities in which they can predict their children's signals. Because the number of signals that parents can predict may be very limited, the range of opportunities that they can engineer for their children may also be restricted. Thus, the development of a child's communication skills may be somewhat restricted due to the limited range and amounts of opportunities provided by parents. It would therefore seem important to assist parents in establishing more effective social interactions and opportunities that will enhance the child's communication development. This is considered important because effective parent-child interactions may form the basis for development of the child social-communication skills (Bates, Camaioni, and Volterra, 1975).

The difficulty parents face in engaging the child in social-communicative interactions stem in part from the child's developmental and physical disabilities. Developmental and physical disability restricts the child's ability to relate to others and interact with the world. The substantial deficits in speech and language development associated with developmental and physical disabilities interfere with parent-child relations in many ways. For one, the parent may have difficulty knowing when and what the child is attempting to communicate. This is due to the fact that in the absence of speech, the child may rely on prelinguistic acts, such as eye contact, gaze shift, facial expression, and general body movements to communication. These types of prelinguistic acts are also seen in typically developing infants before the onset of speech (Brazelton, 1982; Fogel, Diamond, Longhorst, and Demos, 1982; Stern, 1981), but the prelinguistic acts of children with developmental and physical disabilities may be subtle and idiosyncratic and hence difficult for parents to interpret.

Communicative Breakdowns

The communicative function of these prelinguistic signals is often thought to develop as a result of the interpretation that the parents attribute to these acts and the parent's consistency in recognizing and responding to these behaviors (Bruner, 1985; Kaye, 1982). Consequently, if a child's signals are not easily interpreted by the parents as a communicative attempt or if the communicative function of the act is not readily interpretable, then the parent's ability to facilitate the child's transition from the prelinguistic to more advanced stages of communication might be disrupted and delayed (Als, 1979; Pinder, Olswang, and Coggins, 1993). This may also cause frequent communication breakdowns in parent-child communication interaction that may continue to slow the child's communication development and perhaps lead to the emergence of problem behaviors, such as aggression, self-injury, or extreme tantrums (Sigafoos, O'Reilly, Drasgow, and Reichle, 2002).

If the child's communicative attempts are difficult for their parents to interpret, then the acts might also disrupt parent-child relations. That is the child may not be successful in initiating or maintaining social-communicative interactions with the parent. Over time, the child may either stop trying to communicate (Camaioni, 1993) or escalate to more problematic forms of behavior (e.g., screaming, aggression) in an effort to engage the parent into a social-communicative interaction (Baird, Mayfield, and Baker, 1997; Carr and Durand, 1985).

Communicative Attempts

Literature describing the developing interaction between parents and children with developmental and physical disabilities suggests many potential difficulties, which need to be overcome through intervention. For example, these children tend to make fewer communicative initiations and respond less consistently than normally developing children matched on a developmental level (McConachie and Mitchell, 1985). As mentioned before, the child's communicative signals may decrease because parents do not respond to them and the parents may not respond or may not respond in ways that function to strengthen the child's signals, because the signals emitted by the child are subtle or ambiguous, and hence difficult to interpret. Further, the importance of parental responsiveness to children's communicative signals has also been supported theoretically. In their discussion of parental competence, Lamb and Easter-Brooks (1981) reported that appropriate styles of maternal responsiveness are important for communication development.

The Social Context of Communication Development

Social-learning theory has given some responsibility to the child for initiating dyadic interaction and evoking a response from the parent. Woll and Barnett (1998) for example, suggested that the infant's competencies are derived from maternal behavior that is contingent upon the child's own behavior. Similarly, ethologists have theorized that mothers and young children must mutually and actively contribute to their interactive system in order for it to work functionally (Desrchers, Hile, and Williams-Moseley, 1997). Therefore, if one of the dyad members is unable to demonstrate behavior that will be effective in evoking a response from the other, then the dyad is at risk for interactive behavioral anomalies. So when the child can only initiate using subtle and idiosyncratic prelinguistic acts, it would be essential for the parents to be able to recognize and respond appropriately to such acts. In terms of intervention, it would therefore seems essential to identify any behaviors that might be used by the child in an attempt to initiate a social-communicative interaction with the parent. Parents would then be taught to recognize these acts and respond to them so as to maintain the social interaction. Parent must also be taught how to respond to these acts in ways that will also help to foster the child's communication development. That is, in ways that will result in the child developing more effective communicative behaviors over time.

At the beginning stages of intervention it is important for parents to recognize and respond appropriately to the child's prelinguistic acts, even if they are subtle and idiosyncratic. This is important because when such acts are produced by the child, they could signal that the child is motivated to communicate and this is an opportune time for the parent to engage the child in a social-communicative interaction and also the ideal time to teach new communication forms to the child (Iacono, Waring, and Chan, 1996).

Given the potential importance of the child's early communicative signals, and the fact that children with developmental and physical disabilities often exhibit limited, informal, and subtle communication, it is vital that parents learn to recognize anything that the child does that might be a useful and potential communicative act. The approach to collaboration outlined in this chapter includes assisting parents in identifying their child's potential communicative acts.

A major goal in the approach to foster better parent-child is to enhance the communication forms used by the child and increase the number of different communication functions produced by the child. While this approach is focused on the development of intentional communication, it is based on the behavioural-developmental theory that states that communicative development is enhanced by promoting more effective social exchanges between the parent and child. That is, communication must develop in a socio-cultural context. The social context can be made more conducive to communication development by promoting better parent-child interactions.

Focus on Supporting Parents

In recent years, parental participation in communication intervention programs for children with developmental and physical disabilities has been emphasized (Ketelarr, Vermeer, Helders, and Hart, 1998). Parents play an important and active role in motivating, guiding, and enhancing the skill development of their child. The essence of development in this view is the child interacting with his/her parent in an apprenticeship relationship (Rogoff, 1990). Vygotsky (1978) uses the term "zone of proximal development" to describe the child operating on the edge of his/her skill level, guided and supported by the adult (in this case the child's parent) onto a higher plane of development until the child is able to take over at that level.

Brunner (1982) uses the term "scaffolding" to describe the parent's role when the child faces a new and familiar task, again providing maximum support initially, and then decreasing the support as the child is able to take over. Extending this concept into the area of child development, Kaye (1982) uses the term "frames" to describe the interpretations that parents superimpose on the child's behavior, thereby offering the child an organizational framework for his/her actions.

For this approach, parental participation is viewed as collaborating as equal partners with the clinician in all aspects of the intervention; that is, the assessment of their child's communication behavior and the development and implementation of their child's communication intervention program. Further, the literature identifies a number of intervention strategies, which have been implemented for children with developmental and physical disabilities based on the outcomes of assessments of communication behaviors. These include the replacement of unconventional communicative behaviors with socially acceptable ones (Burke, 1990), development of more conventional forms of pre-verbal behavior (Butterfield, 1991), sensitizing caregivers to emerging intentionality (Siegel-Causey and Guess, 1989), and prelinguistic milieu teaching (Yoder and Munson, 1995).

Need for Early Intervention

Children with developmental and physical disabilities often present delayed development in speech and language (Pennington and McConachie, 2001), which can negatively affect parent-child relations. Given this, there would seem to be considerable need and value in developing effective early intervention programs to enhance the communicative interactions between the parent and child. Part of the enhancement process involves working with parents to develop skills that will enable them to recognize and respond effectively to their child's existing communication behaviors. Parents may also benefit form learning how to further enhance and develop the child's communication abilities, so as to move the child beyond the prelinguistic stage. That is, part of the process of this approach involves developing the parents' skills in teaching more effective communication behaviors to their child.

A COLLABORATIVE INTERVENTION APPROACH

Our intervention approach involves close collaboration with parents in the design and implementation of the intervention procedures (Tait, Sigafoos, Woodyatt, O'Reilly, and Lancioni, 2004). The approach includes several features, including (a) a focus on identifying, verifying, and making use of prelinguistic behaviors in the intervention process, (b) use of a non-directive, collaborative consultation approach with parents to develop intervention goals, and (c) application of the logic of functional communication training to enhance the child's prelinguistic repertoire. The approach also includes providing supportive feedback to parents on their implementation of intervention strategies. These features reflect current best practice in communication intervention for children with developmental and physical disabilities (Schlosser, 2003).

The approach involves close collaboration with parents. This particular focus of this collaboration (i.e., between therapist and the child's parent) is important from an applied perspective because parents are the child's primary communicative partners during early development. In addition, including parents in the assessment and intervention process was seen as one way of ensuring that they would value and, hence, perhaps more likely to continue the procedures, which would hopefully lead to greater maintenance of intervention gains.

Empirical Support for the Approach

The intervention approach has been empirically validated in previous research (Keen, Sigafoos, and Woodyatt, 2001; Tait et al., 2004). In the first study, Keen et al. worked with teachers of four non-speaking children with autism. The teachers first identified any existing behaviors that the children used to initiate various types of communicative interactions. To identify these existing communicative acts, the consultant asked the teachers to describe how the children accomplished various communicative functions, such as requesting an object, rejecting an activity, or commenting on the environment. After this, three specific communication acts were selected for child. The intervention objective was to replace the existing act with a more advanced form of communication. For example, if the child requested objects by leading the teacher by the hand, the intervention goals might be to teach the child to request objects using manual signs. In selecting the new form that would be taught, it was important to make sure that these replacement forms would be recognizable and symbolic ways for the child to achieve these same communicative functions. This was considered necessary to ensure that the new forms being taught would in fact be more effective communication signals and thus more likely to evoke an appropriate response from the teachers. After a baseline phase showing that the children did not use the more advanced forms, teachers received in-service training, consultation, and feedback on how to encourage, acknowledge, and react to the replacement forms. During intervention, replacement forms increased and prelinguistic behaviors decreased, suggesting that the teacher-implemented intervention was effective in replacing prelinguistic behaviors with alternative and more advanced forms of functional communication.

The second study (Tait et al., 2004) sought to extend the findings of Keen et al. (2001). Instead of working in schools with teachers of children with autism, Tait and her colleagues worked with mothers in a home-based intervention involving six young children with developmental and physical disabilities. Again the mothers first identified any existing prelinguistic acts (e.g., body movements, facial expressions, and vocalizations) that their children used to initiate various communicative functions (e.g., requesting, rejecting, and commenting). The consultant then assisted the mother in selecting intervention goals that focused on replacing or enhancing the child's existing prelinguistic acts with more formal communication skills, such as use the use of formal gestures or picture-based communication systems. The logic here was that acquisition of more formal skills would enable the child to initiate social-communicative interactions in ways that would be easier for parents to recognize and interpret. As the child acquired these more advanced skills, the social-communicative relations between the parent and child should improve. After an initial baseline phase, the mothers were shown how to teach the new and more formal communication skills. The consultation also provided regular feedback to the parents on their implementation of the procedures. The data show that after the parents had learned to use the intervention procedures, the children's use of the new communication skills increased and there was a collateral reduction in their use of the old prelinguistic acts. These treatment gains were generally maintained at the monthly follow-ups. The results suggest that parents can use the approach to enhance communication skills in children with developmental and physical disabilities.

PHASES OF THE INTERVENTION APPROACH

The intervention approach supported by the findings of Keen et al. (2001) and Tait et al. (2004) involves four phases. In Phase 1, existing prelinguistic behaviors are identified and the communicative functions of these acts are verified through direct observation. The more desired replacement behaviours and the major intervention goals are delineated in Phase 2 as part of a non-directive consultation with parents. In Phase 3, parents are taught to use functional communication intervention to replace and enhance the child's prelinguistic forms with more conventional and symbolic behaviors that serve the same communicative function. Phase 4 is a process of feedback on the parent's implementation of those intervention strategies.

Phase 1: The Identification and Verification of Prelinguistic Behavior

The first step in the intervention process is to identify any behavior that the child currently uses which might have communicative potential. Once identified, there is a need to verify the communicative function, if any, of the child existing behavior. The approach to identification and verification of prelinguistic behavior is based on the hypothesis that the prelinguistic behaviors often serve a communicative function for the child.

Along these lines, parents are asked to identify any prelinguistic acts that their child uses and the communicative function of these acts. This is done by interviewing the parents using a structured protocol, such as the Inventory of Potential Communicative Acts (IPCA) (Sigafoos et al., 2000). For example, the parent is asked to describe any ways that the child can indicate when s/he wants something or does not want something. This is one way of getting at what if any requesting and rejecting skills the child has in his/her repertoire. Parents are also asked how their child comments on aspects of the environment and recruits the parent's attention.

The IPCA is a research-based interview protocol designed for use as with parents, teachers, or therapists (Sigafoos et al., 2000). The protocol is used to gather descriptive information on any informal or idiosyncratic behaviors exhibited by the child that are interpreted by informants, (in this case the child's parents), as forms of communication. The IPCA consists of four sections. The protocol includes questions asking informants to indicate how the child communicates a number of specific functions. The questions cover 10 distinct pragmatic classes. When a behavior is identified as the child's means of indicating a particular pragmatic function, parents are asked to provide an example of specific situations in which the child has been observed to use the identified behavior to communicate that specific function. These examples can then provide the context for intervention.

The IPCA focuses on identifying any potential communicative act (PCA) that might be used by the child. Table 1 provides examples of the types of PCAs observed in children with developmental and physical disabilities. This list is not exhaustive and parents should be encouraged to identify any behaviors that they have observed their child to use in social-communicative interactions with others.

Table 1. Examples of Potential Communicative Acts (PCAs)

Vocalizations	sound/noise, yell/scream, grunt, cry/whine, laugh
Body Movements	moves closer, moves away, tensing, wriggling, reposition, relaxing movement, reach, touch, push/pull, pointing
Face/Eye Movements	purses lips, stare, opens eyes, closes eyes, eye shift, gaze away, gaze toward,
Breathing	rapid, slow, hold, swallow, sigh, blow
Problem Behavior	aggression, tantrum, self-injury, destroy items
Stereotyped movements	use of reflexes, extension, body rocking, spasm
Symbolic acts	speech, manual signs, gestures, head nodding, eye pointing, picture board, AAC

When identifying PCAs, emphasis has been placed on the function of communication behaviors (e.g., requesting, protesting, and commenting), rather than only on the form of communication (e.g., vocal and gestural). The literature is only just beginning to document that some of the PCAs exhibited by children with developmental and physical disabilities may in fact be appropriately classified in pragmatic terms as attempts to request, protest, or comment, for example (Carr and Kemp, 1989; Iacono, Waring, and Chan, 1996). Various classification schemes describing communicative functions from a pragmatic perspective have been proposed (see Reichle et al., 1993 for a review). These schemes and results from the recent empirical studies were used in selecting the pragmatic functions included in the IPCA. The IPCA seeks information on 10 distinct functions that were common to several classification schemes and that have been documented in children with developmental and physical disabilities. These functions are:

- Social convention (e.g., greeting others and responding to own name)
- Attention-to-self (e.g., getting the attention of others)
- Reject/Protest (e.g., rejecting a non-preferred item and indicating no)
- Request an object (e.g., requesting a preferred item)
- Request an action (e.g., seeking help with game or with dressing)
- Request information (e.g., naming of item and asking for clarification)
- Comment (e.g., how does child indicate they are happy or sad)
- Choice making (e.g., choosing between two or more alternatives)
- Answer (e.g., indicating yes or no to a question)
- Imitation (e.g., imitating communicative gestures).

Under each of these 10 general categories, a number of more specific communicative exemplars are included. For example, to assess Requesting an Object, informants are asked to "describe how the child lets you know they want (a) an object (e.g., toy or book), (b) something to eat, (c) more of something, (d) TV or music, (e) other.

The IPCA should not be viewed as a formal or standardized assessment of communication functioning. Instead it was designed to merely document and describe the PCAs of individual children. The information documented with the IPCA is merely the verbal reports from the child's parents and are thus of unknown reliability and validity. This is an important limitation to highlight because the idiosyncratic and often subtle nature of these behaviors means that it is open to possibly varying interpretations.

Our data with respect to the use of the IPCA indicate that parents are often able to identify a number of prelinguistic behaviors that their child uses to request, reject, comment, and call attention to themselves (Keen et al., 2001; Sigafoos et al., 2000; Tait et al., 2004). However, it may be unclear in some cases if parents' responses to such interview questions are sufficient to determine whether the identified PCAs are in fact intentional forms of communication on the part of the child. For example, Stephenson and Linfoot (1996) have indicated that it is possible that parents may over-interpret their children's behaviors and that perhaps the acts are not intentional forms of communication, but rather merely reflexive, orienting, or exploratory responses to environmental stimulation.

Given such plausible alternative explanations, our approach seeks not only to identify these acts but also to verify the communicative potential of these acts. That is, we need to know if the child really using a certain prelinguistic act, such as a body movement, to indicate when he or she wants or does not want something. This verification process requires structured observations. Structured observations need to be conducted to determine if the potential communicative acts identified by a parent could be observed in situations that would support the interpretation of these acts as forms of functional and intentional communication on the part of the child.

Verification involves documenting whether or not the behavior occurred under conditions that would indicate that it served the identified communicative function. Therefore, conditions need to be arranged in an attempt to provide the antecedents that set the occasion for communication involving the identified prelinguistic behavior. The conditions chosen to verify a child's communication behavior needs to be designed to be identical to, or as similar as possible to, the examples provided by the parent as part of the IPCA interview. Specifically, the aim is to determine whether or not a particular PCA would occur consistently in a context and under conditions that would suggest the act was in fact a form of communication. This verification assessment is designed to identify the variables that set the occasion for the occurrence of the communicative behaviors and the consequences that maintain those behaviors (Linfoot, 1994; Wetherby and Prutting, 1984).

For each child, an assessment activity and a target behavior need to be selected based on the examples provided by parents when they are interviewed about their child's prelinguistic behaviors. A number of issues need to be taken into consideration when these selections are made. First, it is advisable to choose target behaviors from at least two communicative functions for a child to provide verification opportunities across different communicative functions. Second, the examples described by the parents in the interview should be chosen for verification only if opportunities related to these examples could be created repeatedly so as to ensure sufficient assessment data would be forthcoming. Third, in an effort to increase the social validity of the intervention, clinicians need to consult the parent about the choice of examples because the subsequent intervention can be conducted in the context of these examples/activities.

An example of possible contexts in which verification assessments may be conducted are (a) playing with an interactive toy, (b) snack time, and (c) socio-dramatic or make believe play (e.g., playing dress-ups, playing peek-a-boo, playing tea parties or shops, etc). In each context, the child should be provided with 10 opportunities to indicate the selected communicative functions. Table 2 describes how the opportunity to exhibit that communicative function may be provided to the same child in each of three separate activities.

A number of factors will influence the choice of the activities as the context for providing opportunities to verify children's selected prelinguistic acts. First, the activities need to be ones in which the child would normally have opportunities to communicate the presumed functions of the selected PCAs. For example, watching TV would not be suitable, as the child would mostly be passive and there would be limited opportunities for the child to communicate with his/her parent. In addition, the activities be more than fleeting and occur at times and in locations that would allow for observation of the particular communicative behaviors nominated.

A structured observation opportunity involves presenting an opportunity to a child as described in Table 2 and then waiting 10 seconds to see if the child will produce the anticipated PCA. For example, from the IPCA, parents might observe that when their son was requesting assistance with something that he would look at his parent and he would say "Ee! Ee! Ee!" to try to get his/her attention. Then the parent would ask, "Do you want some help Alex?" and then the child would say "Yeh!" So, to verify that communicative behavior during a toy play session, the parent would leave an attractive toy near the child, but just out of his reach, wait for 10 seconds and then the clinician and the parent would record what the child did. If the child responded to the situation by trying to gain eye contact with his mother and by saying "Ee! Ee! Ee!" within 10 seconds, then he would be scored as having 'Requested Assistance' using the identified PCA and this would then be an example of an instance of verification for that opportunity.

Table 2. Procedures for Creating Communicative Opportunities

Activity	Function	Description of the Verification Task
Toy play	Request toy	Place an attractive toy just out of the child's reach, but within the visual range of the child. Wait for 30 s. Record what the child does. If he crawls towards the toy, reaches out for it, makes a noise, and points to the toy, then the child is given credit for requesting that toy.
Snack time	Reject/Protest	Offer a non-preferred snack item to the child and ask the child is s/he wants it. Wait 30 s. Record what the child does. If s/he responds to the offer by signing No, or shaking his/her head or vocalizing a "Nah" like sound, then the child is given credit for indicating no or rejecting the item.
Socio-dramatic play	Indicating Choice	Place on the floor near the child two puppets that are within his physical range. Ask child if s/he wants a choice of two puppets. Wait 30 seconds. Record what the child does. If s/he responds to the question by eye scanning both puppets, touching one and ignoring the other, the child is making a choice.

Parents should be involved in this assessment process. Wetherby and Rodriguez (1992) and Iacono, Waring, and Chan (1996) have found that the involvement of parents in structured assessments is valuable not only because of the additional information on the child's skills obtained, but also because it demonstrated to the parents how well their children were using PCAs to communicate their needs.

Phase 2: Non-Directive Consultation with Parents

In this phase parents are assisted to select initial intervention goals for their child. The intent is to ensure parent priorities are addressed and that parents gain ownership and have input in the process. By ensuring parents have input and ownership, they may be more likely to engage the child in the types of social-communicative interactions that are necessary to develop the child's communication skills (Strain, Storey, and Smith, 1991). It is necessary to ensure the parents provide effective opportunities for social interaction because the child's communication development can be viewed as a guided process (Bruner, 1983; Lock, 1978). Parents contribute to the process of communication development by creating opportunities for learning and by responding appropriately to the child's responses to those opportunities (Bakeman and Adamson, 1984; Jones and Adamson, 1987). However, Basil (1992) and Barrera and Vella (1987) noted that when comparing mother child dyads with children with physical disabilities and similar dyads with non-disabled infants, maternal behavior patterns emerged that interfered negatively with the development of communication and independence in the young children with physical impairments. Consequently, parents of children with developmental and physical disabilities may need support to ensure they can provide effective opportunities that will enhance the child's communication development.

Parents should be reminded about the overall intervention. The overall intervention goal is to replace the existing prelinguistic acts with more symbolic form of communication. For this, the parents may need to provide structured opportunities to evoke a communication response on the part of the child and prompt the child to engage in the new communication skill in response to these opportunities. For example, a child who could only cry to get help might be taught to sign HELP to gain the assistance of the parent in reaching a preferred item. In this scenario, the goal was to replace crying with a more appropriate and symbolic form of communication. To teach the sign, the parent is taught how to create a situation where the child will need help. Once the situation is created, the child should be motivated to gain help. At this point is tis most likely that child will use some existing prelinguistic behavior in an attempt to recruit help from the parent. However, the intervention procedure involves pre-empting the prelinguistic form and prompting the child to produce the new form. That is, the child is physically assisted to sign HELP and then the parent gives the necessary help. Over successive opportunities the amount of physical assistance is faded until the child can independently sign help when it is needed. With this procedure, the child should learn to use the manual sign to get help rather than relying on the old prelinguistic form. Once this new and more formal communication skill has been acquired, the child should be better able to initiate a request for help that is likely to be effective from the parent's perspective. This is likely to be the case, because the new form should be easier to the child's communicative partners to recognize and interpret.

In other cases, however, the intervention goal might not involve replacing the prelinguistic behavior, but might instead focus on enhancing the child's existing prelinguistic behavior. For example, a child who used eye gaze as a form of requesting might be taught to alternate her gaze between the toy and her mother rather than merely staring at the toy. Alternating her gaze was considered a more advanced and precise communicative response that would provide a more effective signal to listeners. Another example that follows the logic of enhancement is a situation where a child might shake her head to indicate "NO" but perhaps the shaking motion was so slight that it is easily missed. In tis case the child could be taught to shale her head in a more obvious way.

The parent and consultation therefore need to consider whether an existing prelinguistic act should be replaced with a more symbolic form of communication or enhanced. A number of approaches have been developed to answer this question of enhancement or replacement, in relation to reducing or eliminating challenging behavior (Wickstrom-Kane and Goldstein, 1999). Yet, when determining whether a communicative behavior should be enhanced or replaced, the answer would seem to rely on several issues being addressed. Those are the general readability of the child's current communicative behavior, the consistency of use of that behavior by the child, the child's ability to use a more symbolic form of communication and, the age appropriateness or socially acceptable nature of the current communicative behavior.

In considering these issues, it is important to emphasize that one of the main goals of intervention is to enhance the social-communicative interactions between the parent and the child. IF the parent can read the child signals, then there may be no need to replace the act. However, in the long term, the child's overall development will require that they transition from the prelinguistic stage to the use of more formal and symbolic forms of communication. While the prelinguistic forms of communication behavior identified in the interview may not be problematic for the most part, they may be fairly subtle and idiosyncratic and thus open to possible misinterpretation. It is possible that when a child's communicative attempts are subject to frequent misinterpretation, then there may be escalation to more problematic response topographies in an effort to repair the communicative breakdown (Brady and Halle, 2002). For example, if the child's attempt to request a preferred item by vocalizing (whining) is misinterpreted, then the child may escalate to crying. Early intervention to replace or enhance the child's prelinguistic behaviors may thus help to prevent communicative breakdowns. This in turn may prevent the emergence of problem behaviors as communicative repair strategies, although this is highly speculative.

Further, Pennington and McConachie (2001) found that mothers of infants with cerebral palsy were significantly more commanding than were comparison mothers, and that mothers of infants with cerebral palsy tended to direct and control conversations with their child, resulting in restrictive communication patterns and fewer child initiated conversation exchanges. Consequently, in this approach, it is necessary that the parents be trained to use an intervention strategy so that they have a means by which they can encourage their children to respond freely in a communicative situation using a clear and consistent communicative behavior.

Phase 3: Functional Communication Training

Theoretical and empirical work in applied behavior analysis suggests that aberrant behaviors in children with developmental disabilities often serve a communicative function (Carr, 1977; Carr and Durand, 1985; Durand, 1993; Durand and Carr, 1991). However, in some cases, the topography of the prelinguistic behavior may be unacceptable (e.g., aggression, self-injury, and tantrums). Ultimately, such limited communication skills can restrict the child's ability to express his/her wants and needs and participate in meaningful social interactions with others. Because the approach outlined in this chapter is provided in the home, there is a need for an empirically-validated strategy to support parents in the design and the implementation of communication interventions for their children. In these cases, functional communication training (FCT) can represent a highly effective treatment as it can be used to replace aberrant behaviors with more appropriate communication skills (Didden, Duker, and Korzilius, 1997).

Wacker, Berg, and Harding (2002) described the major components of FCT for replacing aberrant behaviors with socially acceptable communication responses. Briefly, as described in Phase 1 of this approach, an initial functional assessment is conducted to identify the function or purpose of the child's problem behaviors. Next, a more appropriate communication behavior is identified that serves the same function as the problem behavior (as outlined in Phase 2). Third, the communicative alternative is taught under the same conditions that previously set the occasion for problem behavior.

If the communicative alternative is more efficient than the problem behavior (Horner and Day, 1991), then acquisition of the communicative alternative should lead to collateral reductions in problem behavior. Efficiency in this case means that the communicative alternative requires less response effort and is more consistently and immediately reinforced than problem behavior. It is important that problem behavior no longer leads to reinforcement. For example, consider a child who might engage in tantrums to obtain the attention of his parents. Using the logic of FCT, the idea would be to teach this child a better way of getting the parent's attention. For example, the child could be taught to activate a voice output device the produced the pre-recorded phrase "Can you come here please?"

In other cases, however, the child's prelinguistic behaviors might be viewed as acceptable and legitimate forms of communication (e.g., facial expressions, eye gaze, and reaching). While perhaps socially acceptable, these types of prelinguistic behaviors may nonetheless be limiting. For example, it is difficult to communicate about absent objects and past events and to communicate precisely with prelinguistic behaviors.

The FCT approach involves making use of information obtained in the interview and verification phase and then using this in collaboration with parents. For example, when teaching a child to "request more", the parent might chose a play context in which the child is playing with a toy. The parent could interrupt toy play and then prompt the child to use a manual sign to request more. Parents can be taught how to prompt the desired behavior. Prompting might involve the use of verbal instruction (e.g., show me the sign), modeling (the parent models the correct response), or physical guidance (physically assisting the child to make the correct response) (Duker, Didden, and Sigafoos, 2003). The exact type of sequencing of prompts was individualized for each target replacement behavior. For example, if the target replacement behavior were for the child to say a word approximation, verbal instruction and modeling would be used as prompts, whereas if the target replacement behavior was to produce a manual sign, then physical prompting might also be used. Training the parents to implement the intervention plan involves verbal explanation and demonstration by the therapist. Following the in-service, the parents should receive a copy of the relevant plan and be asked to follow the instructions set out in the summary sheet during the session.

With the normally developing child, the parent's role in communication development is that of partner, providing support by scaffolding and modelling as needed by the child. For the child with developmental and physical disabilities, all of those same cognitive and social needs/benefits are present in the relationship with the adult communicating partner, but there is also an additional role for this partner.

The hoped for effect of this approach is that the parent will became the "enabler" as well as the model. In the "enabler" role, the parent was consistently using encouragement to set up the expectation that the child was to communicate with him/her. Then, through the use of acknowledgment, (e.g., " You touched the duck - that tells me that you want the to play with the duck"), the parent would follow the child's subtle cues of changes in direction of eye movement, vocalisation, weight shift (in terms of a hand or head movement) etc., facilitating the child's learning of their replacement communicative behavior.

If no response was made by the child within a prescribed time frame, then the parent would take on the role of "model" (e.g., " Remember, if you want the Duck you have to touch the Duck" or "How can you tell me that you want the duck?") and prompt the child to respond using the individually designed replacement communicative behavior. In this way, the parent was balancing his/her scaffolding with the goal of the intervention program (i.e., to teach the child to use a replacement communicative behavior).

Basil (1992) and Barrera and Vella (1987) have identified that a pattern of dominating parental behavior coupled with the passivity found in many children with cerebral palsy could be partially explained as an example of learned helplessness. Thus, in all cases parents must be trained to recognize that their child's intentions in the social interaction (e.g., the toy play, snack time or socio-dramatic play) must lead the communication that occurs around the scaffolding provided by using the intervention strategy. In this way, both the parent and the child would be active participants in the process.

Phase 4: Feedback

The final phase of this approach involves parents receiving feedback on their child's progress and on their implementation of the plan after each intervention session. Feedback can consist of reviewing the child's data or watching videotapes of the intervention sessions. In providing feedback, the clinician and parent can discuss the progress and review the parent's use of the intervention procedures. Most often there will be a need to troubleshoot the intervention to ensure the child makes adequate improvement. Sometimes this may require that the clinician and parent modify how the intervention is delivered, and how the parent interacts with the child. The clinician may note aspects of the procedures that were implemented correctly as well as aspects of the procedures that need to be implemented more consistently.

Tait (2004) gathered data on parent satisfaction of a similar home-based intervention program as outlined in this chapter. These data indicate that the parents agreed that the program was helpful, effective, easy to implement and that they would recommend it to others. However, there were spin offs from the feedback sessions of this approach that were not anticipated by the researcher. In the first instance, parents indicated that the verbal feedback obtained from the clinician was a very helpful tool that helped them to amend their implementation of the intervention strategy. Specifically, the weekly verbal feedback was a learning tool that taught the parents to hone their communicative interactions with their child so that they were more effective, use the EAR strategy more efficiently, and to offer more authentic communication opportunities for their child.

Secondly, parents of children with severe physical and developmental disabilities must often spend considerable time in caring for their child. Consequently, they are often not in a position to be able to step back and reflect on the small but significant gains made by their child. Several parents indicated in Tait (2004) that the graphs used as feedback tools were the first indication of success and progress that they had ever seen for their child.

Finally, through the video, graphic and verbal feedback strategies of this approach, parents became cognizant of the importance of applying the same intervention goals across the many environments that their child might be encountering (e.g., school, home and community). Parent's comments on satisfaction of the feedback and intervention programs (Tait, 2004) can be seen below:

1) Overall, I found this program very helpful and it has worked for my child. I don't think she would be where she is today without your intervention program. The graphs were good to see, but your coming to us each week and telling us how we had done the week before, was great. I learnt more from speaking to you about it.
2) It is a mind shift. A different way of looking at communication skills for children with cerebral palsy in the sense that it is more positive to look at what they can do

and to work with that. To see the graphs each week showed me the improvement that she is making and that helped, because it is hard to see her progress.

3) I found that perseverance is the key to success. Also, it works well if the intervention is used throughout the child's day to day events, not only at home but at her school and therapy as well.

These comments suggest that the feedback strategies outlined in this approach were considered an important component of the training package by the parents. These encouraging responses from the mothers in Tait's (2004) study seem to indicate that this approach to supporting parents was not only generally effective in developing the child's communication skills, but also valued by and acceptable to the mothers.

CONCLUSION

This chapter has focused on improving the social-communicative relations between parents and their children with developmental and physical disabilities. Evidence suggests that these relations may be difficult owing to the child's failure to develop effective communication skills. In light of this, parents may need to learn how to enhance the child's communicative development. Our approach involves collaborating with parents to identify the child's existing communication acts and then using functional communication training to replace or enhance these acts. Careful implementation of this approach has lead to improvement in the child communication skills (Keen et al., 2001; Tait et al., 2004).

In this approach, parental participation is viewed as making sure that the parents are assisted to collaborate as equal partners with the clinician in all aspects of the approach. In fact, there seems to be a balance of roles, with both infant and adult active in the exchange. Rogoff (1990) terms the concept, "guided participation" to describe the collaborative interaction between children and caregivers. She described the adult as "… building bridges from the child's present understanding to new levels of understanding" (p. 9).

Within this view of a shared responsibility, the child's role as an active participant is supported by research showing the infant's early expectations of what is an appropriate response from their parent and the infant's active attempt to elicit the "right" response (Als, 1982; Fogel, et al., 1982; Tronick, Als, Adamson, Wise, and Brazelton, 1978). There are powerful ramifications of the severity of the child's disability on the child's development in a number of domains related to the development of communicative intent. Those ramifications extend to the adult partner within the social context of development.

Given this situation, intervention assumes a critical position. Because the foundation is being laid at such a young age, intervention should begin early in order to offset the potentially widening effects of the child's disability. In the approach outlined in this chapter, the adult provides guidance and support while the infant becomes increasingly involved through the development of more complex behaviors. Parental involvement is a crucial aspect of a child's development during intervention, for the parents are the primary adults in the child's life. The parents' daily care and interaction with their child provide the social context for consistent feedback and learning for their child. To attempt to view the child's communication development without this context of partnership is to remove development from reality.

The literature identifies a number of intervention strategies, which have been implemented for children with disabilities based on the outcomes of assessments of communication behaviors and which could be implemented by the children's parents. These include the replacement of unconventional communicative behaviors with socially acceptable ones (Burke, 1990); development of more conventional forms of pre-verbal behavior (Butterfield, 1991); sensitizing caregivers to emerging intentionality (Siegel-Causey and Guess, 1989); and prelinguistic milieu teaching (Yoder et al., 1995).

To promote more meaningful and successful communication exchanges between the parent and their child, clinicians can support families of children with a severe communication impairment with home based intervention efforts. Clinicians can do this by (1) assisting parents to identify and verify their child's prelinguistic behaviors, (2) using non-directive collaborative consultation with parents to determine intervention goals; (3) teaching parents to use functional communication training, and (4) providing feedback to the parents on their implementation of the intervention strategies associated with this model. Future efforts must now refine these techniques, to enable children with physical disabilities, developmental disabilities and severe communication impairment to develop more effective means of communicating with their families, teachers and other members of their communities.

REFERENCES

Als, H. (1979). Social interaction: Dynamic matrix for developing behavioral organization. In I. C. Uzgiris (Ed.), *Social interaction and communication during infancy: New direction for dhild development (*pp. 21-41). San Francisco: Jossey Bass.

Bailey, D. B., and Simeonsson, R.J. (1986). Design issues in family impact evaluations. In L. Bickman and D. L. Weatherford (Eds.), *Evaluating early intervention programs for severely handicapped children and their families* (pp. 209-230). Austin, TX: Pro-Ed.

Baird, S., Mayfield, P., Baker, P. (1977). Mother's interpretations of the behavior of their infants with visual and other impairments during interactions. *Journal of Visual Impairment and Blindness*, *91*, 467-483.

Bakeman, R., and Adamson, L. (1984). Coordinating attention to people and objects in mother-infant and peer-infant interaction. *Child Development*, *55* 1278-1289.

Barrera, M. E., and Vella, D. M., (1987). Disabled and non-disabled infants' interactions with their mothers. *American Journal of Occupational Therapy*, *41*, 168-172

Basil, C. (1992). Social interaction and learned helplessness in severely disabled children. *Augmentative and Alternative Communication*, *8*, 188-199.

Bates, E., Camaioni, L., and Volterra, V. (1975). The acquisition of performatives prior to speech. *Merril-Palmer Quarterly, 21*, 205-226.

Brazelton, B. (1982). Joint regulation of neo-nate-parent behavior. In E. Z. Tronick (Ed.), *Social Interchange in infancy: Affect, cognition and communication* (pp. 7-22). Baltimore: University Park Press.

Bruner, J., (1983). *Child's talk.* New York: Norton.

Camaioni, L. (1993). The development of intentional communication: A re-analysis. In J. Nadel and L. Camaioni (Eds.), *New perspectives in early communicative development* (pp. 82-96). London: Routledge.

Carr, E., and Durand, M. (1985). Reducing behavior problems through functional communication training. *Journal of Applied Behavior Analysis, 18*, 111-126.

Cartright, L. and Ruscello. D. (1979). A survey of parent involvement practices in the speech clinic. *ASHA, 21*, 275-279.

Cunningham, C.E, Reuler, E., Blackwell, J. and Deck, J. (1981). Behavioral and linguistic developments in the interaction of normal and retarded children with their mothers. *Child Development, 52*, 62-70.

Desrochers, M., Hile, M., and Williams-Moseley, T. (1997). Survey of functional assessment procedures Used with Individuals who display mental retardation and severe problem behaviors. *American Journal on Mental Retardation, 101*, 535-546.

Dunst, C. J. (1985). Communicative competence and deficits: Effects on early social interactions. In E. T. McDonald and D. L. Gallagher (Eds.), *Social and emotional development in multiply handicapped children (pp. 93-140).* Philadelphia: Home of the Merciful Saviour for Crippled Children.

Fogel, A., Diamond, G., Langhorst, B., and Demos, V. (1982). Affective and cognitive aspects of the two-month-old's participation in face to face interaction with the mother. In E. Z. Tronick (Ed.), *Social Interchange in infancy: Affect, cognition and communication* (37-58). Baltimore: University Park Press.

Goldberg, S., (1977), Social Competence in infancy: A model of parent-infant interaction. *Merrill-Palmer Quarterly, 23*, 163-177.

Hanzlik, J. R. (1990). Nonverbal interaction patterns of mothers and their infants with cerebral palsy. *Education and Training in Mental Retardation and Developmental Disabilities, 25*, 333-343.

Harris, D. (1982). Communicative interaction processes involving non-vocal physically handicapped children. *Topics in Language Disorders, 2*, 21-37.

Harris, M., Jones, D., Brookes, D., and Grant, J. (1986). Relations between the non-verbal context of maternal speech and rate of language development. *British Journal of Developmental Psychology, 4*, 377-394.

Hoff-Ginsberg, E. (1991). Mother-child conversation in different social classes and communicative settings. *Child Development, 62*, 782-796.

Hogg, J., (1996). Communication and learning disability: Briefing and update on developments. *Journal of the Royal Society of Medicine, 89*, 414-415.

Iacono, T., Waring, R., and Chan, J. (1996). Sampling communicative behaviours in children with intellectual disability in structured and unstructured situations. *European Journal of Disorders of Communication, 31*, 106-120.

Jones, C.P., and Adamson, L. (1987). Language use in mother-child and mother-child-sibling interactions. *Child Development, 58*, 356-366.

Kaye, K. (1982). Organism, apprentice, and person. In E. Tronick (Ed.), *Social interchange in infancy: Affect, cognition, and communication* (183-196). Baltimore: University Park Press.

Keen, D., Sigafoos, J., and Woodyatt, G. (2001). Replacing prelinguistic behaviours with functional communication. *Journal of Autism and Developmental Disorders, 31*, 385-398.

Keen, D., Woodyatt, G., and Sigafoos, J. (2002). Verifying teacher perceptions of the potential communicative acts of children with autism. *Communication Disorders Quarterly, 23*, 133-142.

Ketelaar, M., Vermeer, A., Helders, P., and Hart, H. (1998). Parental participation in intervention programs for children with cerebral palsy. *Topics in Early Childhood Special Education, 18*, 109-117.

King, G.A., King, S.M., and Rosenbaum, P.L. (1996). How mothers and fathers view professional care giving for children with disabilities. *Developmental Medicine and Child Neurology, 38*, 397-407.

Kumar, R. (1997). *Research methodology: A step by step guide for beginners*. Sydney: Longman.

Lamb, M.E., and Easter-Brooks, M.A. (1981). Individual differences in parental sensitivity: Origins, components, and consequences. In M. E. Lamb and L. R. Sherrod (Eds.), *Infant social cognition: Empirical and theoretical considerations* (pp. 127-153). Hillsdale, NJ: Erlbaum.

Lennox, D. B, and Miltenberger, R. G. (1989). Conducting a functional assessment of problem behavior in applied settings. *Journal of the Association for Persons with Severe Handicaps*, *14*, 304-311.

Linfoot, K., (1994). Functional communication and the role of context. In K. Linfoot (Ed.), *Communication strategies for people with developmental disabilities: Issues from theory to practice.* (124-155). Sydney: MacLennan and Petty.

Lock, A. (1978). *Action, gesture, and symbol.* London. Academic Press.

Mahoney, G., Boyce, G., Fewell, R., Spiker, D. and Wheeden, C.A. (1998). The relationship of parent-child interaction to the effectiveness of early intervention services for at-risk children and children with disabilities. *Topics in Early Childhood Special Education, 18*, 5-17.

Martin, J. E. and Epstein, L. H. (1976). Evaluating treatment effectiveness in cerebral palsy: Single subject designs. *Physical Therapy, 53*, 285- 294.

McBride, S. L. and Peterson, C. (1997). Home-based intervention with families of children with disabilities: Who is doing what? *Topics in Early Childhood Special Education,* 17, 209-233.

McConachie, H. and Mitchell, D. R. (1985), Parents teaching their young mentally handicapped children. *Journal of Child Psychology and Psychiatry and Allied Disciplines*, 26, 389-405.

McCormick, L., and Noonan, M. (1984). A responsive curriculum for severally handicapped pre-schoolers. *Topics in Early Childhood Special Education, 4,* 79-96.

McDade, H. L. and Varnedoe, D. R. (1987). Training parents to be language facilitators. *Topics in Language Disorders*, 7, 19-30.

Pennington, L. (1996). *The communication skills of severely physically disabled children.* Unpublished doctoral disseration. University College London.

Pennington, L., and McConachie, H., (2001). Predicting patterns of interaction between children with cerebral palsy and their mothers. *Developmental Medicine and Child Neurology, 43*, 83-90.

Pinder, G. and Olswang, L. (1995). Development of communicative intent in young children with cerebral palsy: A treatment efficacy study. *Infant-Toddler Intervention, 5*, 51-70.

Reddihough, D., Bach, T, Burgess, G, Oke, L, and Hudson, I. (1990). Objective test of the quality of motor function of children with cerebral pasly-preliminary study. *Developmental Medicine and Child Neurology, 32*, 902-909.

Rogoff, B. (1990) *Apprenticeship in thinking: Cognitive development in social context.* New York: Oxford University Press.

Sandall, S. R. (1993). Curricula for early intervention. In W. Brown, S. K. Thurman, and L. F. Pearl (Eds.), *Family-centered early intervention with infants and toddlers: Innovative cross-disciplinary approaches* (pp. 129-172). Baltimore: Paul H. Brookes Publishing Co.

Schieffelin, B. B. and Ochs, E. (1986). *Language socialization across cultures.* Cambridge: Cambridge University Press.

Schlosser, R. W. (2003). *The efficacy of augmentative and alternative communication: towards evidence-based practice.* Boston: Academic Press.

Siegel-Causey, E., and Guess, D. (1989). *Enhancing nonsymbolic communication interactions among learners with severe disabilities.* Baltimore: Paul H. Brookes Publishing Co.

Sigafoos, J., and Pennell, D. (1995). Parent and teacher assessment of receptive and expressive language in pre-school children with developmental disabilities. *Education and Training in Mental Retardation and Developmental Disabilities, 30*, 329-335.

Sigafoos, J., Woodyatt, G., Keen, D., Tait, K. J., Tucker, M., Roberts-Pennell, D., and Pittendreigh, N., (2000). Identifying potential communicative acts in children with developmental and physical disabilities. *Communication Disorders Quarterly, 21*, 77-86.

Sigafoos, J., Drasgow, E., Reichle, J., O'Reilly, M., Green, V., and Tait, K. (2004). Teaching communicative rejecting to children with severe disabilities. *American Journal of Speech-Language Pathology, 13*, 31-42.

Stephensen, J., and Linfoot, K. (1996). Intentional communication and graphic symbol use by students with severe intellectual disability. *International Journal of Disability, Development, and Education, 43*, 147-165.

Stern, D.N. (1981). The development of biologically determined signals of readiness to communicate which are language "resistant." In R. Stark (Ed.), *Language behavior in infancy and early childhood* (45-62). New York: Elsevier.

Strain, P., Storey, K., and Smith, D. J. (1991). Quality of life outcomes for young children with disabilities: Legislative and service delivery implications. *Early Education and Development, 2*, 40-53.

Sugarman, S. (1984). The development of preverbal communication: Its contribution and limits in promoting the development of language. In R. Schiefelbusch and J. Pikar (Eds.), *Communicative competence: Acquisition and intervention* (pp. 23-67). Baltimore: University Park Press.

Tait, K. (2004) *The identification and enhancement of communication behavior in very young children with cerebral palsy.* Unpublished doctoral disseration, University of Queensland: Brisbane, Australia.

Tait, K., Sigafoos, J, Woodyatt, G. O'Reilly, M. and Lancioni, G.E. (2004). Supporting parents in designing and implementing communication interventions for children with developmental and physical disabilities. *Disability and Rehabilitation,* 26, 1241-1254.

Tannock, R., and Girolametto, L. (1992). Reassessing parent-focused language intervention programs. In S. F., Warren and J. Reichle (Eds.), *Causes and effects in communication and language intervention* (pp. 49-79). Baltimore: Paul H. Brookes Publishing Co.

Throp, E .K. and McCollum, J. A., (1994). Defining the infancy specialization in early childhood special education. In L. J. Johnson, R. J. Gallagher, M. J. LaMontague, J. B. Jordon, J. J.Gallagher, P. L. Huntinger, and M. B. Karnes (Eds.), *Meeting early intervention challenges: Issues from birth to three* (pp. 167-183). Baltimore: Paul H. Brookes Publishing Co.

Van der Pijl, D.J. (2000). Ongoing developments in augmented communication and computer use. *Journal of Intellectual Disability Research, 44*, 408- 429.

Vygotsky, L. (1978). *Mind in society: The development of higher psychological processes.* Cambridge, MA: Harvard University Press.

Wehman, T. and Gilkerson, L., (1999). Parents of young children with special needs speak out: perceptions of early intervention services. *Infant-Toddler Intervention, 9*, 137-167.

Wetherby, A., and Prutting, C. (1984). Profiles of communicative and cognitive-social abilities in autistic children. *Journal of Speech and Hearing Research, 27*, 364-377.

Wetherby, A.M., and Rodriguez, G.P. (1992). Measurement of communicative intentions in normally developing children during structured and unstructured contexts. *Journal of Speech and Hearing Research, 35*, 130-138.

Westwood, P. (1998). *Commonsense methods for children with special needs: strategies for the regular classroom.* New York: Routledge.

Wickstrom-Kane, S. and Goldstein, H. (1999). Communication assessment and intervention to address challenging behavior in toddlers. *Topics in Language Disorders, 19*, 70-89.

Woll, B., and Barnett, S., (1998). Toward a sociolinguistic perspective on augmentative and alternative communication. *Augmentative and Alternative Communication, 14,* 200-211.

Yoder, D., and Munson, L. (1995). The social correlates of co-ordinated attention to adult and objects in mother-infant interaction. *First Language, 15*, 219-230.

Zarcone, J.R., Rodgers, T.A., Iwata, B.A., Rourke, D.A., and Dorsey, M. F. (1991). Reliability analysis of the Motivation Assessment Scale: A failure to replicate. *Research in Developmental Disabilities,* 12, 349-360.

In: Parent-Child Relations: New Research
Editor: Dorothy M. Devore, pp. 197-205 ISBN 1-60021-167-4

Chapter 11

PREDICTORS OF MIDDLE SCHOOL YOUTH EDUCATIONAL ASPIRATIONS: HEALTH RISK ATTITUDES, PARENTAL INTERACTIONS, AND PARENTAL DISAPPROVAL OF RISK

Regina P. Lederman*[1]*, Wenyaw Chan and Cynthia Roberts-Gray
University of Texas Medical Branch, USA

ABSTRACT

School-wide surveys in five middle schools were used to measure educational aspirations, attitudes toward sexual health risk behaviors and drug use, and perceptions of parental interactions and disapproval of risk behavior and one year later. Participants were male and female students of Black (n = 222), Hispanic (n = 317), White (n = 216), and Asian or other heritage (n = 85), ages 11 to 14. Analyses were performed for three factors with Cronbach's alpha coefficients ≥ 0.65 (youth's attitudes, discourse with parents, and parents' disapproval of risk behavior), and three single items inquiring about use of alcohol, use of marijuana, and sexual behavior. Generalized Linear Model (GLM) with logit link was used to evaluate the contribution of these measures at baseline as predictors of educational aspirations at the one-year follow-up. Results showed race/heritage ($p < .001$), attitudes toward health risk behaviors ($p < .01$), extent to which youth talked with parents about use of drugs and other health risk behaviors ($p < .05$), and perceptions of their parents' disapproval of risk behavior ($p < .05$) each made significant contributions in predicting educational aspirations. Gender did not contribute to the prediction of educational aspiration nor did self-report of actual risk behavior. These results indicate that youths' interactions with parents regarding health risk behaviors is worthy of further exploration to develop interventions to reduce adolescent health risks and increase educational aspirations.

---

[1] Contact Author: Regina P Lederman, PhD, University of Texas Medical Branch, 301 University Blvd., Galveston, TX 77555-1029, Phone: 713 666 0172, 409 772 6570, email: rlederma@utmb.edu

INTRODUCTION

Parent-child relations occupy important positions in pathways linking education and health. Parental encouragement for educational attainment is, for example, closely linked to youths' educational aspirations (Looker & Thiessen, 2004; Goyette & Xie, 1999). Educational aspirations of youth (Trusty & Harris, 1999) and parental involvement in their children's education (Trusty, 1999) are linked to educational attainment. Lack of educational attainment and low educational aspirations in turn are associated with a variety of health and health behavior problems, including substance abuse (Caetano, 2002) and rates of teenage birth (Pamuk, Makuc, Heck, Reuben, & Lochner, 1998). The association of poor education and poor health is a consistent finding from domestic and international research in economics, epidemiology, and sociology (Blane, 2003; Morowsky & Ross, 2003).

In some formulations of the pathways linking education and health, education is identified as a health-protecting factor (see Hannum & Buchman, 2003). Because of the abundant empirical evidence that better educated people lead longer, healthier lives, those who espouse the health protection formulation recommend investment in programs and practices that promote educational attainment as a means for improving health and reducing health inequalities. At a local program level, such an initiative might include parenting education and supportive services to assist families in encouraging their children to aspire to and achieve higher educational attainments, anticipating that positive health outcomes will accrue.

Other analyses demonstrate that good health in adolescence predicts both higher educational attainment and better adult health (Chandola, Clarke, Blane & Morris, 2003). Recommendations for action from this perspective focus on interventions to help families encourage healthy behaviors in childhood and adolescence with the expectation that better educational and adult health outcomes will follow.

In this chapter we examine a secondary analysis of data from a prevention research project exploring relationships among the educational aspiration of middle school youth, their health risk attitudes and behaviors, and interactions with their parents regarding risk behavior. The data, originally obtained to test the effectiveness of an innovative parent-child program for the prevention of sexual health risk behaviors (see Lederman, Chan, & Roberts-Gray, 2004; Lederman & Mian, 2003), were collected in school-wide surveys at five middle schools during a baseline period and again the next school year. The purpose of this secondary analysis of the data is to explore the possibility that, in addition to putting the health of youth at risk, negative health attitudes and behaviors distract youth from the pursuit of educational goals and thereby constrain educational aspirations, while appropriate parental involvement in discouraging youth negative health behaviors can contribute to higher educational aspirations. We hypothesized that middle school youth involvement in and attitudes toward health risk behaviors, and their perceptions of interactions with their parents/guardians regarding health risk behaviors would be predictive of educational aspiration measured during the subsequent school year.

RESEARCH DESIGN AND METHODS

This study analyzed data collected in school-wide surveys over two successive school years from students in five middle schools in two school districts in coastal Texas. The written survey questionnaire provided self-report measures of: (1) sexual involvement and the use of alcohol and other drugs; (2) attitudes toward sexual health risk behavior; (3) the frequency and breadth of discourse with parents about sexual health topics; (4) perceptions of parents' disapproval of the youth's involvement in sexual and other health risk behaviors; and (5) educational aspiration. The protocol was approved by the Institutional Review Board of the University of Texas Medical Branch at Galveston. Active assent of students and consent of parents was obtained and documented.

Participant Recruitment

Participants were recruited in four steps. First, we sent invitations through the mail and through presentations at conferences to all urban school districts located in and near Galveston, Texas. Leaders in two school districts indicated willingness to have their schools participate in the prevention intervention research project. The next step was meeting with principals and counselors at middle schools in the consenting districts. Two out of the three middle schools in one district and three of the four middle schools in the second district agreed to participate. The third step was partnership with the consenting schools to invite families to participate. A cover letter, consent form, and informational flyer were sent to parents via the students and through the mail informing them about the program and providing details regarding the research protocol. The school principals at each of the participating schools endorsed the program and signed the letters to parents, which were written in both English and Spanish.

The participating schools represented diversity in school size, ethnic heritage of the student body, and performance characteristics. Two of the schools had approximately 500 students, two had between 700 and 1,000 students, and one had more than 1,200 students. Across the five schools, the percent of students of different heritage ranged from 0.0 to 3.4 Asian, 7.0 to 54.3 African American, 32.8 to 85.8 Hispanic, and 5.2 to 52.1 White. Three of the schools had more than two-thirds of the student body identified as economically disadvantaged. The percent of students with special circumstances ranged from 3.7 to 23.6 with limited English proficiency, 4.5 to 13.6 participating in gifted and talented programs, and 2.2 to 4.3 percent with disciplinary placement. Total enrollment across the five schools was 3,881. Informed consent and actual participation in the survey was obtained for 848 youth.

Demographic Characteristics of the Participating Youth

More than half of the students were in sixth grade at the time they completed the baseline survey. There were approximately equal numbers of females and males. The majority was youth of color with nearly 40% indicating Hispanic/Latino/Mexican ethnicity. These data are displayed in Table 1.

Table 1. Demographic Characteristics of Survey Participants

Youth characteristics	Number of Youth	Percent
GENDER		
Male	383	45%
Female	465	55%
RACE/ETHNICITY		
Hispanic/Latino/Mexican	317	38%
Black/African American	222	26%
White – not Hispanic	216	26%
Asian or Mixed or Other	85	10%
GRADE LEVEL		
Sixth	480	60%
Seventh	249	31%
Eighth	76	9%

Survey Administration

Students completed the survey questionnaire during a special assembly at the school. The survey items originally were selected to be relevant in evaluating outcomes of prevention education interventions to reduce sexual health risk behaviors and prevent teen pregnancy and the spread of HIV and other sexually transmitted infections (STI). Adapted from the National Youth Survey (Elliot, Huizinga, & Ageton, 1985) and a middle school survey developed by ETR Associates (Kirby et al, 1997), the 9-page, 94-item survey questionnaire was divided into sections asking: "What do your parents think?," "What do you think?," "What do you do?," and "Do you talk with your parents?" Students typically completed the survey in 30 to 45 minutes. Unique identifying codes were marked on the survey forms so that records could be matched from year to year without disclosing individual identifying information.

Measures

Survey items addressing a common content domain (e.g., youth attitudes toward risk behaviors) and having similar response options (e.g., strongly agree to strongly disagree) were combined to produce domain scales which then were tested for internal consistency. Those obtaining a Cronbach alpha of 0.65 or greater were retained as scales. The scales and survey items used in the current analyses are described as follows.

- *Educational Aspiration* was measured with a single item asking, "How far do you think you will go in school?" Response options were assigned ordinal codes of 1 = "Won't graduate from high school," 2 = "Will finish high school," 3 = "Will go to trade, vocational, or business school after high school," 4 = "Will attend college."

Youth involvement in and attitudes toward risk behaviors were measured with two sets of survey items, one that counted the number of self-reported risk behaviors and the other a scale measuring perceived acceptability of "someone my age" having sex.

- *Health Risk Behaviors* was measured with three single items: (1) "In the last 30 days, did you drink alcohol such as beer, wine, wine coolers or hard liquor?," (2) "In the last 30 days, did you use marijuana?," and (3) "In the last 6 months, did you try to get someone to have sex with you?" Response options were coded 1 = No and 0 = Yes.
- *Attitude Toward Sexual Health Risk Behavior* was measured with a 14-item domain scale asking about conditions under which it is acceptable to have sex. Sample items are: "I believe it's OK for someone my age to have sex with someone they like, but don't know well," "I believe people my age should always use a condom if they have sex," and "If my boyfriend or girlfriend wanted to have sex and I didn't, it would be OK to say 'no'." Response alternatives were "Strongly agree," "Agree," "Disagree," and "Strongly Disagree," coded 1 through 4 with more desirable responses receiving a higher numerical score. Cronbach's alpha for the baseline sample was 0.76.

Interactions with parents regarding risk behaviors was assessed with two domain scales, one measuring the frequency and breadth of youths' discourse with parents about sexual health topics and the other measuring youths' perceptions of whether or not parents or guardians would disapprove of the youth engaging in risk behaviors.

- *Discourse with Parents about Sexual Risk Behavior* measured how often in the last three months youth had talked with their parents about five topical items: menstruation, the risk of getting pregnancy or getting someone pregnant, being a teenage parent, different kinds of birth control, and sexually transmitted diseases (STDs) or AIDS. Response options were coded 0 = "Never," 1 = "1-3 times;" and 2 = "More than 3 times." Cronbach's alpha for this domain scale at baseline was 0.73.
- *Parental Disapproval of Risk Behavior* was measured by asking if the parent or guardian would "approve" or "disapprove" if the youth engaged in six types of risk behavior: used alcohol; sniffed paint or glue or used marijuana; used hard drugs such as heroin, cocaine or crack; had sex (made love, went 'all the way'); got pregnant or got someone pregnant; and failed a grade in school. Responses were coded 1 and 0. The Cronbach alpha for this scale at baseline was 0.65.

A study reported elsewhere (Lederman, Chan, & Roberts-Gray, 2004) showed the domain scales selected for the predictive model tested in the current study were independent of one another. The obtained inter-domain correlations were low with Pearson correlation coefficients of r = 0.10 for Discourse and youth Attitude, r = 0.04 for Discourse and perceived Parental Disapproval, and $r = 0.29$ for youth Attitude and perceived Parental Disapproval.

Data Analyses

Generalized Linear Model with logit link was applied to evaluate the contribution of the baseline measures of interactions with parents and youth involvement in and attitudes toward risk behaviors as predictors of youths' educational aspirations measured in the subsequent school year. Additional variables included in the statistical models were students' age (11 and 12 versus 13 and 14), self-reported ethnic heritage, and gender. A limitation of this study is that all analyses assume the data are taken from random samples. Like many studies reported in the research literature, this study cannot verify this assumption. Generalization of the results should be cautious.

Results

Educational Aspirations

Virtually all (99%) of the middle school students that participated in the survey indicated they plan to finish high school. Ten percent indicated completion of high school is the highest level of education they expect to attain. The vast majority of the students (86%), however, indicated they plan to attend college.

Predictors of Educational Aspirations

Race/heritage ($p < .001$), youth attitudes toward sexual health risk behaviors ($p < .01$), discourse with parents about health risk behavior ($p < .05$), and perception of parental disapproval of youth involvement in risk behavior ($p < .05$) each made significant contributions in predicting educational aspirations. The full model is displayed in Table 2. Neither age nor gender made significant contributions in predicting educational aspirations, nor did actual risk behaviors. Excepting the exclusion of actual risk behavior, the hypothesized model fit the data well (Chi-Square = 735.19, $df = 740$).

Lower educational aspiration was predicted by higher levels of discourse with parents about sexual health risk behaviors and with being Hispanic/Latino/Mexican. Higher educational aspiration was predicted by youth holding attitudes less accepting of sexual activity and perceiving that their parents/guardians disapprove of their being involved in risk behaviors.

Table 2. Generalized Linear Model with PREDICTORS Measured at Baseline and the Criterion Variable EDUCATIONAL ASPIRATION Measured the Subsequent School Year

Predictors	*Beta Weight*	*SE*	*Chi Square*	*p-value*
Gender	0.1835	0.2376	0.60	NS
Age (11-12 versus 13-14)	0.4917	0.3779	1.69	NS
Race/Ethnicity				
Hispanic / Latino, including Mexican	-1.3867	0.4196	10.92	<.01
Black / African American	0.1924	0.4792	0.16	NS
White – not Hispanic	-0.0617	0.4722	0.02	NS
Asian or Mixed or Other	0	.	.	
Health Risk Behaviors				
Use alcohol	-0.1672 -	0.2894	0.33	NS
Use marijuana	0.1890	0.4317	0.19	NS
Try to get someone to have sex	-0.3618	0.4139	0.76	NS
Parental disapproval of risk behaviors	2.0630	1.0186	4.10	<.05
Discourse with parents about risk behaviors	-0.7926	0.3454	5.27	<.05
Attitudes about acceptability of having sex	2.0928	0.6970	9.02	<.05

CONCLUSION

This analysis demonstrates that the attitudes of middle school youth toward health risk behaviors and their perceptions of interactions with their parents/guardians regarding health risk behavior are useful in predicting educational aspiration measured during the subsequent school year. Youth who are at baseline less accepting of involvement in sexual activity and who perceive that their parents disapprove of their involvement in risky behaviors are more likely than those with more tolerant attitudes and perceptions to continue into the next school year with high educational aspirations. The finding that perceived parental disapproval of health risk behavior predicts youths' educational aspiration is consistent with other research indicating that maternal connectedness may facilitate the development of a positive future time perspective by young adolescents (Aronowitz & Morrison-Breedy, 2004).

An unexpected finding in the current analyses was that frequency and breadth of youths' discourse with their parents about sexual health topics showed a negative relationship with youths' educational aspirations. Youth who reported more discourse with parents about sexual health topics were significantly more likely than their peers to report lower educational aspirations. This finding underscores conclusions presented in Healthy People 2010 (U S Department of Health & Human Services, 2000, Chapter 25) regarding the need to give further attention toward helping parents impart information about sexual health risks. The research literature suggests there is no simple, robust relationship between parent-adolescent communication about sexuality and subsequent adolescent sexual health behaviors (Miller, 1998; Dittus & Jaccard, 2000). A hypothesis for exploration in future research is the possibility that young adolescents talk with their parents about risk behavior only when their behavior has created a predicament that forces discussion between parent and child. Another possibility is that more discussion about risks and protection may have a normalizing effect on the youth's perceptions of risk behavior. Yet another possibility is that more discourse about risk behavior occurs in families where parental control experienced as excessive or coercive, and impels the youth toward acting out and/or toward a more negative future time perspective (Tiongson, 1997).

The current study indicates that the interactions of youth with parents regarding health risk behaviors is worthy of further exploration and the development of interventions to improve adolescent health, and educational and adult health outcomes. There is a clear need for additional research to identify ways to marshal, nurture, and work in concert with parental efforts to reduce adolescent health risks and encourage educational attainment.

REFERENCES

Aronowitz, T., & Morrison-Breedy, D. (2004). Comparison of the maternal role in resilience among impoverished and non-impoverished early adolescent African American girls. *Adolescent & Family Health*, 3(4), 155-163.

Blane, D. (2003). Commentary: Explanations of the difference in mortality risk between different educational groups. *International Journal of Epidemiology*, 32, 355-356.

Caetano, R. (2002). *Education, psychiatric diseases and substance use/abuse.* Presentation made at conference on Education and Health: Building a Research Agenda. National Institutes of Health. Available to read online: *www.wws.princeton.edu/chw/conferences /conf1002/session/Caetanofiles/frame.html*

Chandola, T., Clarke, P., Blane, D., & Morris, J. (2003). *Pathways between education and health: A causal modeling approach.* University College London (UCL). Published online: *www.ucl.ac.uk/epidemiology/Chandola/healtheducation.htm*

Dittus, P., & Jaccard, J. (2000). The relationship of adolescent perceptions of maternal disapproval of sex and of the mother-adolescent relationship in sexual outcomes. *Journal of Adolescent Health*, 26, 268-278.

Elliot, D., Huizinga, D., & Ageton, S. (1985). *Explaining delinquency and drug use.* Beverly Hills, CA: Sage.

Goyette, K., & Xie, Y. (1999). Educational expectations of Asian-American youth: Determinants and ethnic differences. *Sociology of Education*, 71, 24-38.

Hannum, E., & Buchman, C. (2003). *The consequences of global educational expansion: Social science perspectives.* Cambridge, MA: American Academy of Arts & Sciences. Available to read online: *www.amacad.org*

Kirby, D., Korpi, M., Adivi, C., & Weissman, J. (1997). An impact evaluation of SNAPP, a pregnancy- and AIDS-prevention middle school curriculum. *AIDS Education Prevention,* 9(Suppl A), 44-67.

Lederman, R., Chan, W., & Roberts-Gray, C. (2004). Sexual risk attitudes and intentions of youth age 12-14 years: Survey comparison of parent-teen prevention and control groups. *Behavioral Medicine*, 29(4), 155-163. Available to read online: *www.findarticles.com /p/articles/mi_m0GDQ/is_4_29/ai_n6192603*

Lederman, R., & Mian, T., (2003). The Parent-Adolescent Relationship Education (PARE) Program: A curriculum for prevention of STDs and pregnancy in middle school youth. *Behavioral Medicine*, 29, 33-41.

Looker, D., & Thiessen, V. (2004). *Aspirations of Canadian youth for higher education.* Learning Policy Directorate, Strategic Policy & Planning, Canada. Available to read online: *www.pisa.gc.ca/SP-600-05-04E.pdf*

Miller, B. (1998). *Families matter: A research synthesis of family influences on adolescent pregnancy.* Washington, DC: National Campaign to Prevent Teen Pregnancy.

Morowsky, J., & Ross, C. (2003). *Education, Social status, and Health.* New York: Aldine de Gruyter.

Pamuk, E., Makuc, D., Heck, K., Reuben, C., & Lochner, K. (1998). *Socioeconomic Status and Health Chartbook. Health, United States, 1998.* Hyattsville, MD: National Center for Health Statistics, Table 9, page 185 of 464. Available to read online: *www.cdc/nchs/data/hus/hus98.pdf*

Tiongson, A. (1997). Throwing the baby out with the bathwater: Situating young Filipino mothers and fathers beyond the dominant discourse on adolescent pregnancy. In: M. Root (Ed*), Filipino Americans: Transformation and Identity*, Thousand Oaks, CA: Sage.

Trusty, J. (1999). Effects of eighth-grade parental involvement on late adolescents' educational expectations. *Journal of Research and Development in Education*, 32, 224-233.

Trusty, J., & Harris, M. (1999). Lost talent: Predictors of the stability of educational aspirations across adolescence. *Journal of Adolescent Research*, 14, 359-382.

U S Department of Health & Human Services. (2000). *Healthy People 2010: Understanding and Improving Health* (2nd ed). Washington DC: US Government Printing Office.

INDEX

A

D

E

N

O

P

Q

R

T